# Digital Surveillance in Africa

**Digital Africa series, edited by Tony Roberts**

Digital Africa explores how digital technologies have opened new spaces for the exercise of democratic rights and freedoms in Africa, as well as how repressive regimes have used digital technologies to monitor, diminish, or remove those rights. The series foregrounds vital new research from across the continent that combines empirical rigor with theoretical sophistication in order to offer new, more nuanced perspectives on the interactions between digital technology and social life on the continent. In so doing, it offers an important, in-depth corrective to existing studies of the relations between digital technologies and social and political power, studies that have overwhelmingly focused on the Global North.

Each volume is co-edited by the series editor in collaboration with an established scholar in the field, and each features comparative and rich case studies authored by ECRs and other African scholars involved in the African Digital Rights Network. Thanks to contributors' diverse disciplinary and professional backgrounds, each chapter offers uniquely practical suggestions for policy, legislation and practice.

Titles include:

*Digital Citizenship in Africa: Technologies of Agency and Repression*
*Digital Disinformation in Africa: Hashtag Politics, Power and Propaganda*
*Digital Surveillance in Africa: Power, Agency, and Rights*

# Digital Surveillance in Africa

*Power, Agency, and Rights*

Edited by Tony Roberts and Admire Mare

## ZED

LONDON • NEW YORK • OXFORD • NEW DELHI • SYDNEY

ZED Books
Bloomsbury Publishing Plc
50 Bedford Square, London, WC1B 3DP, UK
1385 Broadway, New York, NY 10018, USA
29 Earlsfort Terrace, Dublin 2, Ireland

BLOOMSBURY and Zed Books are trademarks of Bloomsbury Publishing Plc

First published in Great Britain 2025

Series design by Toby Way

A catalogue record for this book is available from the British Library.

A catalog record for this book is available from the Library of Congress.

ISBN:    HB:      978-1-3504-2208-7
         PB:      978-1-3504-2207-0
         ePDF:    978-1-3504-2210-0
         eBook:   978-1-3504-2209-4

Series: Digital Africa

Typeset by Integra Software Services Pvt. Ltd.
Printed and bound in Great Britain

*This book is dedicated to the memory of our friend and colleague Dr Sam Phiri who sadly passed away on 25 May 2024. Dr Phiri was a former Permanent Secretary in Zambia, a tireless campaigner for media freedom, and a founding member of the African Digital Rights Network. He was one of our most prolific and knowledgeable contributors and he will be missed greatly. May he rest in peace.*

# Contents

# Contributors

**Kiss Abraham** is an activist, researcher, artist, and media practitioner. Kiss is a founding member of the African Digital Rights Network (ADRN) and is passionate about civic space, the use of art in civic action, and promoting dialogue on development issues. Kiss is the Director of NewZambian Innovations, a Zambian NGO. Kiss wrote 'The names in your address book: Are mobile phone networks effective in advocating women's rights in Zambia?' in *African Women and ICTs: Investigating Technology, Gender and Empowerment* (2009) with Sam Phiri. He co-authored 'Zambia Digital Rights Landscape Report' for the ADRN report 'Digital Rights in Closing Civic Space' (2021), as well as the chapter 'Digital citizenship and cyber activism in Zambia' in the first book in the Digital Africa series *Digital Citizenship in Africa: Technologies of Agency and Repression.*

**Afef Abrougui** is a researcher, writer, and consultant with more than ten years' experience researching and writing on technology and human rights. She is the owner of Fair Tech, a consultancy based in The Hague, with the mission to protect human rights in the digital space through the provision of research services, advice to nonprofits and funders, community organizing, and knowledge sharing. She holds a Media Studies MA (Track: New Media and Digital Culture) from the University of Amsterdam and a BA in English Language from the Higher Institute of Human Sciences in Tunis. Afef has regional expertise across the Middle East and North Africa, in addition to experience leading editorial projects covering Sub-Saharan Africa and editing stories on digital rights from other regions, particularly South Asia, Southeast Asia, and Eastern and Central Europe.

**Gifty Appiah-Adjei** is Senior Lecturer and Head of Department of Journalism and Media Studies at the School of Communication and Media Studies in the University of Education, Winneba in Ghana. She has a PhD degree in Applied Communication from the University of Ibadan, Nigeria (2018) and a postgraduate degree in Communication and Media Studies from the

University of Education, Winneba (2011). Her research interests include: digital security of journalists; press freedom; media and democracy; media and gender; and journalism education. She is affiliated to the Communication Educators Association of Ghana (CEAG), Journalism Safety Research Network (JSRN), Network of UNESCO Chairs in Communication, and International Association for Media and Communication Research (IAMCR). She is also an honorary member of Media Action Nepal.

**Jane Duncan** is Professor of Digital Society at the University of Glasgow where her work focuses on strengthening public oversight of intelligence-driven surveillance. Before that, she was a Professor at the University of Johannesburg (UJ). Before joining UJ, she held the Chair in Media and Information Society in the School of Journalism and Media Studies at the university currently known as Rhodes. She was also Co-Director of the Highway Africa Centre, devoted to promoting digital media in Africa. She comes from a civil society background, having worked for the Freedom of Expression Institute for fifteen years. She has published widely academically, in popular publications and in the media, on issues relating to freedom of expression, democratic space, the right to protest, and surveillance, and has authored four peer-reviewed books: *The Rise of the Securocrats* (2014); *Protest Nation* (2016); *Stopping the Spies* (2018); and *National Security Surveillance in Southern Africa* (2022).

**Judy Gitahi** is a Kenyan researcher interested in digital development and its impact on the economic growth of low- and middle-income countries. She has a background in economics and holds a master's in Development Studies from the Institute of Development Studies at the University of Sussex, where her dissertation analysed how digital lender regulation in Kenya, or lack thereof, increased the use of predatory lending models and thus reduced the agency of borrowers using digital lending applications. Judy also has experience as a development consultant and currently works at a research organization providing analytics and advisory to governments, philanthropists, and other NGOs through various services like impact evaluations, process evaluations, and capacity building.

**Jimmy Kainja** is Senior Lecturer in Media, Communication, and Cultural Studies at the University of Malawi. He is also Communication and Public

Relations Coordinator at the Centre for Resilient Agri-Food Systems, University of Malawi. He is an adjunct research fellow at the Institute of Public Opinion and Research, an editorial team member for the University of Malawi's *Kachere Series*, and a mentor for the University of Malawi's *Journal of Humanities* mentorship programme. Kainja is a Digital Rights Coalition (Malawi) African Digital Rights Network member. He has published widely in the following areas of interest: media and communications policy, journalism, new media, digital rights, freedom of expression, access to information, and the intersection of media, democracy, and development. He is Freedom House's country researcher and analyst (Malawi) for the 'Freedom on the Net' report. His list of publications is on ORCID and Google Scholar.

**Muthuri Kathure** is a human rights lawyer, researcher, campaigner, and policy expert based in Nairobi. His interest areas are civic space and technology, law, and society. Until recently he led Article-19's civic space and digital programmes in Eastern Africa. His expertise lies in civic participation and digital rights policy, steering advocacy, research, and capacity building efforts for online and offline communities. Previously, as Legal Aid Manager at Justice Defenders (formerly African Prison Project) in Kenya, Gambia, and Uganda, he established twelve prison-based legal aid clinics and trained over 150 officers and inmates as paralegals. He has received awards from Amnesty International and was nominated for the Under 35 Award by Kenya Youth Agenda for his work on human rights. Muthuri is a regular columnist with the *Star Newspaper* and is currently a policy fellow with the Tech Global Institute.

**Admire Mare** is Associate Professor and Head of the Department of Communication and Media at the University of Johannesburg, South Africa. He was previously Deputy Head of the Communications Department at the Namibia University of Science and Technology. His research focuses on global platform studies, global disinformation studies, global surveillance studies, and the nexus between technology and society. He has co-authored *Participatory Journalism in Africa* for Routledge and is the co-editor of *Media, Conflict and Peacebuilding in Africa* (also Routledge). He holds a PhD from Rhodes University, Makhanda. Admire is co-editor of the collected edition *Digital Surveillance in Southern Africa* with Allen Munoriyarwa. His full list of publications is available on Google Scholar and ORCID 0000-0002-9329-4030.

**Nana Nwachukwu** is a technology lawyer with over fourteen years of expertise, specializing in governance and regulatory frameworks across Africa, the Middle East, and Europe, with a focus on AI ethics and emerging technology policies. At Saidot, she simplifies and makes policies accessible, ensuring practical application and responsible AI use for clients. Nana holds a law degree from Abia State University, a master's degree in Intellectual Property and Technology Law from the University of Liverpool, another in International Humanitarian Affairs from the University of York, and another in Digital Media and Communications from Teesside University. Her published papers are on SSRN, Google Scholar, and arXiv.

**Oyewole Adekunle Oladapo** is Lecturer in the Department of Communication and Language Arts, University of Ibadan, Nigeria. He received his doctoral degree in 2018 from the University of Ibadan. His doctoral thesis examined variations in online and offline audiences' deconstruction of newspaper representation of Nigeria's unity. Oyewole's areas of interest include media and development, protests and politics on social media, and media and identity. He has authored and co-authored book chapters and articles in both local and foreign journals. His publications include the 'Digital Landscape Report on Nigeria' for the African Digital Rights Network report 'Digital Rights in Closing Civic Space: Lessons from Ten African Countries' (2021).

**Sam Phiri** was a senior academic at the University of Zambia where he headed the Department of Media and Communication Studies. His research focused on national politics, political communication, and political organizations and parties. Projects included: 'Research in Communications: Focus of Mass Communication Teaching at the University of Zambia' and 'Person Not Profit – an Africanist Approach to Corporate Social Responsibility Theory'. His publications included the 'Zambia Digital Rights Landscape Report' (with Kiss Abraham) for the African Digital Rights Network report 'Digital Rights in Closing Civic Space' (2021); 'Media Development Aid and the Westernisation of Africa: The Case of the Open Society Initiative for Southern Africa' (2016); 'Political Dis-Empowerment of Women by ICTs: The Case of the Zambian Elections' (2011); and 'Youth Participation in Politics: The Case of Zambian University Students' (2019).

**Tony Roberts** is a Research Fellow at the Institute for Development Studies (IDS), UK. After a period as Lecturer in Innovation Studies at the University of East London, Tony founded and led two international development agencies working in Central America and Southern Africa. When he stood down as CEO of Computer Aid International, he completed a PhD in the use of digital technologies in international development (University of London). After one year working as a research fellow at the United Nations University in Macao, China, Tony joined IDS where his research focuses on digital development and digital rights. He co-founded the African Digital Rights Network for whom he has edited reports including 'Mapping the Supply of Surveillance Technologies to Africa'. He is the series editor of the Zed Books 'Digital Africa' series, and co-editor of the collected editions *Digital Citizenship in Africa* and *Digital Disinformation in Africa*.

**Anand Sheombar** is a senior researcher from the Digital Together expertise group at the HU University of Applied Sciences Utrecht, the Netherlands. Before joining academia, he worked as an IT advisor for a university medical centre and as an IT procurement officer for the Dutch National Research and Education Network organization. He holds a master's in Informatics from HU University of Applied Sciences Utrecht, and MRes and PhD from Manchester Metropolitan University, UK, on the use of social media in international development by NGOs. His research covers the societal impact of ICTs, such as eHealth, ICT for education, digital civil society, online hate speech detection, social media, digital transformation, digital sustainability, and digital development. His post-doc research focused on digital transformation maturity and international development NGOs. He has co-authored the ADRN publication *Mapping the Supply of Surveillance Technologies to Africa*.

**Sebastian Klovig Skelton** is the data and ethics editor at *Computer Weekly*. Seb is interested in the social, political, and economic implications of technology, and writes extensively about the use of data-driven technologies like artificial intelligence and facial recognition. In January 2024, Seb took on responsibility for *Computer Weekly*'s new data and ethics beat, where he writes and commissions reports on the practical consequences of how technology is being deployed. In 2019, Seb was nominated alongside colleagues for a British

Press Award under the 'Technology Journalism' category, for work reporting on a trove of internal documents leaked from Facebook. In 2021, Seb received an MHP '30 Young Journalists to Watch' award for his work on the role tech firms play in the extraction of minerals from the DRC and the unlawful use of hyperscale public cloud services by UK police. Seb previously studied History at Queen Mary University before completing an MA in Investigative Journalism at City University.

# Foreword

Thank you for having taken the time and trouble to open this book, which focuses on digital surveillance in Africa as a means of exercising power and social control. It examines the fundamental human rights that are impacted in the process, and the citizen agency that has been exercised, or needs to be exercised, to call those to account who abuse this power and violate these rights. This book, which is an edited volume of chapters by leading academics and activists, offers new knowledge about the global trade in the digital technologies that enable surveillance (or spyware), and opens new possibilities for action on these issues. In this Foreword, I will explain why I think this book is important and why you should read it.

In 2013, a contractor for the United States signals intelligence agency responsible for bulk surveillance of electronic signals, the National Security Agency (NSA), Edward Snowden, shocked the world by leaking classified intelligence documents. These documents detailed how an alliance of countries with some of the most powerful bulk surveillance capabilities in the world, the Five Eyes alliance, abused these capabilities. They showed how members of the alliance (the United States, the United Kingdom, Canada, Australia, and New Zealand) used these capabilities far beyond the claimed purpose of protecting global security (Five Eyes Ministerial 2018), and conducted espionage against their own citizens, and the citizens of other countries. More relevant for readers of this book though, they spied on the trade negotiators, political and business leaders of African countries to gain competitive advantages over them in trade negotiations and business deals. These countries did so to protect their economic interests on the continent, and in doing so, they practised imperialism by other means, reinforcing existing economic inequalities between Africa and the centres of global economic power, with the United States as the apex (Piel and Tilouine 2016).

In response to the Snowden leaks, organized civil society in the Five Eyes countries and beyond pushed back against bulk surveillance, attempting to force the offending governments to reform the laws governing this intelligence practice. They also put pressure on countries with arms industries that manufacture and export spyware to other countries, to limit exports to authoritarian governments where the potential for abuse was high. These efforts led to some reforms in how particularly powerful dual use surveillance technologies – or technologies that have military and civilian uses – are exported, with the most important reform being greater transparency in reporting on these exports.

The spyware industry is dominated overwhelmingly by arms companies in the Global North, although Israel and China are becoming more prominent as suppliers on the continent, too. In contrast, most African countries are importers of spyware. As a result, these countries are vulnerable to technological dependency and espionage as data can be extracted and exploited through backdoors by the arms-producing countries. Yet, despite these vulnerabilities, with potential repercussions for these countries' national security, evidence from the available export control data points to African governments being enthusiastic buyers of this spyware.

However, reforms to the global trade in spyware have not been adequate (Amnesty International 2019: 5; Bromley 2018: 21), and poorly regulated surveillance continues across the world. You should read this book because its authors demonstrate in graphic detail just how inadequate these reforms have been for, and in, Africa. They expose the implications of these failures for basic human rights on the continent, and the ability of citizens to exercise agency to change how these societies are organized, for the better.

Governments of the major arms exporting countries are reluctant to limit markets for spyware as they are so profitable. Most of the major arms-exporting countries have signed up to the Wassenaar Arrangement on Export Controls for Conventional Arms and Dual-Use Goods and Technologies, which requires them to be more transparent in their exports of spyware. But they also know that the Arrangement is a toothless tiger.

As former UN Special Rapporteur on the Promotion and Protection of the Right to Freedom of Opinion and Expression, David Kaye has pointed out, the Arrangement does not require these countries to consider the human rights implications of their exports, as the system is voluntary. Only if export controls are domesticated in law can controls be enforceable, and these domestication efforts have been inadequate (Amnesty International 2019: 5). This gap in the export control regime for spyware led Kaye to conclude that '[It] is insufficient to say that a comprehensive system for control and use of targeted surveillance technologies is broken. It hardly exists' (Kaye 2019: 14). Consequently, Kaye called for an immediate moratorium on the sales of surveillance technologies until such safeguards were introduced (Kaye 2019: 14–15).

You should read this book because it demonstrates how – by failing to develop such a system that restrains exports to rights-abusing countries – these governments are complicit in human rights abuses. The book provides the material necessary to hold these governments to account for putting profits before people. It is extremely difficult to document the violence that surveillance enables as it is less visible than that caused by conventional arms. In the case of the latter, causal links can be drawn between the sales of arms and deaths and injuries in recipient countries, which in turn can fuel public outrage and action. Anti-war and peace movements have become important elements of the political landscape, but these have confined themselves largely to mobilizing around disarmaments involving conventional arms. The problem with tackling the less visible violence that poorly regulated spyware makes possible – such as the harassment, or worse, of journalists and activists – is how does one expose this violence in ways that galvanize the public to do something about it?

This book helps to make that violence more visible as it examines the actors most at risk of surveillance and surveillance impacts. Africa has had its own surveillance scandals, where evidence has come into the public domain of surveillance overreach, and these scandals suggest that surveillance targets are often change agents that threaten the status quo, such as investigative journalists, political and civil society activists, and opposition movements. At the same time, governments typically provide limited to no empirical evidence of surveillance having brought down crime or protected national security.

Where legal and policy frameworks fail to protect citizen rights, surveillance abuses are a near certainty, and even a cursory glance at the legal frameworks discussed in this book show just how woefully inadequate they are. This book is important because it shows up the lack of due diligence of the major arms exporters, and they need to be called to account where their due diligence has been inadequate to non-existent.

You should read this book because it acts as an important corrective to so much of the recent literature on surveillance. Since 2013, this field of study has grown massively – however, with a bias towards the Five Eyes countries and Global North (Shiraz and Aldrich 2019: 1313–29). There has been little systematic effort to document and understand the extent of the problem in more peripheral and volatile parts of the global economy, including Africa. This gap exists despite the documented evidence that African governments have been enthusiastic consumers of spyware, while having limited protections in place to shield the populace from surveillance abuses.

You should also read this book because it expands the focus on bulk surveillance beyond internet-protocol (IP) surveillance, or the kind of surveillance practised by the signals intelligence agencies of the Five Eyes countries. Few African countries are known to possess these extremely expensive and powerful capabilities, with only South Africa having publicly admitted to using them (Ministry of State Security 2017: 58). In a welcome departure from surveillance literature from the Global North, the authors focus on the diversity of bulk surveillance practices that African governments and private companies resort to. In this regard, the authors focus on five practices: internet interception, mobile interception, social media monitoring, public space surveillance, and digital-identity systems. This helps the reader to understand the depth of the problem. Relatedly, it would be a mistake to limit export controls to IP-based bulk surveillance systems, which is where so much of the debate around export controls has focused. This is because African governments are likely to respond to any such limitations – even if they could afford the spyware – by ratcheting up their reliance on other forms of bulk surveillance that are even more poorly regulated than IP-based surveillance.

This book is the latest in a series of publications produced by the African Digital Rights Network, and coordinated from the Institute for Development Studies, based at the University of Sussex. The work of the network, supported by the Institute, provides an important example of a scholarly community committed to having positive, real-world impacts, rather than confining knowledge to the often-rarefied world of academia. This book has its origins in a research project initiated in 2020, at the height of the COVID-19 pandemic. The project involved establishing a network of researchers from twelve African countries. Not only has the project and the network that underpins it survived one of the most trying periods in recent history, but it has grown in scale and impact, which is a testament to its strong leadership and rootedness.

In its formative stages, the project focused on the extent to which civic space was opening or closing. The first book focused on democratic openings, examining the ways in which citizens of African countries used digital technologies to expand civic space and practise citizenship from below through activism.

This book focuses much more on democratic closures, where governments, aided and abetted by corporations, ramped up their surveillance capabilities to limit citizen agency. It examines extant surveillance practices and traces their roots in colonial intelligence practices to suppress indigenous liberation movements, as well as emergent authoritarian tendencies in those movements. It grew out of a 'sousveillance' project, which mapped the supply chains of dual-use technology producing countries based mainly in the Global North, and the uses to which these technologies were being put, including the social control of increasingly restive African populations. It acknowledges the fact that digitization has turbo-charged surveillance, greatly enhancing their capabilities to conduct surveillance.

Helpfully, though, its authors have not fallen victim to surveillance realism (Dencik 2018: 31–43). In other words, they have resisted the temptation to become resigned to a fate where no reasonable expectation of privacy exists. They do not assume that the potential for abuse of these extremely powerful spying capabilities is a given. They believe that the social appropriation of spyware can and should be contested, and that ordinary citizens do have the ability to exercise counter-power on these matters and bring about more just and equitable digital societies. One of the ways in which this counter-power is being exercised is through mapping the production and exportation of spyware and preventing their exportation at their source.

Exploring opportunities for agency on these issues also means examining the fractured, youth-orientated societies so evident across Africa, where formal politics does not reflect the social base sufficiently. There is a yawning disconnect between older political movements with their roots in struggles against colonialism, which are unable to take their societies forward, and the young social base that feels increasingly unrecognized and unrepresented. Governing parties across Africa were shaken by the 2010–12 Arab Spring. Less well known is the fact that the Arab Spring rippled across the rest of Africa to different degrees, galvanizing protest movements from Nigeria to Mozambique and Lesotho. The political ferment provided these parties with the motivation and opportunities to ramp up surveillance. However, it also provided opportunities for those under surveillance to expose abuses when they occurred (Duncan 2022: 1–7). The challenge these movements continue to face is to link surveillance to broader efforts to open democratic space and change the highly exploitative and unequal social relations that continue into the post-colonial period.

It is extremely difficult to conduct empirical research on surveillance, owing to high levels of secrecy in how governments and corporations use or abuse spyware, particularly for law enforcement and national security purposes. Doing so is even more difficult in authoritarian societies where, all too often, national security is reduced to security of the state, the ruling party, or factions of the ruling party and the vested interests they represent. Researching, writing, and advocating around surveillance is inherently dangerous as powerholders could consider these activities as subversive, and frame them as national security threats. Authors that are on the ground in the affected countries are more likely to ferret out sources of information that pierce the veil of secrecy on these issues and shed light on the supply and demand sides of surveillance. That is precisely what the authors of this book have set out to do.

You should read this book and take note of the work of the network because it brings together academics with journalists and civil society practitioners who are at the heart of the problem they are writing about. It combines the skills sets of people who know how to find the information with the people who can do something about these problems. The book also extends existing literature beyond southern Africa into Africa (Duncan 2022; Munoriyarwa and Mare 2023). Several countries examined in this book are regional hegemons. In other words, they have the geostrategic power to influence how surveillance is regulated and overseen beyond their own borders, which is why it is especially important to understand the trajectories of surveillance in these countries and how to change them if needed.

I am confident that the African Digital Rights Network will continue generating new and important knowledge on these issues. This book is another milestone on a journey to put Africa at the centre of the debate on more just and equitable digital futures.

Jane Duncan

# References

Amnesty International. (2019). 'The Surveillance Industry and Human Rights: Amnesty International Submission to the UN Special Rapporteur on the Promotion and Protection of Freedom of Opinion and Expression', 22 February. https://www.ohchr.org/Documents/Issues/Opinion/Surveillance/AMNESTY%20INTERNATIONAL.pdf

Bromley, M. (2018). 'Export Controls, Human Security and Cyber-Surveillance Technology' (Report), Stockholm: Stockholm International Peace Research Institute. https://sipri.org/sites/default/files/2018-01/sipri1712_bromley.pdf

Dencik, L. (2018). 'Surveillance Realism and the Politics of Imagination: Is There No Alternative?', *Krisis: Journal for Contemporary Philosophy*, 1: 31–43.

Duncan, J. (2022). *National Security Surveillance in Southern Africa: An Anti-Capitalist Perspective*, London: Zed Books.

Five Eyes Ministerial. (2018). Official Communiqué on National Security. https://www.homeaffairs.gov.au/about-us/our-portfolios/national-security/securitycoordination/five-country-ministerial-2018

Kaye, D. (2019). 'Surveillance and Human Rights: Report of the Special Rapporteur on the Promotion and Protection of the Right to Freedom of Opinion and Expression'. Presented to the forty-first session of the Human Rights Council, 28 May. https://www.ohchr.org/EN/HRBodies/HRC/RegularSessions/Session41/Documents/A_HRC_41_35.docx

Ministry of State Security, the Office for Interception Centres, the National Communications Centre and the State Security Agency. (2017). *amaBhungane Centre for Investigative Journalism and Stephen Patrick Sole v The Minister of Justice and Correctional Services and Nine Others*: Second, Seventh, Eighth and Tenth Respondent's Answering Affidavit, case number 25078/2017.

Munoriyarwa, A. and Mare, A. (2023). *Digital Surveillance in Southern Africa: Policies, Politics and Practices*, London: Palgrave Macmillan.

Piel, S. and Tilouine, J. (2016). 'British Spying: Tentacles Reach Across Africa's Heads of State and Business Leaders', *Le Monde*, 8 December 2016. https://www.lemonde.fr/afrique/article/2016/12/08/british-spying-tentacles-reach-across-africa-s-heads-of-states-and-business-leaders_5045668_3212.html (accessed 10 February 2024).

Shiraz, Z. and Aldrich, R.J. (2019). 'Secrecy, Spies and the Global South: Intelligence Studies beyond the "Five Eyes" Alliance', *International Affairs*, 95(6): 1313–29. https://doi-org.ezproxy.lib.gla.ac.uk/10.1093/ia/iiz200

# Acknowledgements

This book is a product of the African Digital Rights Network (ADRN), a group of more than sixty activists, analysts, and academics from over twenty African countries. The network has provided a wonderful platform of deep contextual knowledge and analytical expertise. This book series could not have been produced without the inspiration of their prior work and kind support. The authors of this book would like to acknowledge the leadership and generous assistance and advice from surveillance scholars like Edin Omanovic, Jane Duncan, and the rest of the team at the University of Johannesburg who have contributed so much to the study of surveillance in Southern Africa: Dércio Tsandzana, Sarah Chiumbu, Allen Munoriyarwa, Arsène Tungali, and Frederico Links. We also wanted to thank those analysts who were kind enough to present their work at our online meetings: Victoria Ibezim Oheri and Smith Oduro-Marfo. We are grateful also to Amy Cowlard at the Institute of Development Studies and to Blossom Carrasco and Judy Gitahi who put in such important work on the project management, design, and editing work for the preliminary report 'Mapping the Supply of Surveillance Technologies to Africa' by the African Digital Rights Network that informs this book. In this book, and throughout this Digital Africa series, we are indebted to Nick Wolterman and Olivia Dellow at Zed Books for steering the project and to the unnamed reviewers who provided invaluable feedback on the initial book proposal and manuscript draft.

# Critical approaches to digital surveillance in Africa

Tony Roberts and Admire Mare

## An introduction to this collected edition

African governments spend billions of dollars on digital technologies to surveil their own citizens. These digital surveillance technologies are often used in ways that violate citizens' fundamental human rights that are guaranteed in national constitutions, international conventions, and domestic laws. The use of digital surveillance to intercept emails, monitor mobile phones and social media use, and to track citizens' movements and transactions provides governments and corporations with unprecedented capacity for panoptic real-time surveillance of citizens' private lives. The rapid expansion of rights-violating surveillance and its use to surveil peaceful protest, independent journalism, opposition politicians, judges, and activists is contributing to a closing of civic space that inhibits citizen agency from freely participating in democratic deliberation, political discourse, and inclusive decision making.

Paradoxically, citizens have good reason to value both the narrow surveillance of the most serious criminals *and* the fundamental human right to privacy of all citizens. In this volume we argue that it is in citizens' interests that surveillance is carried out on terrorists and other serious criminals but only when authorized by a court and when subject to independent oversight. Such warranted surveillance is the mechanism by which we can be sure that any surveillance is lawful, necessary, and proportionate and that no unwarranted surveillance violates fundamental human rights. At the same time as valuing narrow surveillance of the most serious criminals, citizens also have good reason to value privacy in their homes, in their business correspondence, and in their private communication.

The right to privacy is valuable in its own right, but it is also instrumental in enabling other rights that are central to democracy, including freedom of speech, freedom of association, and political affiliation. For these reasons, privacy rights are clearly protected in African constitutions, in international human rights conventions, and in domestic laws. Our previous research has detailed how in legislation and in practice it is possible to balance the need for narrowly focused surveillance of terrorists while guaranteeing the privacy rights of the majority of citizens (Roberts et al. 2021; Munoriyarwa and Mare 2023).

Surveillance is an ancient practice, but digitalization has dramatically expanded its reach, depth, and impact. Historically, surveillance was a laborious manual process of human intelligence gathering, including physically following people and intercepting their postal communications. Over time these human intelligence processes were augmented by signals intelligence, including the interception of telegraph and telephone communications via 'wiretapping' and codebreaking of encrypted transmissions. The high unit cost of manual surveillance and decryption provided a practical limit to the number of people who could be surveilled. Once these analogue forms of communication were digitalized, it became possible to automate the interception and analysis of mobile and internet traffic using algorithmic keyword searches and artificial intelligence pattern recognition to conduct 'signals intelligence' on millions of messages per second. Automated monitoring for keywords and the use of artificial intelligence pattern recognition make it affordable to conduct surveillance on a scale and at a depth that was previously unimaginable. Corporations, governments, military, and security agencies can now automate the remote surveillance of citizens' precise location, mobile communications, instant messages, posts and likes, and map their network of contacts dynamically in real-time.

Mass surveillance using digital technologies violates the privacy rights of citizens. Digital surveillance makes possible the routine surveillance of all citizens who use mobile or internet technologies. Mass surveillance using for example deep-packet inspection of internet traffic and deep learning artificial intelligence enables dragnet surveillance that trawls through everyone's private communication looking for 'suspicious' activity patterns. These new forms of dragnet mass surveillance and automated activist surveillance violate citizens' rights as they do not meet the international legal thresholds of being 'lawful, necessary, and proportionate' (EFF 2014). These new digital abuses of surveillance power were brought to public attention via three global news stories: Cambridge Analytica's use of social media surveillance to distort democratic elections (Ekdale and Tully 2020); the Snowden revelations about state mass surveillance (Snowden Archive 2019) and the Pegasus spyware story documenting the widespread use of mobile phone malware to spy on journalists, opposition politicians, judges, and peaceful activists (Amnesty 2021).

The market for digital surveillance technologies in Africa has grown exponentially. African governments are now spending billions of dollars per year on new surveillance capabilities. This rapid change is taking place in the absence of adequate legal frameworks, rights protections, or independent oversight. Our previous study across ten African countries documented over fifty examples where digital surveillance technologies have been used in ways that contravene constitutional, international, or domestic laws, or violate fundamental human rights (Roberts et al. 2023). In most cases, this happens with impunity but as the chapters in this book document, citizens are not without agency in the face of these violations, and are organizing to push back, claim their rights, circumvent surveillance, and hold governments accountable. Each chapter in this book includes a section on forms of resistance to mitigate or overcome rights-violating surveillance. The growing use of digital surveillance in Africa – the associated abuse of power, its impact on citizens' fundamental human rights, and new forms of citizen agency to resist these developments – is the focus of this book.

Most research on digital surveillance has focused on the Global North. Relatively little was known about the use of digital surveillance in Africa until very recently. The excellent research that has begun to emerge in the last few years has focused primarily on South Africa and on Southern Africa more generally (Duncan 2018; Munoriyarwa and Mare 2023; Yingi and Benyera 2024). This is the first book to provide a platform for African researchers from across the continent to document surveillance practices in their own countries, and draw upon their own deep contextual knowledge of local history, politics, and culture to analyse how digital surveillance is affecting citizens' rights and what interests it serves.

## Our research approach

This is the first pan-African power analysis of digital surveillance practices. The book expands the existing geographical coverage of digital surveillance beyond Southern Africa to provide rich case studies from North, West, East, as well as Southern Africa. The book sets out to address a range of related questions: what factors are driving the explosion in digital surveillance in Africa, whose rights are affected, who benefits and what power interests are being served by surveillance, and what needs to be done by whom in order to reassert citizen agency, rights, and equitable political participation?

Building on our preliminary mapping of which companies, from which countries, are supplying which digital surveillance technologies to African governments (Roberts et al. 2023), this book examines five categories of digital surveillance technologies being used by Africa governments, namely: internet interception; mobile interception; social media monitoring; public space surveillance; and digital-ID systems. In addition to documenting the landscape of surveillance technologies in each country, this book adds a level of conceptual analysis assessing the impact of digital surveillance through the lens of digital rights, power interests, and the agency of citizens actively avoiding, resisting, and challenging surveillance practices. To help translate research into action, each chapter contains a section analysing the active means by which citizens are resisting surveillance such as strategic litigation, advocacy, and the use of virtual private networks, and concludes with recommendations to inform future policy, practice, and further research.

The book contributes new knowledge, analysis, and recommendations. By documenting data about which companies are supplying surveillance technologies we contribute new knowledge about the dimensions of digital surveillance in Africa. By providing contextual and conceptual analysis we reveal the power relationships and interests that drive digital surveillance. By detailing market size and documenting key actors, we foreground the role of the private sector in expanding the use of rights-violating digital surveillance.

And by providing rich case studies we build on previous research to provide a platform for comparative analysis and theory-building so that other scholars can build an African theory of change and provide practical guidance for the social action that is needed to enable citizens to exercise, defend, and expand their rights and agency to secure social justice.

The remaining sections of this introductory chapter are organized as follows. After some background information for the reader who is unfamiliar with surveillance issues, and after attending to some definitional issues, we provide a review of the existing scholarship on digital surveillance in Africa before conducting a review of the conceptual literature on digital rights, power analysis, and citizen agency to provide a conceptual frame for analysis. We then provide a brief summary of the issues covered by each of the case study chapters before concluding with some tentative suggestions for a framework for critical surveillance studies in Africa.

## Background

Surveillance is as at least as old as nation-states themselves. Governments have always spied on external enemies, as well as on internal dissidents. Over time they have gathered increasingly sophisticated data on populations to aid taxation and service provision, and to manage and control the population. In Africa, institutionalized state surveillance systems were introduced by colonial administrations to further their imperial interests in the economic and political exploitation of Africa.

Colonial governments often created surveillance agencies to monitor and undermine national liberation movements (Rid 2020; Browne 2015; Roberts et al. 2021; Munoriyarwa and Mare, 2023). In many anglophone African countries under colonial administration surveillance was the responsibility of the police Special Branch. The UK Special Branch was formed in 1887 to conduct surveillance on Irish opponents of British colonial rule in Ireland and conducted surveillance on suffragettes and labour movement leaders (Wilson and Adams 2015). It was then exported to its colonies where it was also responsible for intelligence gathering on political opposition to colonial power (Woodman 2018). However, not all African surveillance has colonial roots: Ethiopia, which was alone in Africa in never being formally colonized, independently developed one of the most intensive political surveillance systems in Africa called 5:1 where every fifth person was responsible for monitoring their family and neighbours and reporting back intelligence data to the state.

After independence, colonial surveillance agencies were often retained. The Special Branch continued to operate in many anglophone African countries decades after liberation. Although its name was sometimes changed, its capabilities and political spying function remained to serve new power interests. The surveillant gaze was often retrained on external and internal opposition to post-independence governments and new technologies were introduced. Pass-book IDs and fingerprint biometric surveillance technologies were updated over the decades (Browne 2015; Kwet 2023), but it is the current digitalization processes that have brought the most dramatic expansion of surveillance capabilities and privacy violations. Since the millennium, African governments have invested billions in procuring digital surveillance technologies and putting in place a legal framework for the expansion of mass surveillance (Roberts et al. 2021; Roberts et al. 2023).

Companies from the Global North have used Africa as a surveillance technology testing ground. Researchers have begun documenting how new technologies of surveillance such as biometric fingerprinting (Breckenridge 2019) and social media monitoring (Nyabola 2018) have been trialled in Africa where regulation is relatively weak before being used internationally. This book expands the documentation of the supply of surveillance technologies to Africa by foreign powers, but it is importantly also about the growing domestic capability and interest of African governments to expand their use of surveillance to further their own power interests.

African governments have spent at least $2.7 billion buying digital surveillance technologies from companies in Europe, USA, China and Israel with Nigeria alone having spent more than $1 billion (Roberts et al. 2023). Private companies sit at the centre of many state surveillance systems. Whereas surveillance was once primarily the preserve of state agencies, it is increasingly conducted on corporate platforms and by private companies with state surveillance companies sourcing large volumes of personal data from the private sector. In each African country that we studied we found that governments were making it mandatory for mobile phone companies to collect personal identification details of anyone using a mobile phone SIM card. We also found that African governments were introducing legislation to require telecoms and internet service providers to capture and save records of citizens' private communications and make them available to government agencies. This expands data protection and data security risks. As Susan Landau (2010: 3) has argued, 'Embedding surveillance capabilities deeply into communications infrastructures squarely pits surveillance against security and may in fact endanger us far more than it secures us'. This introduction of mass surveillance by corporations was introduced without citizen consultation or participation and elevates the interests of corporations and states above the constitutional rights and freedoms of citizens.

Mass surveillance has become the business model of Big Tech companies. The indiscriminate capture, processing, and trading of personal information by Big Tech companies and powerful actors have become not just routine but ubiquitous. Zuboff (2022) argues that the 'surveillance capitalism' business model first developed by Google and Facebook has since been adopted by many of the world's largest and most powerful companies including global monopolies Apple, Amazon, Alphabet, Microsoft, and IBM from the United States as well as TenCent and Alibaba from China. For these companies, surveillance of online traffic to harvest and sell citizens personal data is a core business function. In Africa too, companies are engaging in invasive targeted advertising. Platform companies cooperate with credit card companies and commercial data brokers to extract personal data and build detailed digital profiles on citizens using the thousands of data points that they have about each person's identity, location, browsing history, online purchases, likes and follows, and network of contacts (Srnicek 2017). In many cases, this may result in foreign companies having more detailed information on citizens and populations than African states: a form of data extractivism some call digital colonialism (Kwet 2019). Those foreign companies are often beyond the regulatory and governance reach of African governments. As Jimoh (2023) notes, the use of surveillance in Africa is becoming widespread, yet the legal and regulatory protections urgently need to be updated to keep pace with these changes. Insufficient information is known about the scale of surveillance in Africa and the international trade in the data.

The authors in this book 'follow the money' of digital surveillance contracts. They document which companies from which countries are supplying which rights-violating technologies to which Africa governments. They do so on the basis that without a detailed understanding of the supply and demand for digital surveillance technologies it is not possible to adequately design social action to cut off that supply or to curtail the demand. In documenting the growing size of the surveillance market in Africa, the authors in this volume also expand our understanding of the role that the private sector plays in providing the surveillance technologies on which this rights-violation relies. The task of this book is urgent: to document and analyse digital surveillance practices across Africa and to use that analysis to produce practical recommendations to achieve the defunding and abolition of rights-violating digital surveillance and the reassertion of citizens' rights, power, and agency.

Our researchers use five categories of technology and three main lens to organize their analysis. The documentation of digital surveillance contracts is organized in five categories identified during a previous study: (1) internet interception, (2) mobile interception, (3) social media monitoring, (4) public space surveillance, and (5) biometric digital-ID systems. In the first category, researchers evidenced contracts to supply technologies that enable the interception of internet communication including private emails and instant messages such as the use of 'deep packet inspection' to enable the interception and inspection of packets of data. We also document contracts supplying technologies to intercept private mobile phones, including by using fake cell phone towers. The surveillance of social media was famously provided as a commercial service by the UK companies Cambridge Analytica and Bell Pottinger, but our research shows that African governments have now procured the technology to conduct this form of surveillance locally 'in-house'. This book also documents the procurement of hundreds of millions of dollars' worth of public space surveillance technology in the form of thousands of closed-circuit television (CCTV) cameras equipped with facial recognition technology enabled by artificial intelligence. The fifth and final category of surveillance technology that this book documents is the procurement of biometric digital-ID systems, which have the potential to enable the integration of all of the other surveillance technologies by linking data verifiably to an individual citizen. If or when these five forms of surveillance are combined by government agencies or corporations, they provide the potential for real-time panoptic surveillance capabilities, making it possible to geo-locate citizens in real-time and monitor their calls, transactions and associations, in ways that violate fundamental human rights and exceed what is legal, necessary and proportional.

The case studies documented in this volume are analysed primarily through the lens of digital rights, power interests, and citizens agency. The book takes an historical and political approach to contextualize current surveillance practices. The authors in this collected edition preface each chapter by providing the reader with a section on the political history of the country in the belief that surveillance practices and citizen agency can only be adequately understood in the light of the colonial, cultural, and political context that gives rise to particular surveillance practices. The book takes a critical historical approach that not only maps and documents the landscape of surveillance technologies and citizen resistance in each country but analyses how they are deployed to serve particular power interests. As the title implies, the overarching research questions include documenting and analysing experiences of digital surveillance in Africa through the lens of digital rights, power, and agency. Before looking at these concepts in some depth, the next section first attends to some definitional issues.

## Defining surveillance

The word sur-veillance comes from the French and literally means over-watching. The definition of surveillance has been debated in the field of surveillance studies. Dandeker (1990: vii) defines surveillance as 'the gathering of information about, and the supervision of, subject populations'. David Lyon (2007: 14) defines surveillance as 'the focused, systematic, and routine attention to personal details for purposes of influence, management, protection, or direction'. These open and inclusive definitions of surveillance allow for realities in which surveillance can be socially positive or negative (Giddens 1995; Allmer 2012) depending on the actions of those doing the watching and actioning the data. Defined, thus, surveillance can refer to the collection of data for pandemic management, allocation of government social services, or to control and persecute minorities. Indeed, the word surveillance could refer to the loving over-watching of an infant by a parent.

As this book is focused primarily on documenting and analysing rights-violating surveillance carried out by the state and corporations, we define surveillance as the systematic observation and monitoring of individuals, groups, places, or activities by public and private agencies with the rationale of maintaining social and political order.

Unequal power relationships are a core feature of all such surveillance practices. In all of the above definitions and examples of surveillance there exists a power relationship. The act of conducting surveillance furthers some interests often at the expense of others, and in doing so reflects, reproduces, and amplifies existing power inequities. The decision about which data to collect or ignore is already a political decision with potentially huge implications. Surveillance data is used for social sorting including determining who qualifies as a citizen with rights, who is entitled to government services, who is credit-worthy or a credit risk, and so forth. From this perspective, power analysis to isolate the particular interests that are advanced by specific applications of surveillance are a legitimate line of enquiry, as are the varying kinds of meaning-making and forms of resistance that accompany its spread. Surveillance practices have traditionally been conducted with the aim of influencing, managing, protecting, or directing human behaviour. Although surveillance also has positive and benign applications, it remains the case that surveillance is often used as a means of control and influence. As the chapters in this volume will show, surveillance has been used extensively by colonial and post-colonial governments in Africa. It has also been deployed by both democratic and authoritarian regimes, for managing social service provision, influencing beliefs and behaviours, maintaining law and order, and repressing peaceful opposition and critical voices.

## Digital surveillance

Digital surveillance makes possible new forms of power. Digital surveillance is the use of internet or mobile technologies to monitor, intercept, or exploit sensitive data, information, or communication. We use the concept of digital surveillance throughout this book for reasons of coherence despite being aware that other scholars use terms including electronic, online, or cyber-surveillance as well as dataveillance. There are strong continuities between pre-digital and digital surveillance but in this book we argue that digital surveillance makes possible qualitatively distinct forms of surveillance and new forms of power relationships. Lyon (2007) argues that 'digital devices only increase the capacities of surveillance or, sometimes, help to foster particular kinds of surveillance or help to alter its character'. This book documents how digital technologies are making possible new forms of mass surveillance, digital profiling, targeting, and manipulation of beliefs and behaviour that were previously beyond the scope of African governments. We also show how private companies and global corporations have become key surveillance actors. We argue that these changes are giving rise to new risks and impacts on citizens' rights, and that new forms of corporate and state power are emerging. Finally we ask how citizens agency is being affected and how it can best resist and overcome unjust and repressive impacts of surveillance.

Digitalization makes the automation of algorithmic surveillance possible. This in turn makes possible pervasive mass surveillance. Graham and Wood (2003) argue that analogue surveillance tended to be bureaucratic and electromechanical and that the digitalization of surveillance allows the displacement of human discretion and the relegation of operatives to the tasks of programming, supervising, and maintaining systems. Digitization of surveillance practices has brought significant quantitative (in terms of size, coverage, speed, and intensity) and qualitative transformations (claimed ability to infer a person's sexuality, menstrual cycle, susceptibility to influence, and trigger issues). Quantitively, the number of persons and the categories of information that it is possible to collect on each person (datapoints) has been exponentially extended.

The reach of digital surveillance continues to expand. The scope of digital surveillance is being continually extended in terms of storage capacity and data processing speeds as well as by automated and algorithmic surveillance (Introna and Wood 2004), amplifying the capabilities and power of those conducting surveillance (Norris and Armstrong 1999). This has allowed state surveillance agencies to 'do two things: (a) conduct mass surveillance of all citizens' digital communications, and (b) micro-target individual digital citizens for in-depth surveillance by drawing together in multiple data sets from mobile calls, email and messaging, global positioning system (GPS) location, and financial transactions' (Roberts et al. 2023). These transformations in the surveillance ecosystem 'represent a step change in the relationship between the state and those subject to its jurisdiction' (Murray et al. 2023: 2). They create numerous possibilities where the state has the capacity 'to monitor the minutiae of individuals' day-to-day lives, to generate patterns of life, to identify "unusual" or "suspicious" behaviour, and to make individually-focused decisions on this basis' (ibid.).

Digital surveillance makes citizens machine-readable to the state. Unlike analogue surveillance which was largely 'invisible and subtle', digital surveillance 'makes visible' citizen activities and preferences (Taylor 2017: 4). Digitalization means that it is possible to surveil multiple data formats including text, audio, video, likes, follows, location data, biometrics, and meta-data. Key to synthesizing this potentially bewildering array of datapoints is the digital format of all of the information set and the use of verifiable unique identifiers like a person's biometric digital-ID, SIM-card registration, and banking account details. Once surveillance agencies have these three core identifiers in place it is relatively easy to add other datasets (vehicle, medical, tax, social media, store cards, fitness trackers etc.) to build up rich data profiles using otherwise disparate means (Roberts et al. 2023).

Pervasive surveillance is eroding citizen rights and agency. In many cases, state surveillance and corporate surveillance are complementary in profiling citizens to micro-target them for commercial advertising and for identifying their political preferences, sexual identities, and psychological vulnerabilities. States and corporations may feel that they have a shared interest in combining state data (digital-ID, census, medical, education, driving licence, taxation records) with commercial data (social media, GPS location, fitness trackers, virtual assistants, store cards, SIM card, mobile money/banking data) to provide the potential for panoptic real-time surveillance of citizens. Munoriyarwa and Mare (2023) call this trend 'pervasive surveillance'. Dencik and Cable (2017) have written about 'surveillance realism': how this experience of ubiquitous surveillance is becoming normalized to the extent that many people cannot imagine the world being otherwise – eroding citizens' sense of the right to privacy.

Documenting the dimensions and drivers of digital surveillance in Africa is essential to protect digital rights. It is impossible to adequately develop appropriate policy responses without clarity about which companies, from which countries, are supplying which digital surveillance technologies to which African countries. A growing range of digital surveillance technologies are being sourced from companies and states in the Global North by government agencies across Africa. According to the CIPESA (2021) report, several African countries now deploy spyware, drones, and video surveillance (CCTV), as well as social media monitoring, mobile phone location tracking, and the hacking of mobile phones, messaging, and email applications.

## Gaps in African surveillance studies

Despite the emerging literature on digital surveillance in Southern Africa (Duncan 2018; 2022; Munoriyarwa and Mare 2023), there has been a geographical imbalance in the research to date. There have been relatively few studies of digital surveillance in other regions of Africa, and Africa is underrepresented in the literature when compared to other continents. Recent studies in Southern Africa have addressed the implications of surveillance law on citizens' rights, the introduction of public space surveillance, resistance strategies by those targeted by surveillance, and the use of policing technologies for surveillance (Murray and Mare 2020; Duncan 2018; Munoriyarwa and Mare 2023; Munoriyarwa and Chiumbu 2020). While these authors clearly document specific surveillance technologies in Southern Africa, there has been relatively little analysis in other regions of the continent (see, however, Spaces for Change in Nigeria (Ibezim-Ohaeri et al. 2021)). This edited volume will make a much-needed contribution to filling that gap by providing rich case studies and analysis from each of Africa's main geographical regions; however, further research is needed especially in francophone Africa and in the most authoritarian regimes which we were unable to include in this volume.

The size of the African market for surveillance technologies has not been documented until recently and we lacked clarity on who the main suppliers were in each sector. As Jili (2022) notes, 'both supply and demand factors contribute to the growing proliferation of surveillance tools'; however, there has been relatively little analysis to date of which companies are supplying which surveillance technologies to which actors in Africa. Surprisingly little is known about the dynamics or dimensions of the surveillance economy in Africa. This book builds on unique preliminary research carried out by members of the African Digital Rights Network, mapping the supply lines of surveillance technologies from companies in the Global North to governments across the African continent (Roberts et al. 2023). That research shows that most surveillance technologies are supplied to African governments by companies from the United States, China, Europe, and Israel.

Researching surveillance is challenging, partly because the export, import, and use of surveillance technology in Africa is shrouded in secrecy and lacking transparency (Duncan 2018). Although private companies supplying surveillance technologies from Europe are supposed to conduct human rights assessments prior to the conclusion of deals with African governments, this is often not done and these voluntary self-policing measures have failed to prevent the repeated violation of citizens' fundamental human rights (Roberts et al. 2023).

The African Digital Rights Network provides a valuable platform for African researchers. This is the first book to contain rich case studies by African authors from across the continent about digital surveillance in their own countries. By working with established and emerging African scholars from the countries that they are writing about they are able to use their deep contextual knowledge to produce situated interpretations of these rapid technological developments in light of specific cultural and political contexts. Each chapter begins with a section on the relevant political and economic history before presenting documentary information about the categories of surveillance technologies and the companies supplying them, and then conducting conceptual analysis through the lens of digital rights, power, and agency. This allows authors to analyse the drivers of state surveillance of citizens, identify which demographic groups are (dis)advantaged, and what interests are served.

This is the first book to analyse surveillance in Africa through the lens of digital rights, power, and agency. As editors we wanted to avoid being narrowly prescriptive in imposing specific conceptual framings on authors. The diverse background of authors, the wide variety of contexts across Africa, the distinct drivers and dynamics of surveillance practices, and the range of power interests that surveillance reflects and (re)produces mean that authors need latitude in selecting concepts that are relevant to their research question, case studies, and interests. At the same time, we wanted the book to have coherence, so we provided a range of concepts from which authors were free to draw and to build on. These are reviewed in the next section.

## Rights, power, and agency in surveillance studies

This book documents which surveillance technologies are being used to violate citizens' rights, but it does more than document the growing procurement of surveillance technologies by African governments. It also analyses the impact of expanding surveillance on human rights, examines what power interests are being served by surveillance of citizens, and asks what forms of citizen agency are needed to mitigate and overcome associated harms. To ground this framing in existing scholarship, the next three sections review the conceptual literature on rights, power, and agency.

### Rights and surveillance

All mass surveillance of citizens by states and corporations violates fundamental human rights. The Universal Declaration of Human Rights (United Nations 1948) outlines a set of foundational rights agreed in principle by all countries. Article 12 of the declaration states that no one shall be subjected to arbitrary interference of their privacy, family, home, or correspondence. Article 18 provides the right to freedom of opinion and Article 19 protects freedom of speech and expression. As the UN Special Rapporteur on freedom of expression concluded in his report (UNGA 2013), the rights to privacy and freedom of opinion and expression are indivisible because the right to privacy is instrumental in achieving the rights to freedom of association, freedom of opinion, and freedom of speech, which are central to free and open participation in democratic life and the conduct of business. All state surveillance violates the right to privacy and, while it may on occasion be necessary to violate the privacy of the most serious criminals, this should not be at the expense of other citizens' rights (Roberts et al. 2021). The rapid expansion of surveillance capabilities and practices has eroded the right to privacy (Friedewald et al. 2017; Jimoh 2023). In Southern Africa, digital surveillance practices and cultures have been shown to contribute significantly towards the erosion of right to privacy (Munoriyarwa and Mare 2023; Jili 2022).

## Power and surveillance

Surveillance is always an expression of power (Lyon 2007). It takes place across relationships of power difference including those of class, age, ethnicity, race, and gender. In doing so surveillance (re)creates power relationships between those that watch and those who are watched. Those who surveil often combine watching with other operations of power including categorizing and discrimination. Surveillance power is thus often employed to assign differential outcomes based on surveillance categorization such as who will be promoted, where to police, or who to target with disinformation. Thus, surveillance reflects, (re)produces, and amplifies power asymmetries between the surveiller and the surveilled. Surveillance practices can also stimulate counter-power if those subject to rights-violating surveillance resist through circumvention, legal challenges, and everyday forms of resistance. Power analysis of surveillance in Africa is under-developed in the existing literature (see, however, Duncan 2022; Munoriyarwa and Mare 2023). In this book, we argue that there is a need for research that goes beyond explaining how surveillance works, and what rights are affected, to apply a critical and conceptual lens to understand who benefits from surveillance in Africa and what power interests it serves.

Surveillance practices are employed to further specific power interests. Surveillance is expensive and must deliver commensurate benefits. Research on the supply lines of surveillance technologies has revealed that African governments are spending billions of dollars annually to conduct surveillance on their own citizens (Roberts et al. 2023). Surveillance is conducted to serve specific colonial, political, economic, military, gender, and ethnic power interests, but these have not always been analysed in the literature. The chapters in this book detail and analyse who benefits from the shrinking of civic space caused by pervasive surveillance. In seeking to answer these questions we argue that it is important to distinguish between the first-order and second-order effects of surveillance. From this perspective the first-order effects are the immediate outcomes, and the second-order effects are the downstream impacts caused by those outcomes. For example, repressive governments use surveillance to harass journalists and activists causing a 'chilling effect' that closes the civic space for democratic speech (first-order effect). If repressive governments are successful in silencing opposition, the second-order effect can be to enhance incumbent power and weaken opposition. Our intention in this book is both to document first-order effects and to analyse the second-order effects using the lens of digital rights, power interests, and citizen agency.

Power is an essentially contested concept (Lukes 1974) and a comprehensive review is beyond the scope of this chapter. However, in analysing how power operates in digital surveillance systems, one useful distinction is between approaches that view power as a structural resource that states wield over citizens, and alternative post-structuralist approaches that view power as more diffuse and relational, operating everywhere, and in all social relations (Hayward 1988). From this perspective, power is a capacity that all persons have in all situations (in varying forms and to varying degrees). Our review begins with the more structural approaches that emphasize the power of the state before moving on to more agency-based approaches.

**Panoptic power:** Michel Foucault is a foundational theorist in surveillance studies. His 1975 book *Surveiller et Punir*, translated into English as *Discipline and Punish* (1977) is about surveillance as a 'disciplinary mechanism' of control and punishment. Foucault examined historical modes of discipline in which subjection within social institutions such as prisons or hospitals resulted in the modification of citizens' behaviour. He argued that through such disciplinary mechanisms the need for external coercive power was partly replaced by citizens internalizing what was expected of them by those in power and modifying their behaviour in a form of self-discipline.

Foucault uses Jeremy Bentham's 'panopticon' prison as the model for modern disciplinary societies. The panopticon employs an invisible *surveillant* in an observation tower who has a panoptic view of all aspects of prisoners' life. As a result of knowing they can potentially be observed at any moment, Foucault argued that those subjected to the disciplinary mechanism of panoptic surveillance modify their own behaviour without further need of coercive power.

**Societies of control:** Giles Deleuze (1992) argued that Foucault's 'disciplinary society' is being increasingly superseded by what he terms 'societies of control'. Deleuze contrasts the bricks and mortar place-based disciplinary institutions (such as prisons, hospitals, schools) with the less tangible networked society in which digital mobile and internet technologies make possible pervasive systems of online surveillance. In this conception, the surveillance tower of the panopticon is replaced by the power to automate mass surveillance across all communication media and digital platforms. Prison walls are replaced by mobile and internet systems capable of tracking citizen movement, utterances, financial transactions, 'likes', and 'follows', placing them in a state of continual uncertainty about who is watching them and why (Lyon 2007). These 'societies of control' are mediated by what Shoshana Zuboff (2018) calls 'surveillance capitalism', whereby digital companies track and monitor citizens' real time digital footprints of users using analytic systems and cookies.

**Surveillance state:** The conceptions of panoptic power in Foucault often underpin studies of the 'surveillance state'. The Snowden revelations lifted the veil on mass surveillance by the United States and United Kingdom governments on a scale that Giroux (2014) points out was unthinkable to previous generations even in dystopian fiction like Orwell's classic *1984*. Giroux (2014) has argued that it is important to go beyond identifying and documenting structural power abuse to analyse why the modern surveillance state has flourished and how to overcome it. This book will continue the work of documenting state surveillance across Africa but aims to go beyond descriptive accounts to analyse what power interests give rise to the current expansion of digital surveillance and what forms of collective power can overcome it. We do so in the belief that studying why and under what conditions powerholders conduct rights-violating surveillance, and why, and under what condition citizens acquiesce or resist surveillance, is central to informing future action to mitigate and overcome the abuse of surveillance powers.

**Power interests:** It is common to talk of governments pursuing their power interests without specifying whether those interests are, for example, economic, political, gender, or racial power interests. Analysis is complicated by the fact that holders of political power have other kinds of power interests. The notion of intersectionality as elaborated in Crenshaw's (1989) seminal text highlights the complex intersection of (dis)advantage along dimensions including gender, race, class/caste, and sexuality. In their power analysis some scholars use one form of power as their primary lens to provide in-depth understanding about that specific power interest. Other scholars choose as their analytic focus the intersection of two or more dimensions of power (hooks 1997; 2000) reminding us that power systems are often interlocking systems, and that analysis therefore also needs to be intersectional (Davis 1981; Hill Collins 1990).

**Digital colonialism:** Some scholars have found digital colonialism (or data colonialism) to be a useful lens for analysing the interests served by multinational platform companies (Pinto 2018; Kwet 2019; Couldry and Mejias 2019). This perspective sees the extraction of data from Africa to serve the interests of foreign capital as an analogue of previous forms of colonialism that extracted slaves or minerals. Kwet (2019) argues the extraction of data from the Global South to the United States 'violates the sanctity of privacy and concentrates economic power into the hands of US corporations – a system of global surveillance capitalism'. He points out that Global North intelligence agencies partner with their private corporations to conduct mass and targeted surveillance in the Global South, intensifying imperial state surveillance. Abeba Birhane (2020) has written about the 'Algorithmic Colonisation of Africa', the process by which digital surveillance remotely and automatically extracts value across power divides. She argues (ibid.: 391) that whereas the historical colonization of Africa involved the violent extraction of humans and mineral to benefit foreign powers, 'In the age of algorithms, this control and domination occurs not through brute physical force but rather through invisible and nuanced mechanisms such as control of digital ecosystems and infrastructure'.

These structuralist conceptions of power are extremely useful for analysing how power operates in states and through military and corporate institutions. However, they often fail to account for everyday forms of resistance and the novel ways in which the targets of surveillance express their agency to exercise and defend their rights, such as Mann et al's (2003) concept of sousveillance in which citizens turn the tables and monitor police and state actors. To analyse citizen action to resist surveillance and to think through how to build the necessary counterpower to challenge, disrupt, or overcome state surveillance, it may prove useful to also employ more agency-based conceptions of power including those reviewed below.

## Agency in resisting surveillance

Concepts of power and agency are inherently linked. Agency is a person's ability to act in pursuit of their goals (Sen 1999). A person's ability to act is always constrained by social structures including laws and regulations, social norms and values, and by institutional disciplinary mechanisms. A person's agency is shaped by power relations of gender, ethnicity, class, and by their relation to the means of production, policymaking, and institutions of social control. Agency can change over time and is contextual and relational, meaning that a person's ability to act may be different in different settings and at different points in their life. Some theories define empowerment as increases in agency by individuals or groups that have previously lacked that agency (Alkire 2008; Kabeer 1999). In this dynamic view of agency, a person has different degrees of agency at different times and in different aspects of their life. Even the prisoner in solitary confinement has agency about how to react: whether to acquiesce or resist (Sartre 1943).

**Powercube:** Gaventa (2006; 2019) provides the 'powercube' as a model for conducting a three-dimensional analysis of the levels, spaces, and forms of power operating in any setting. In this model, visible power refers to the known and public rules and processes, whereas hidden power refers to the back-room form of power that operates out-of-view and which often determines who gets a seat at the table and what issues make it onto the agenda for public discussion (Batliwala 2019). Invisible power is the most insidious form of power and refers to the effect of dominant norms being internalized in ways that limit what people feel free to say and do (VeneKlasen and Miller 2002). Hidden and invisible power may be useful concepts in analysing how algorithmic surveillance is hidden from view and how pervasive surveillance creates a chilling effect, leading to citizens feeling unfree to speak out on important issues in a form of self-censorship. The normalization of pervasive surveillance and aquiescence had led to some scholars talking about 'surveillance realism' (Dencik and Cable 2017). In his more recent work Gaventa (2019) has cautioned against viewing any space as characterized exclusively by one form of power, and has also recommended dynamically combining the forms, spaces and levels of power in the powercube (Figure 1.1).

**Affordances:** Not a concept of power per se, affordances are nonetheless useful for analysing what is qualitatively distinct about digital surveillance when compared to preceding forms of analogue and manual surveillance. Affordances are the new action possibilities that a novel technology enables, invites, or facilitates (Gibson 1977; Norman 1988). Internet messaging *affords* citizens the new action possibility of sharing text, voice, and video with any number of recipients, globally, instantly, repeatedly at negligible marginal cost. Affordances make new actions possible, but they do not determine them (Hutchby 2001); users can appropriate and adapt technologies in creative ways. Technologies have interpretive flexibility (Feenburg 2002) allowing them to be appropriated for purposes not envisaged by the designer. Surveillance cameras are deployed by law enforcement, but they can also be used by activists to capture footage of police violence in forms of 'sousveillance' (underseeing),

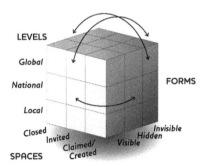

**Figure 1.1** Gaventa's three-dimensional powercube.
Source: Gaventa (2006).

as a form of citizen power to resist police abuse of power (Mann et al. 2003). The concept of affordances helps us to answer the question of what is 'digital' about digital surveillance: what qualitative difference exists between 'traditional' telephone 'wiretap' surveillance when compared to automated mass surveillance using artificial intelligence.

## What issues do the chapters address?

The chapters in this book provide a range of rich case studies to underpin future analysis of digital surveillance in Africa. Each chapter addresses its own research question about that country's experience of digital surveillance. Authors begin by locating their research within the country's specific political history and surveillance landscape, documenting which companies, from which countries, are supplying which kinds of digital surveillance technologies to the government. The chapter authors then use a variety of conceptual frames to analyse the implication of digital surveillance for digital rights, power relations, and citizen agency. This book takes a critical historical approach that not only maps and provides typologies of surveillance technologies but also analyses how they are deployed to serve specific power interests. Each chapter also comments on existing forms citizen agency used to evade, challenge, and resist state and corporate surveillance practices and asks, given the unique context of each country, what strategies hold promise for overcoming or abolishing rights-violating surveillance of citizens.

In Chapter 2, Gifty Appiah-Adjei and Oyewole Adekunle Oladapo focus on incidents of rights-violating surveillance in Ghana. The chapter contains powerful illustrations of the lived experience of citizens who have been personally targeted by state actors using digital surveillance to disrupt their journalism and defend the power interests of the incumbent government. Their chapter identifies the main actors, human rights impacts, and motivations for the growing use of digital surveillance in Ghana. The authors assess how surveillance has affected the lives of those targeted by police and security agencies and asks: how can the rights-violating surveillance of citizens be mitigated and overcome? Through interviews with purposively selected journalists, digital rights activists, and top officials in the main opposition party, Appiah-Adjei and Oladapo used Gaventa's powercube to investigate the forms, spaces, and levels through which power operates to provide concrete recommendations to end rights-violating digital surveillance of citizens.

In Chapter 3, Afef Abrougui shifts the gaze towards North Africa and discusses digital surveillance practices in Egypt. Since the Arab Spring revolution in 2011, the return to authoritarianism has taken a digital turn, with the government making large investments in surveillance technologies to intercept mobile and internet communications, monitor social media, and roll-out a huge expansion of closed-circuit surveillance of public spaces in 'smart city' projects. Abrougui documents this new digital surveillance landscape and analyses the first-order impact on closing civic space and digital rights but also the second-order impacts limiting the power of civil society and entrenching the power of incumbent governments. The chapter illustrates how digital surveillance technologies have helped the military regime of Sisi to intensify his crackdown on critics, freedom of expression, media freedoms, and the rights to privacy, protest, and assembly through coordinated state surveillance.

In Chapter 4, Sam Phiri and Kiss Abraham interrogate the relationship between state surveillance and digital rights in Zambia. The authors trace the origins of state surveillance from the colonial era to the present post-colonial state where political power is in the hands of Zambians. They argue that, although the hands of the levers of political power may have changed over the past seventy-five years, and surveillance technologies have evolved and expanded, the motivation and final outcome of surveillance remains retention of power by those in control. Phiri and Abraham show how post-independence regimes in Zambia have used state surveillance to spy on their own citizens and repress people's agency, which has negatively impacted their fundamental human rights.

In Chapter 5, Jimmy Kainja analyses changes and continuities in state surveillance in Malawi. His chapter shows that instead of ruptures with the colonial architecture of state surveillance, post-colonial Malawi has witnessed continuity of the application of surveillance to serve incumbent power. Although surveillance continues to serve political objectives, new technologies have recently turbo-charged the state surveillance capabilities. Kainja shows that the Malawian government has implemented mandatory mobile phone

SIM card registration and biometric national digital-ID, and established a national data centre. Although these programmes have been welcomed by some sectors of society, they have also raised concerns in civil society about the implications for human rights in Malawi. Drawing on Michel Foucault's panopticon theory, Kainja argues that growing state surveillance has created chilling effects and self-disciplinary censorship, and the shrinking of civic space.

In Chapter 6, Judy Gitahi and Muthuri Kathure explore digital surveillance practices and cultures in Kenya. Their chapter demonstrates that in Kenya there has been rapid acquisition of surveillance technologies by different state and non-state actors with no clear justification for their use and without adequate legal and regulatory frameworks. The introduction of the national biometric digital-ID system is a focal case: the *Huduma* Namba system provides a unique digital-ID to every citizen along with the promise of easing access to government services and entitlements. However, in the absence of an adequate legal framework, it also provides the potential for panoptic surveillance if linked to citizens' mobile and banking activities. The rapid acquisition of mass surveillance potential without judicial oversight or accountability mechanisms has prompted resistance from citizens and civil society actors. Using the Foucauldian concept of panoptic power, Gitahi and Kathure provide a fascinating case study of how power is being contested in Kenya's rapidly expanding digital spaces.

In Chapter 7, Nana Nwachukwu describes the contours of the Nigerian digital surveillance landscape which at $2.7 billion is the largest documented digital surveillance market in Africa. The chapter scrutinizes the impact of this trade on citizens' rights and agency, and analyses the power interests that give rise to and sustain the proliferation of rights-violating digital surveillance. The chapter addresses several compelling questions: what forces drive the expansion of digital surveillance; how can legitimate surveillance and digital rights be reconciled, and how can citizens' agency and civil society organizations keep the power of the state in check? The chapter shows that digital surveillance practices that were institutionalized in Nigeria during the colonial era were retained by post-colonial governments before being expanded and digitalized. The author argues that digital surveillance must be warranted and be subject to independent oversight to ensure that state responsibility for national security can be balanced with constitutional guarantees to protect fundamental human rights.

In Chapter 8, Anand Sheombar and Sebastian Klovig Skelton analyse which companies, from which countries, are supplying which surveillance technologies to African governments. This concluding chapter is significantly different from the chapters that precede it. It focuses on the supply side of the equation rather than on the demand side: on the companies and countries supplying digital surveillance technologies to African governments. The chapter provides an overview of the distinct specializations of each of the main supplier countries in Europe, the United States, China, and Israel, and analyses the forces shaping this multi-billion-dollar market. The authors use the powercube to think through the political, economic, and diplomatic interests driving the market in digital surveillance technologies and use this analysis to identify key leverage points for resistance to disrupt and end this pernicious trade.

# Conclusion

This book provides the most extensive documentation and analysis to date of digital surveillance practices across Africa's main geographical regions. It reveals a multi-billion-dollar trade in digital technologies to intercept citizens' internet messaging and mobile phone and social media communication, as well as the use of facial recognition surveillance of public spaces and the risks attending biometric digital-ID systems. These digital technologies make possible (but do not determine) mass surveillance and the targeting of journalists and peaceful activists. The case studies in this book illustrate how digital technologies reflect, (re)produce and amplify existing geographic, economic, and political power imbalances. The authors show how the supply lines of surveillance technologies echo patterns of colonial power relations and emanate predominantly from the world's top arms-exporting countries. The power relations of surveillance are not determined by the affordances of new digital technologies but more accurately reflect the power relations of coloniality, capitalism, and the desire to retain political power by repressing the ability of opposition groups to organize and hold power to account. Although it is possible to see old colonial relationships mirrored in the supply-line of digital surveillance technologies, this interpretation is strongly challenged by the entry of Chinese, Israeli, and US companies into this market. China's provision of facial recognition CCTV as part of the 'safe city' surveillance and Israel's mobile spyware are two cases in point.

Reading across the country case studies, it appears to be the case that the political openings of the millennial decades have been eclipsed in many countries by declining political freedoms, closing civic space, and a descent into digital authoritarianism. However, the surveillance landscape of each country is distinct. The country case studies illustrate how diverse post-colonial political settlements and the distinctive practices of African political institutions mean that digital surveillance in Africa has both important continuities and discontinuities with colonial surveillance practices, making it impossible to analyse African surveillance realities adequately without taking these situated realities into account.

The authors argue that surveillance is always an expression of power in the pursuit of specific interests but that the unique features of each country mean that the impact of state surveillance is playing out differently across the continent and that the practical options available in each country to disrupt, challenge, and overcome surveillance injustice are different in each country. To enable a situated analysis of surveillance we recommend the following critical approach to surveillance studies in Africa.

## Critical surveillance studies in Africa

To date research on most of Africa's regions has been underrepresented in the existing surveillance studies literature. It is not uncommon for reviews of the surveillance literature to contain few if any examples from Africa (Allmer 2011). Existing analysis has been based overwhelmingly on Western studies, Western theory, and researchers from the Global North and is applied primarily in contexts of Western industrial and post-industrial capitalism. It would not therefore be legitimate or productive to impose it on African authors studying digital surveillance in Africa. Our own research to date does not go nearly far enough in addressing these gaps, omitting as it does Francophone and Lusophone countries, many of the most authoritarian countries, and many of the largest economies in Africa. Much more work needs to be done to develop African theories of surveillance. Providing these case studies is only one small step on that journey.

However, it is important to deepen as well as widen surveillance studies in Africa. Understandably much of the initial research has been descriptive and documentary, but we want to conclude with some modest and tentative proposals for a more critical approach to surveillance studies in Africa – an open proposal on which others can build. In doing so we borrow in part from Kuo and Marwick's (2021) 'critical disinformation studies' framework, that we developed in the previous book in this series *Digital Disinformation in Africa* (Roberts and Karekwaivanane 2024).

As we have tried to in this book, we encourage African researchers of surveillance to first ground their empirical studies in African post-colonial history and to situate their analysis in local political, economic, and cultural relationships. We encourage researchers to be attentive to the continuities and discontinuities between analogue and digital surveillance practices. We argue that any comprehensive analysis of digital surveillance needs to include but also go beyond documentation of the immediate 'first-order effects' of surveillance such as impacts on rights and civic space and also capture the 'second-order effects' on power relationships domestically and internationally. For this reason, we argue that any comprehensive analysis of digital surveillance in Africa should also ask who benefits and what power interests are served by expanding digital surveillance. Finally, we argue that critical surveillance studies should take a normative position against rights-violation, in favour of social justice, and for that reason our research should provide practical guidance for action to mitigate and overcome rights-violating surveillance.

Put otherwise, we argue that African critical surveillance studies should distinguish itself in six ways:

1. **Context.** It should begin by grounding each study in the local historical, political, economic, and cultural context to make evident the contextual factors driving surveillance practices.
2. **Affordances.** It should analyse the affordances provided by specific technologies and surveillance practice without succumbing to

technological determinism. The above grounding in political economy should mitigate against this fallacy.

3. **Power.** Analysis of surveillance practices should consider who is (dis)advantaged including along lines of coloniality, race and ethnicity, gender, age, class, and sexuality.

4. **Interests.** Analysis of surveillance practices asks what power interests are being served: political, economic, ecological, social, technological, cultural, and organizational.

5. **Justice.** Research should have clear normative commitments to rights, equity, and social justice.

6. **Action.** Research should provide practical recommendations that can guide concrete action to mitigate and overcome rights-violating surveillance practices.

# Bibliography

Alkire, S. (2008). *Concepts and Measures of Agency*, Working Paper 9. Oxford: OHPI.

Allmer, P. (2011). *Critical Surveillance Studies in the Information Society.* https://www.researchgate.net/publication/277032378_Critical_Surveillance_Studies_in_the_Information_Society (accessed 7 February 2023).

Allmer, P. (2012). *Towards a Critical Theory of Surveillance in Informational Capitalism*, Frankfurt: Peter Lang.

Amnesty International (2021). *Forensic Methodology Report: How to Catch NSO Group's Pegasus*, London: Amnesty International Forensic Laboratory.

Batliwala, S. (2019). *All About Power: Understanding Social Power and Power Structures, CREA.* https://reconference.creaworld.org/wp-content/uploads/2019/05/All-About-Power-Srilatha-Batliwala.pdf

Birhane, A. (2020). 'The Algorithmic Colonisation of Africa', *Scripted*, 17(2). https://script-ed.org/article/algorithmic-colonization-of-africa/

Breckenbridge, K. (2019). *Biometric State: The Global Politics of Identification and Surveillance in South Africa, 1850 to the Present*, New York: Cambridge University Press.

Browne, S. (2015). *Dark Matters: On the Surveillance of Blackness*, Durham, NC and London: Duke University Press.

CIPESA (2021). *State of Internet Freedom in Africa 2021: Effects of State Surveillance on Democratic Participation in Africa, Kampala.* Collaboration on International ICT Policy for East and Southern Africa.

Couldry, N. and Mejias, U. (2019). 'Data Colonialism: Rethinking Big Data's Relation to the Contemporary Subject', *Television and New Media*, 20(4). https://journals. sagepub.com/doi/abs/10.1177/1527476418796632?journalCode=tvna

Crenshaw, K. (1989). 'Demarginalizing the Intersection of Race and Sex: A Black Feminist Critique of Antidiscrimination Doctrine', *University of Chicago Legal Forum*, 140: 139–67.

Dandeker, C. (1990). *Surveillance, Power and Modernity*, New York: St Martin's Press.

Davis, A. (1981). *Women, Race and Class*, New York: Random House.

Deleuze, G. (1992). 'Postscript on the Societies of Control', *October*, 59: 3–7.

Dencik, L. and Cable, J. (2017). 'The Advent of Surveillance Realism: Public Opinion and Activist Responses to the Snowden Leaks', *International Journal of Communication*, 11: 763–81.

Duncan, J. (2018). *Stopping the Spies: Constructing and Resisting the Surveillance State in South Africa*, Johannesburg: Wits University Press.

Duncan, J. (2022). *National Security Surveillance in Southern Africa: An Anti-Capitalist Perspective*, London: Zed Books.

EFF (2014). 'Necessary and Proportionate: Principles on the Application of Human Rights Law to Communications Surveillance', Electronic Frontier Foundation. https://necessaryandproportionate.org/principles/ (accessed 9 March 2023).

Ekdale, B. and Tully, M. (2020). 'African Elections as a Testing Ground: Comparing Coverage of Cambridge Analytica in Nigerian and Kenyan Newspapers', *Journal of African Journalism Studies*, 40(4): 27–43.

Feenburg, A. (2002). *Transforming Technology: A Critical Theory Revisited*, Oxford: Oxford University Press.

Foucault, M. (1977). *Discipline and Punish: The Birth of the Prison*, New York: Vintage Books.

Friedewald, M., Burgess, J. P., Cas, J., Bellanova, R., and Peissl, W. (eds). (2017). *Surveillance, Privacy and Security: Citizens' Perspectives*, New York: Routledge.

Gaventa, J. (2006). 'Finding the Spaces for Change: A Power Analysis', in R. Eyben, C. Harris and J. Pettit (eds), *Exploring Power for Change, IDS Bulletin*, 37(6): 23–33.

Gaventa, J. (2019). 'Using the Powercube to Explore Forms, Levels and Spaces', in R. McGee and J. Petit (eds), *Power, Empowerment and Social Change*, 117–38, London: Routledge.

Gibson, J. (1977). 'The Theory of Affordances', in R. Shaw and J. Bransford (eds), *Perceiving, Acting, and Knowing*, 127–37, London: Oxford University Press.

Giddens, A. (1995). *A Contemporary Critique of Historical Materialism*, Stanford, CA: Stanford University Press.

Giroux, H. (2014). 'Totalitarian Paranoia in the Post-Orwellian Surveillance State', *Cultural Studies*, 29(2): 108–40. https://www.tandfonline.com/doi/full/10.1080/09 502386.2014.917118 (accessed 4 April 2023).

Graham, S. and Wood, D. M. (2003). 'Digitizing Surveillance: Categorization, Space, Inequality', *Acoustics, Speech, and Signal Processing Newsletter, IEEE* 23(2): 227–48. https://doi.org/10.1177/0261018303023002006 (accessed 2 June 2023).

Hayward, C. (1988). 'De-facing Power', *Polity*, 31(1): 1–22.

Hill Collins, P. (1990). *Black Feminist Thought: Knowledge, Consciousness, and the Politics of Empowerment*, Boston, MA: Unwin Hyman.

hooks, b. (1997). 'Culture, Criticism and Transformation, Media Education Foundation'. Transcript. https://www.mediaed.org/transcripts/Bell-Hooks-Transcript.pdf (accessed 23 August 2023).

hooks, b. (2000). *Feminist Theory: From Margin to Centre*, London: Pluto Press.

Hutchby, I. (2001). 'Technologies, Texts and Affordances', *Sociology*, 35(2): 441–56.

Ibezim-Ohaeri, V., Olufemi, J., Nwodo, L., Olufemi, O., Juba-Nwosu, N., and TIERS (2021). *Security Playbook of Digital Authoritarianism in Nigeria*, Lagos: Action Group on Free Civic Space. https://closingspaces.org/the-security-playbook-of-digital-authoritarianism-in-nigeria/ (accessed 28 December 2023).

Introna, L. D. and Wood, D. (2004). 'Picturing Algorithmic Surveillance: The Politics of Facial Recognition Systems', *Surveillance & Society*, 2(2/3): 177–98.

Jili, B. (2022). 'Africa: Regulate Surveillance Technologies and Personal Data', *Nature*, 607(7919): 445–8. https://doi.org/10.1038/d41586-022-01949-9

Jimoh, M. (2023). 'The Place of Digital Surveillance under the African Charter on Human and Peoples' Rights and the African Human Rights System in the Era of Technology', *African Journal of Legal Issues in Technology & Innovation*, 1: 113–30.

Kabeer, N. (1999). 'Resources, Agency, Achievements: Reflections on the Measurement of Women's Empowerment', *Development and Change*, 30(3): 435–64.

Kuo, R., and Marwick, A. (2021). 'Critical Disinformation Studies: History, Power, and Politics'. Harvard Kennedy School (HKS). *Misinformation Review*, https://misinforeview.hks.harvard.edu/article/critical-disinformation-studies-history-power-and-politics

Kwet, M. (2019). 'Digital Colonialism: US Empire and the New Imperialism in the Global South', *Race & Class*, 60(4): 3–26.

Kwet, M. (2023). 'Surveillance in South Africa: From Skin Branding to Digital Colonialism', in J. Vagle and M. Kwet (eds), *The Cambridge Handbook of Race and Surveillance*, Cambridge: Cambridge University Press.

Landau, S. (2010). *Surveillance or Security: The Risks Posed by New Wiretapping Technologies*, Cambridge, MA: MIT Press.

Lukes, S. (1974). *Power: A Radical View*, London: Bloomsbury.

Lyon, D. (2007). *Surveillance Studies: An Overview*, Oxford: Polity Press.

Mann, S., Jason, N. and Wellman, B. (2003). 'Sousveillance: Inventing and Using Wearable Computing Devices for Data Collection in Surveillance Environments', *Surveillance & Society*, 1(3): 331–55.

Munoriyarwa, A. and Chiumbu, S. H. (2020). 'Big Brother Is Watching: Surveillance Regulation and Its Effects on Journalistic Practices in Zimbabwe' (Special issue: Practices, Policies and Regulation in African Journalism), *Ecquid Novi African Journalism Studies*, 1(1): 1–17. https://doi.org/10.1080/23743670.2020.1729831

Munoriyarwa, A. and Mare, A. (2023). *Digital Surveillance in Southern Africa*, London: Palgrave Macmillan. https://doi.org/10.1007/978-3-031-16636-5_1

Murray, D., Fussey, P., Hove, K., Wakabi, W., Kimumwe, P., Saki, O. and Stevens, A. (2023). 'The Chilling Effects of Surveillance and Human Rights: Insights from Qualitative Research in Uganda and Zimbabwe', *Journal of Human Rights Practice*, 16(1): 397–412. https://doi.org/10.1093/jhuman/huad020

Murray, H. and Mare, A. (2020). *A Patchwork for Privacy: Mapping Communications Surveillance Laws in Southern Africa*. A Report for the Media Policy and Democracy Project. https://www.mediaanddemocracy.com/uploads/1/6/5/7/16577624/patchwork_for_privacy_-_communication_surveillance_in_southern_africa.pdf (accessed 1 March 2024).

Norman, D. (1988). *The Design of Everyday Things*, New York: Basic Books.

Norris, C. and Armstrong, G. (1999). *The Maximum Surveillance Society: The Rise of CCTV*, Oxford: Berg.

Nyabola, N. (2018). *Digital Democracy, Analogue Politics: How the Internet Era Is Transforming Politics in Kenya*, London: Zed Books.

Pinto, R. A. (2018). 'Digital Sovereignty or Digital Colonialism: New Tensions of Privacy, Security and National Policies', *Sur*, 15(27): 15–27.

Rid, T. (2020). *Active Measures: The Secret History of Disinformation and Political Warfare*, London: Macmillan.

Roberts, T., Mohamed Ali, A., Farahat, M., Oloyede, R. and Mutung'u, G. (2021). *Surveillance Law in Africa: A Review of Six Countries*, Brighton: Institute of Development Studies. https://opendocs.ids.ac.uk/opendocs/handle/20.500.12413/16893 (accessed 22 February 2024).

Roberts, T. and Karekwaivanane, G. (2024). *Digital Disinformation in Africa: Hashtag Politics, Power and Propaganda*, London: Zed Books. https://www.bloomsburycollections.com/monograph-detail?docid=b-9781350319240&pdfid=9781350319240.0015.pdf&tocid=b-9781350319240-chapter9 (accessed 2 May 2024).

Roberts, T., Gitahi, J., Allam, P., Oboh, L. Oladapo, O., Appiah-Adjei, G., Galal, A., Kainja, J., Phiri, S., Abraham, K., Klovig Skelton, S. and Sheombar, A. (2023). *Mapping the Supply of Surveillance Technologies to Africa: Case*

*Studies from Nigeria, Ghana, Morocco, Malawi, and Zambia*, Brighton:
     Institute of Development Studies. https://opendocs.ids.ac.uk/opendocs/
     handle/20.500.12413/18120 (accessed 3 March 2024).

Sartre, J.-P. (1943). *Being and Nothingness*, London: Routledge.

Sen, A. (1999). *Development as Freedom*, Oxford: Oxford University Press.

Snowden Archive (2019). *Snowden Digital Surveillance Archive*, Toronto: York
     University.

Srnicek, N. (2017). *Platform Capitalism*, London: Polity.

Taylor, L. (2017). 'What Is Data Justice? The Case for Connecting Digital
     Rights and Freedoms Globally', *Big Data & Society*, 4(2). https://doi.
     org/10.1177/2053951717736335

United Nations (1948). *Universal Declaration of Human Rights*, New York: United
     Nations. https://www.un.org/en/about-us/universal-declaration-of-human-rights
     (accessed 2 November 2023).

UNGA (2013). *Promotion and Protection of the Right to Freedom of Opinion and
     Expression*, New York: United Nations General Assembly. https://documents-dds-
     ny.un.org/doc/UNDOC/GEN/N13/464/76/PDF/N1346476.pdf?OpenElement
     (accessed 12 October 2023).

VeneKlasen, L. and Miller, V. (2002). *A New Weave of Power, People and Politics*,
     Oklahoma: World Neighbours.

Wilson, R. and Adams, I. (2015). *Special Branch: A History 1883–2006*, London:
     BiteBack Publishing.

Woodman, C. (2018). 'Spycops in Context: A Brief History of Political Policing in
     Britain'. CCJS_SpecBrief1_4Dec18.qxp (crimeandjustice.org.uk) (accessed 12
     December 2023).

Yingi, E. and Benyera, E. (2024). 'The Future of Democracy in the Digital Era:
     Internet Shutdowns, Cyber Laws and Online Surveillance in Zimbabwe',
     *Alternatives: Global, Local, Political*. https://doi.org/10.1177/03043754241259878

Zuboff, S. (2018). *The Age of Surveillance Capitalism: The Fight for a Human Future at
     the New Frontier of Power*, London: Profile Books.

Zuboff, S. (2022). 'Surveillance Capitalism or Democracy? The Death Match
     of Institutional Orders and the Politics of Knowledge in Our Information
     Civilization', *Organization Theory*, 3: 1–79.

# 2

# Power, resistance, and the experience of digital surveillance in Ghana

Gifty Appiah-Adjei and Oyewole Adekunle Oladapo

## Introduction

Under Ghana's Fourth Republic (1993–present), governments have invested at least $184 million in digital surveillance technologies from China, Greece, Israel, Taiwan, Switzerland, and the United Kingdom (Oladapo and Appiah-Adjei, in Roberts et al. 2023). This chapter focuses on the implications for citizens' rights of the rapid expansion of digital surveillance in Ghana and explores the forms of civic agency being used to resist state use of rights-violating surveillance and the contestation of power in digital spaces. The chapter considers the surveillance experiences of victims targeted by government investments in surveillance technologies and the enactment of statutes that support and expand government's surveillance power. Specifically, it examines power and resistance in the context of rights-violating digital surveillance.

Through interviews with purposively selected journalists and human right activists, data was gathered and analysed through the lens of a powercube framework to answer the following questions: What are the experiences of victims of rights-violating digital surveillance in Ghana? Who are the architects behind the acts of surveillance and what are their motivations? What strategies do victims adopt to cope with rights-violating digital surveillance?

This chapter begins with the historical experience of surveillance to provide the context for the description of Ghana's current digital surveillance landscape. After a review of the existing literature, we present our framework for analysing the case study and answering our research questions. We use

Gaventa's powercube model to analyse how government surveillance power affects citizens' rights and the experiences of victims and their agency in resisting rights-violating surveillance.

## Historical context of surveillance in Ghana

Surveillance in Ghana can be traced to the Gold Coast era (1482–1957) when the colonial government felt a need to reorganize the internal security following widespread pre-independence riots in February 1948. Surveillance is one of the trade-offs from the riots that was used to gather intelligence to stall and avoid repetition of the riots (Eshun 2022). After the riots, the need to augment the security duties of the Gold Coast Police Force (GCPF) and Gold Coast Regiment (GCR) became apparent. Hence, from February 1948 to 1957, intelligence-gathering agencies such as the Special Branch (SB), Reserve Unit, Wireless and Communications Unit, and Central Security Committee were set up to acquire the needed intelligence to circumvent any possibility of riots (ibid.).

Upon independence, surveillance of citizens continued. Kwame Nkrumah retained and reformed these security agencies into the Ghana Police Service, the Ghana Armed Forces, and National Security (consisting of Criminal Investigation Department (CID), SB, Military Intelligence Unit (MIU), Foreign Service Research Bureau and an African Affairs Secretariat). Following the assassination attempts on Nkrumah, he established several security and intelligence agencies that ran parallel to the existing National Security and 'were tasked to undertake intelligence work and … report directly to the President' (Eshun 2022: 18) to control dissidents.

Upon the overthrow of Nkrumah in 1966, the military government abolished, dissolved, and reorganized existing security and intelligence agencies. For example, Foreign Service Research Bureau (FSRB) was renamed the Research Bureau (RB) and its personnel were reshuffled and assigned to gather foreign intelligence to protect the regime from Nkrumah's allies abroad. With assistance from Western intelligence agencies, the Special Executive for Counter Espionage (SECE) was set up to mount surveillance 'across the African continent to counter threats posed by Nkrumah loyalists based in other African countries' (Eshun 2022: 18). Various democratic and military governments from 1969 to 1981 maintained these fundamental structures of the national security architecture despite changes made to the top of the echelon of almost all the national security agencies. The SECE was disbanded (Eshun 2022).

The Provisional National Defence Council (PNDC) military era (1981–93) came with a significant transformation of the architecture of national security under the leadership of President Rawlings (1981–92) – the National Security apparatus was dissolved and rebuilt completely. Aside from disbanding MIU, dismantling SB, and reshuffling CID, the Defence Intelligence (DI) and Bureau for National Investigations (BNI) were created. A Special Services Division (SSD) was also created to handle all national intelligence and security-related matters. Through physical surveillance and infiltration, this military regime extended its surveillance tentacles to every part of Ghana by decentralizing National Security activities to regions, district capitals, and local levels (Eshun 2022). These offices inductively gathered and forwarded intelligence to the National Security Secretariat for assessment and, later, on deductive dissemination of feedback for necessary actions. The PNDC era is known as the era of the culture of silence because surveillance and the abuse of human rights with impunity were pervasive, due to intelligence gathered on journalists, citizens, and Civil Society Organisations (CSOs) (Temin and Smith 2002).

The preceding paragraphs show that systems of state surveillance were employed during the colonial, post-colonial, and military regimes to monitor citizens. Physical and social surveillance systems were retained after independence and were regularly revised and restructured to mount surveillance to suppress dissidents' voices and perceived political opponents. Though pre-digital governments used surveillance to fight crime and maintain order, they also used it to serve and protect their political interests and to retain power.

## Ghana's digital surveillance landscape

Ghana's 1992 Constitution guarantees privacy of communication and correspondence as a fundamental human right in Article 18 Clause 2, but this right is subjected to exceptions 'as may be necessary in a free and democratic society' (Republic of Ghana 1992: 22). The Constitution permits and justifies limitations on privacy rights to protect the health, morals, freedoms, and rights of others and to prevent disorder and crime when necessary. However, qualifying the provision with 'as may be necessary in a free and democratic society' creates a poorly defined legal framework that allows illegal surveillance of citizens (Roberts et al. 2021). This broadens the scope of and allows government to enact laws and policies that impact citizens' privacy and facilitate illegal surveillance.

The preceding has severe implications for free expression in Ghana. The 2021 Summary Report on Mapping and Analysis of Privacy Laws and Policies in Africa indicates that rights to anonymous communication and without fear cannot be guaranteed without effective protection of privacy rights (CIPESA 2021). This may account for recent retrogression of Ghana's rankings on the Rule of Law and Press Freedom indices (Freedom House 2022). As national security concerns grow, countries expand their security architecture to include state-of-the-art technologies. African countries have been found to exploit bilateral and multilateral relationships with the Chinese, some European and American governments, and surveillance technology suppliers located in China and Israel to acquire digital surveillance technologies (Roberts et al. 2023). Ghana has recently acquired digital surveillance technology capabilities that could be exploited for perpetrating rights-violating surveillance of citizens. In our previous study we analysed five types of digital surveillance technologies: internet interception, mobile interception, social media monitoring, safe city public space surveillance, and biometric digital-ID systems (Roberts et al. 2023). The main findings of that research are summarized in the following five sections.

**Internet interception:** There is no evidence that Ghana has procured internet interception technologies to surveil citizens' internet communications. However, Ghana's Cybersecurity Act mandates all internet service providers to record and retain the contents of citizens' communications to facilitate investigations by state security agencies (Freedom House 2022). This provision could be exploited by security agencies for targeted/mass surveillance of citizens. Ghana also made two user information requests to Google in 2013 but the company refused both requests (CIPESA 2017). It is apparent that

Ghana's government is interested in what its citizens do on the internet. With its possession of sophisticated surveillance technologies, refusal from platform companies might not be able to stop the country from conducting targeted interception operations. The Ghanaian government threatened twice, in 2016 and 2020, to shut down the internet but backed down both times due to pressure from civil society organizations (Akwei 2016; Christian 2020). Although Ghana remains one of the African countries without a history of internet shutdown or denial of access to social media platforms, the spectrum is not completely clear.

**Mobile interception:** In Ghana, three laws give power to top officials and senior security officers to intercept mobile communications: the Anti-Terrorism Act 2008, the Electronic Communications Act 2008, and the Cybersecurity Act 2020. In terms of technological capabilities, Ghana possesses the hacking software, Pegasus, acquired from the Israeli company NSO Group for $5.5 million in 2016 (Dadoo 2022; Dogbevi 2022), and digital forensics technology used for decrypting encrypted devices from Cellebrite, another Israeli surveillance company (Freedom House 2022). The country also possesses spyware technologies from Quadream and Mer Group and a telecommunication interception technology from an unnamed Swiss company (Roberts et al. 2023). In addition to the growing mobile interception technologies, government agencies seem to enjoy undefined power to request subscriber information from telecoms operators (Media Foundation for West Africa 2021).

**Social media monitoring:** In 2014, Ghana used the services of Cambridge Analytica for health policy planning (Ghana Web 2020). Cambridge Analytica is infamous for illegally accessing social media data to influence election results in many countries. The company's notoriety together with the secret dealings in surveillance technologies by the Ghanaian government allow for only a cautionary acceptance of the official explanation of the terms of engagement of Cambridge Analytica's services. Although no evidence was found that the company engaged in social media monitoring in Ghana, Facebook data harvesting for election-related marketing campaigns could not be ruled out (Romano 2018). In 2020, Ursula Owusu-Ekuful, Ghana's Communication Minister, directed social media companies to self-regulate or have the government regulate them (Adepoju 2021).

**Smart city/safe city:** Ghana has recently spent hundreds of millions of dollars on 'safe city' projects. Ordinarily, safe cities are supposed to make citizens feel safe in their countries, but governments in some countries have exploited the technologies to subject citizens to rights-violating mass surveillance (Nkwanyana 2021). Ghana's Integrated National Security Communications Enhancement Network project (ALPHA) comprises Huawei's AI-powered facial recognition CCTV cameras installed around its capital city Accra, regional capitals, entry ports, and other state infrastructures. Phase I of the project implemented in 2012 was worth $176 million. Phase II of the project contracted in 2018 was worth $235 million (Roberts et al. 2023). Besides the CCTV cameras, the project covers fifty automatic number plate recognition (ANPR) devices installed 'at checkpoint sites, expansion of an existing data centre and establishment of a backup data centre, a video transmission network, and an intelligent video analysis system' (Roberts et al. 2023: 74).

**Biometric digital-ID:** Ghana has multiple biometric identification systems that require citizens to provide facial recognition or fingerprint biometrics. Besides the country's national passport, Ghana introduced a biometric means of identification called the Ghana Card. Between 2017 when the registration began and February 2023, 17 million people were registered with a Ghana Card (Akata 2023). Phase II of the Ghana Card registration exercise started on 4 September 2023 for all Ghanaians of fifteen years and above (Business Ghana 2023). From 31 March 2023, all children born in Ghana would be issued a Ghana Card (Hersey 2023). From 1 July 2022, the Ghana Card became compulsory for accessing mobile telecommunication and banking services for citizens and permanent residents of the country (Bank of Ghana 2022; Kuuire 2022), further enhancing the state's capability to monitor digital interactions.

Together, these technologies show that Ghana is developing an enormous capacity for digital surveillance of its citizens. The secrecy that surrounds the procurement of surveillance technologies, as in the case of Pegasus, suggests that Ghana appears to have mastered the art of distracting the world from its growing arsenal of digital surveillance technologies, using its celebrated democratic profile.

Having documented the growing range of digital surveillance technologies employed by the government of Ghana, the next section reviews existing conceptual literature to produce a framework for analysing it.

# The powercube

The powercube is a conceptual tool developed by John Gaventa (2006) and colleagues at IDS (see Figure 2.1). It is used to analyse and understand power and its interrelations in processes of governance, social relationships and organizations. It is a valuable lens through which the various aspects of power and their interconnectedness are explored. It 'presents a dynamic understanding of how power operates, how different interests can be marginalized ... and the strategies needed to increase inclusion' (Luttrell et al. 2007: 1). Through three dimensions of power consisting of spaces, forms, and levels, the powercube is used for understanding power relations in participation and engagements within social and political spaces and to ensure social change.

The powercube is often used to analyse how power operates in the spaces used for decision making. From this perspective, all spaces for participation and civic engagement are shaped by the power relations within and around such spaces (Cornwall 2002). The powercube has been used to analyse political spaces (Webster and Engberg-Petersen 2002), policy spaces (McGee 2004), and democratic spaces (Cornwall and Coehlo 2006).

The powercube characterizes the *spaces* of power using three concepts: closed spaces, invited spaces, and created spaces (Gaventa 2006). Policy spaces are often characterized as 'closed spaces' because participation and engagement is the preserve of the elites only. Political and democratic spaces are more often characterized as 'invited spaces' because the elites invite the powerless to these public arenas but with boundaries and rules limiting participation

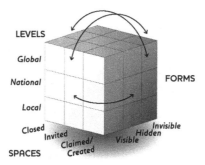

**Figure 2.1** Gaventa's three-dimensional powercube.
Source: Gaventa (2006).

(Gaventa 2019). 'Created spaces' refer to spaces that the powerless claimed from the elites or created for themselves. Created spaces are outside of the institutionalized policy arena (Gaventa 2019) and 'may come into being as a result of popular mobilisation', or may consist of spaces in which 'like-minded people join together in common pursuits' (Cornwall 2002: 24). This is because such collective actions afford the mobilized group the power and agency to take collective action to make claims to closed/policy spaces (Gaventa 2006).

A second dimension to the powercube model is *forms* of power. This dimension reflects how power is manifested in different forms in different spaces, namely, visible power, hidden power, and invisible power. Visible power is the public process and transparent rules by which decisions are made. Hidden forms of power are 'used by vested interests to maintain their power and privilege by creating barriers to participation, by excluding key issues from the public arena, or by controlling politics backstage' (Gaventa 2006: 11). Invisible power is the most insidious form of power and involves individuals' unconscious internalization of unequal power relations in ways that shape the extent of their agency to take part in decision making. Invisible power manifests itself in 'ways in which awareness of one's rights and interests are hidden through the adoption of dominating ideologies, values and forms of behaviour by relatively powerless groups themselves' (ibid.: 12).

The third dimension of the powercube recognizes that power can operate at different *levels*, including local, national, and global levels. In the area of public spaces for participation, levels of power are deliberated on from the local, national, and global tangent and the focus has been on which of these levels 'critical social economic and political power resides' (Gaventa 2006: 27). Some analysts have concerned themselves with which level is most important but Gaventa (2019) posits that a growing body of literature supports deviation from such contestations because 'the interrelationships of these levels of power with one another suggest that the challenge for action is not only how to build participatory action at differing levels, but how to promote the democratic and accountable vertical links across actors at each level' (ibid.: 28).

The concept of power (powercube) is 'central to understanding agency' and how power offers 'different possibilities … for agency to emerge' (Spencer and Doull 2015: 903). Agency refers to 'the ability of individuals to operate, through their own active will, regardless of wider social structures that may otherwise limit the choices that they may possess' (Dedman 2011: 511). This implies that within closed spaces, hidden powers persist and influence decisions taken at international or national levels, leading to invisible power and limited or no agency among the masses, due to the acceptance of the status quo. However, closed spaces can be opened or turned into created spaces when resistance to hidden power results in agency for the masses.

For this chapter, the powercube offers a valuable model for investigating the inter-relation of levels, spaces, and forms of power in the rapidly expanding digital surveillance landscape in a young and thriving democracy like Ghana. Also, the concept of rights and agency offers insights into the analysis of the coping strategies employed by the victims of rights-violating surveillance.

## Methodology

A qualitative approach was employed to enable us to understand the significance and meanings study subjects ascribe to rights-violating digital surveillance in Ghana (Creswell and Creswell 2018) and a case study design was employed to conduct an extensive analysis of the phenomenon (Yin 2018). Interviews were conducted with five purposively selected participants with experiences of rights-violating digital surveillance in Ghana and were willing to participate in the study. The observations made from the interviews were thematically analysed through the lens of the powercube model (Gaventa 2005; 2006; 2019).

Researching rights-violating surveillance raises a number of ethical concerns and places a burden of care upon us. Our major ethical consideration in this study was the risks to which both the participants and the researchers could be exposed in the process. As proactive measures, the following decisions were taken to reduce the harm that could result from participating in the study: (i) The nature and implications of the study were explained to the interviewees to secure their informed, voluntary participation; (ii) face-to-face interviews were conducted to avoid the risk of digital surveillance; (iii) interview locations were decided by the interviewees to guarantee their safety; (iv) the contents of the interviews were handwritten (not recorded on any electronic devices); (v) no personally identifying information was recorded in the notes; and

(vi) pseudonyms are used in presenting the data to safeguard interviewees' identity. Therefore, 'P5' and 'YYYY' in the section below are devices employed to safeguard the interviewees' identity because their identity could be inferred not only from their names but from the subjects they discuss. The experience of being subjected to rights-violating surveillance is presented in the next section.

# Findings and discussion

Despite growing intolerance of political dissent in Ghana (Freedom House 2022) and huge investments in digital surveillance technologies (Roberts et al. 2023), evidence of rights-violating digital surveillance appears to be non-existent in Ghana due to secrecy surrounding the use of these technologies (Roberts et al. 2023). Therefore, to answer the first research question, 'what are the experiences of victims of rights-violating digital surveillance in Ghana?', we identified individuals with direct experience of digital surveillance and used interviews to document their experiences.

Sharing his experience, interviewee 'P5' recounted several experiences where he was suspicious that his phone had being bugged due to feedback noise on his phone when making or receiving calls. However, he became very certain when he received an anonymous call from a security official asking him questions about a privately held phone discussion with a source for an on-going investigative project. The security official further informed him that he was on their surveillance radar so anytime he mentioned YYYY topics or Mr ZZZZ in his conversations, it automatically triggered the monitor and caused them to start monitoring him. Therefore, he scanned his computer, and discovered that his email had been compromised and so he started using Authenticator.[1] The other four interviewees in this study shared similar experiences. They noted that, when they were suspicious that their phones were compromised, they used a phone hacking verification short code (*#62#) or checked the settings of their social media accounts, and realized their accounts were linked to unknown devices and their calls and SMS messages were being automatically forwarded to unknown numbers.

The interviewees also revealed that, upon their arrest and detention, their digital devices were seized by security officials. 'P2' recounted that immediately he was 'marched into the room, the first thing the officers seized' was his mobile phone. Other interviewees recounted the same experience. However, upon release from detention, the interviewees were informed by colleagues/family members that they (interviewees) were constantly online throughout the detention period. This made them suspicious that the security officials might have accessed their confiscated phones, so they checked the settings of their social media accounts and used the phone hacking verification short code to scan their phones. They realized that their social media accounts, calls and SMS had been linked or forwarded to unknown numbers and devices. Thus, 'the setting of my WhatsApp account showed that my account has been linked to an unknown computer' (P3).

The fact that the interviewees did not set up the call-forwarding feature on their phones themselves but that a covert call-forwarding feature was activated after they had been held in police custody made them draw the logical conclusion that this was a covert surveillance mechanism used to monitor their private communications.

Moreover, interviewees with no prior contact with security agencies believed that officials were using the Pegasus[2] spyware to monitor or access their digital content because they discovered after scanning that their devices had been remotely bugged. Reinforcing the Pegasus spyware hypothesis and his bugging experience, P5 claimed that the anonymous call proved that officials were able to remotely monitor his conversation anytime he mentioned YYYY topics or Mr ZZZZ in his conversation because the Pegasus spyware enabled the officials to listen to his calls remotely and access his chats or view photos and videos on his phone.

Another interviewee made inferences from the circumstances surrounding the theft of digital devices to conclude that they were under surveillance. When they were in the middle of planning a protest against government, the location used for storing their digital communication devices was broken into after a phone discussion to keep their devices at a different location. Besides, only their 'computers, external hard drives and other digital devices were stolen, in spite of other valuable properties in the room' (P4). P3 noted that his political sources in opposition parties refused to use any digital devices because (having previously been in government) they knew that 'security officials were remotely monitoring [his] phone [using] Pegasus spyware' (P3).

In instances of rights-violating digital surveillance, insights from the recounted experiences show the use of both power and authority to abuse participants' privacy rights, especially when the 2017 landmark High Court order indicates that, without a warrant, the Ghana police have no authority to access the contents of phones during arrest or detention (Bannaseh 2017). Therefore, placing an interviewee who is not a crime suspect on radar and remotely monitoring his phone without a court warrant demonstrate the abuse of power due to poorly defined legal provision on privacy rights in the 1992 Constitution and the Security and Intelligence Act 2020, which encourages officials to mount illegal surveillance on participants (Gwagwa and Wilton 2014).

Using Gaventa's concepts, these situations demonstrate that state security officials were operating in a closed space in which the power to conduct surveillance was done without transparency and in the absence of discussion or debate (Gaventa 2005; 2019). Hence, Gaventa (2006: 16) avers that decisions 'are made by a set of actors behind closed doors' (15) with little broad consultation or involvement. This is the case of decisions on intelligence gathering without a warrant in Ghana. Acts of surveillance without a warrant are the preserve of the security officials only (Gaventa 2005; 2019) because power and rights-violating surveillance behaviour are embedded in the 'closed space' systems of state security institutions. These closed spaces afford the officials the ability to exceed their legal powers to access interviewees' private phones without court warrants, thereby violating their rights to freedoms from surveillance and to private and secured communication (Tsui and Lee 2019). The foregoing exhibits power as negative traits that enable officials to hold power and exercise control over the interviewees through surveillance. Unfortunately, the interviewees are unable to prevent the officials from illegally violating their privacy rights because they are denied agency by the status quo (Gaventa 2006).

## Architects and motivations of surveillance

The second research question guiding this chapter is: 'Who are the architects behind the acts of surveillance and what are their motivations?'. The interviewees explained that, upon the discovery that their mobile communications were being surveilled or their devices were stolen, they were uncertain about the specific security agency conducting the surveillance. However, they indicated that the state actors were the architects behind their experiences. P5 used his experience of algorithmic and automation surveillance as explicit evidence of state actors being the perpetrators behind his experience. Thus, the phone call from the official in which the mention of topic YYYY or Mr ZZZZ in his conversation automatically triggered the monitor to record his conversation was his reason for citing state actors as the perpetrators.

> I am often exposing the wrong actions and inactions of people in government so if I detect that my phone has been bugged or it is being monitored after my detention and this same government has purchased Pegasus spyware, who is the likely suspect?
>
> (P4)

In the interview P4 stated that his phone was clean before his detention but was found to be infected with spyware when re-checked immediately after detention, hence, providing strong evidence that state actors infected the phone. Only these actors had the motive, opportunity, and capabilities to effect the surveillance.

Sharing their perspectives on the perpetrators, interviewee P1 mentioned 'state actors'. P2 indicated 'national security operatives' and P3 noted that 'it is obviously the state'. Besides their personal experiences, they also outlined a number of reasons for implicating state actors in their rights-violating surveillance experience. The government's purchase of Pegasus mobile phone spyware, the high cost of digital surveillance technologies, and the technical capacity to use these technologies served as the basis for making their implications.

They supported their responses by citing the government's purchase of the Pegasus spyware, a technology that NSO claims it only sells to governments and it had been used in Ghana (Benjakob 2022). One interviewee posited that 'no businessman or individual [had] the financial muscle to invest huge sums of money in digital technologies just to monitor or scrutinize what goes on in [his] phone. Definitely, the taxpayers' money can …' (P1). Some interviewees also used the ability to use such technologies illegally and with impunity as their basis. They argued that only National Security Agencies have the ability to use such surveillance technologies to bug or hack their devices illegally without risk of arrest and since there was no record of any arrest of individuals for using digital surveillance technologies in Ghana, it was evident the state was behind their experiences.

Although it is true that the above assertions are inferences, they can be justified based on the fact that, despite NSO denials that Pegasus was operational in Ghana, NSO employees admit to having trained Ghanaian officials in its use and some Ghanaian journalists, CSO activists, and opposition members allege they were targets of the spyware (Benjakob 2022).

Regarding the motivation for illegal surveillance of the interviewees, the themes that emerged from the analysis were information gathering, fear, and impunity. The interviewees believed state actors wanted information on their online activities in order to serve the interests of the state (by using their power to determine which information should be hidden). Also, access to such information would enable the state actors to decide whether they needed to stop them from exposing an issue they were investigating. For instance, one interviewee noted that: 'information is power so people in government always want to be ahead in order to know what is about to happen to be able to stop people like me or my colleagues' (P4). Linked to the preceding is the theme of fear. The interviewees suggested that state actors were often afraid of unfavourable exposure of events and issues that would make them unpopular. Hence, P3 indicated that they used 'surveillance to monitor and maintain checks' on people of interest to 'safeguard the interests of the government' (P3).

Four interviewees also identified impunity to be a feature of their experience of rights-violating digital surveillance. They argued that using the guise of national security, state actors knew that they could get away with rights-violating surveillance without injurious consequences. According to P1, this emboldened them to 'mount surveillance on people' (P1). To this effect, national security becomes a social belief on which the interviewees base their state of powerlessness and inability to demand accountability.

The above findings align with Gaventa's (2006) concept of hidden and invisible forms of power. For Gaventa (2006: 11), hidden powers 'are used by vested interests to maintain their power and privilege by creating barriers to participation, by excluding key issues from the public arena, or by controlling politics backstage'. Therefore, rights-violating digital surveillance affords the perpetrators a hidden form of power to have backstage control over the information being gathered by the interviewees or voices of dissidents. In addition, they are able to obtain advance warning about issues/events that could damage their power interests, thereby gaining the opportunity to prevent the issue ever getting onto the public agenda. In this way, they secure their privilege of being in a position to keep information they prefer hidden from the public arena (Gaventa 2005; 2019). Again, hidden power through the guise of national security emboldens the perpetrators to carry out these acts with impunity and widely use surveillance powers intended to narrowly target the most serious crime (Roberts et al. 2021).

Gaventa (2006: 12) avers that invisible power 'involves the ways in which awareness of one's rights and interests are hidden through the adoption of dominating ideologies, values and forms of behaviour by relatively powerless groups themselves'. In our analysis of the evidence from Ghana we argue that the privacy rights of interviewees and their interest in privately secured communication with others are hidden through the abuse of the adoption of the dominating norms that privacy rights enshrined in the Constitution can be over-ridden by police and security forces. Thus, the guise of national security becomes 'a dominating ideology' that acts to hide the interviewees' awareness of their right to private communication and represses their propensity to make rights claims and redress for the injurious consequences of rights violations. This creates an environment where the interviewees are denied the ability to challenge security officials and change the existing status quo on illegal digital surveillance (denied of agency), therefore, rendering them relatively powerless (Gaventa 2006; 2019) and with repressed agency.

## Resistance

Our third research question asked: 'What strategies do victims adopt to cope with rights-violating digital surveillance?' Ghanaians have not been passive in the face of growing rights-violating surveillance. They exercise their agency by taking a range of actions to forbear surveillance power, protect their right to privacy, and hold power to account.

Our findings showed that to resist digital surveillance, the interviewees changed the manner of usage of their devices in attempts to evade surveillance. The interviewees disclosed that they used digital security conscious strategies like *#002#,[3] Authenticator, VPN, checked the settings of their social media handles regularly or used software (e.g. Avast, Norton 360, Mobile Verification Toolkit by Amnesty International) to protect their devices from digital surveillance. Hence, an interviewee indicated that his team had 'received a software from a French NGO [for Pegasus detection] and we use it to [conduct forensics] of our digital devices regularly to ensure that they are not compromised' (P4). Another participant also revealed that he changed his 'phone number every six months' and had 'installed software with double shields to protect' him against 'illegal digital surveillance' (P5). Another participant indicated that it was 'a matter of constantly being on the lookout and finding another means to outwit' the perpetrators anytime he discovered that his device had been hacked or bugged because the perpetrators never stopped monitoring him (P4). P1 also noted that he had multiple numbers that he used from time to time to avoid being monitored. These findings point to the theme of resistance.

The above findings indicate a power struggle in digital space between the interviewees and the perpetrators of digital surveillance. The interviewees want to resist the dominance of the perpetrators who use surveillance to maintain authority over them. This aligns with Gaventa's (2006) assertion that the powerful rarely 'give up their power easily' and this 'often involves conflict and power struggle'. Also, the findings are in consonance with Gaventa's (2006) levels of power. In this study, levels of power refer to decisions taken by formal institutions to surveil serious crimes, protect online privacy, and safeguard free expression at international, national, and local levels. Therefore, the perpetrators, by virtue of operating from a national level of power (Gaventa 2006), are mandated to mobilize formal institutions (police, security, law, and treasury) to practise narrow monitoring of suspects and uphold online privacy and free expression. Yet in Ghana, our findings show that decisions at national level make the perpetrators powerful because they operate within a closed space of power where security officials make decisions to mount rights-violating surveillance free from oversight and with impunity from accountability. The result undermines the constitutional right to privacy and free expression.

However, once they had discovered the rights-violating surveillance, the interviewees created a 'claimed space' outside of the institutionalized policy arena of rights-violating surveillance where they (interviewees) claimed their right to private and secured communication by adopting a range of noted security-conscious strategies to ward off the perpetrators and claim back their right to private and secured communication.

Findings also revealed that intimidation or fear resulting from the discovery of being monitored limited their agency and caused unnecessary delays in the execution of the project/event/issue the participants were working on. Four interviewees indicated that fear of rights-violating surveillance necessitated the need to either re-strategize or 'go cold' on a project/issue for a while in order to avoid or outwit monitoring, which resulted in interruptions/postponement of the proposed completion date of such projects. Also, the discovery of being under surveillance compelled some team members to give up on the project/ issue/events out of fear. Besides, the interviewees noted that rights-violating digital surveillance denied them the constitutional right to communicate privately and to store private information on their digital devices. Hence, one interviewee noted that he resorted to physical meetings with his sources rather than using his phone. Such rights-violating surveillance violates their rights and undermines their efforts to bring to light and critique the actions and inactions of people in power. It is also direct evidence of a 'chilling effect'.

The preceding shows the effect of digital surveillance in crippling and silencing the voices of dissidents (Buchi et al. 2022) in a young but thriving democracy like Ghana, and slowing the interviewees down from holding the government accountable to its citizens. Rights-violating surveillance encourages self-censorship and restrains free expression (Stevens et al. 2023) because it caused the interviewees to refrain from discussing certain topics or issues over their digital devices.

## Recommendations

In this study, all the interviewees acknowledged citizens' low awareness around rights to privacy issues and the misguided assumption that only individuals involved in crime were monitored. Hence, both remotely monitored interviewees and those who had encounters with security officials were monitored on their blind side until the anonymous call from the security official or observations of constant online presence. This calls for sensitization and awareness raising to equip individuals to better understand the problem and be digitally vigilant to resist rights-violating digital surveillance. Public education on such issues comes with sensitization and awareness raising that enhances the power and agency of citizens to challenge the hidden power of security officials (Gaventa 2006). Also, common concerns and awareness due to power within the victims of surveillance/citizens will cause them to have serious considerations about issues surrounding privacy intrusion and challenge the existing status quo about illegal digital surveillance in the country (Gaventa 2006: 2019). This has the potential to contribute to building citizens' power through mobilization around shared concerns. To challenge rights-violating surveillance effectively, the collective action of citizens is necessary to open up the closed spaces and demand accountability from the security officials who conduct surveillance (Gaventa 2006; 2019).

Our findings also suggest that it is state actors who are the apparent perpetrators of rights-violating digital surveillance, due to their interest in repressing investigative journalism and critical voices. The poorly defined nature of the existing laws indirectly empowers security officials to digitally monitor individuals illegally and with impunity. As a result, the interviewees became afraid, intimidated, suspicious of their environment, and suffered privacy intrusions upon discovery that they were victims of illegal digital surveillance. This has repercussions because it restrains free expression, encourages self-censorship (Stevens et al. 2023), and shows attempts to cripple and silence the voices of dissidents (Buchi et al. 2022) in a young but thriving democracy like Ghana. Hence, the study recommends a review of the existing security and intelligence laws to address or block rights-violating digital surveillance and a check on the conduct of security officials regarding these laws. Furthermore, we call for an independent body with the mandate to oversee the application and implementation of existing laws and conduct of security officials in a democratically accepted manner to protect public interest against rights-violating surveillance. This would allow narrow surveillance of the most serious criminals while simultaneously protecting constitutional rights to privacy and free expression. Ghana needs to improve transparency and public accountability to open up the civic spaces currently closed to citizens, prevent rights-violating surveillance, and end the impunity surrounding it. In this way power can be used in a positive sense to bring about progressive desired change (Gaventa 2006).

## Conclusion

This chapter analysed the experiences of victims of rights-violating digital surveillance in Ghana. It identified the architects of that surveillance and examined their motivations. It also documented the coping strategies of Ghanaians who have been subjected to rights-violating digital surveillance. The study adopted Gaventa's (2006) powercube model, consisting of spaces, forms, and levels of power. Findings revealed discovery of rights-violating digital surveillance after interviewees had scanned their devices. Also, state actors were identified as the perpetrators of the rights-violating digital surveillance, due to information gathering interests in the activities of the interviewees and the impunity surrounding surveillance. However, awareness of such surveillance acts caused the interviewees to adopt digital security-conscious strategies to resist surveillance actions from state actors.

Analysis of these findings through the lens of Gaventa's (2006) powercube shows that power operating in closed spaces enables rights-violating surveillance. The ability of state security actors to exercise hidden power in closed spaces affords them the power to mount rights-violating surveillance with impunity. The surveillance decisions made in closed spaces result in the normalization of these relations and their internalization in what Gaventa calls 'invisible power' that enables the perpetrators to mount rights-violating digital surveillance with impunity. However, those subject to digital surveillance in Ghana are not passive victims – there is an on-going power struggle between them. Thus, as state actors abuse their ability to mobilize bias through state institutions to surveil and maintain dominance over investigative journalists, they (the interviewees) moved to claim new spaces, gain agency, resist the dominant power interests, and reclaim their rights to private and secured communication through adoption of digital security-conscious strategies.

# Notes

1   Authenticator is a software for securing sign-ins for online accounts with multi-factor authentication.
2   Pegasus is a form of mobile phone malware used to enable surveillance of calls and messages.
3   *#002#: A code to disable call forwarding on a phone; VPN: Stands for virtual private network and is a service that creates encrypted tunnels to protect online data and identity by hiding the IP address.

# Bibliography

Adepoju, P. (2021). 'Ghana's Mixed Track Record with Social Media Regulation'. IT Web, 15 May. https://itweb.africa/content/lwrKx73Kao87mglo (accessed 11 November 2023).

Akata, D. A. K. (2023). 'Ghana Card: Over 17 Million Ghanaians Registered as of February – Prof Attafuah'. My Joy Online, 25 February. https://www.myjoyonline.com/ghana-card-over-17-million-ghanaians-registered-as-of-february-prof-attafuah/ (accessed 12 November 2023).

Akwei, I. (2016). 'Ghana Stands to Lose if Internet Is Shut Down on Election Day', *Africanews*, 12 June. https://www.africanews.com/2016/12/06/ghana-stands-to-lose-if-internet-is-shut-down-on-election-day/ (accessed 10 January 2023).

Bank of Ghana (2022). 'Use of Ghana Card for All Financial Transactions', https://www.bog.gov.gh/wp-content/uploads/2022/01/BOG-Notice-BG-GOV-SEC-2022-01-Notice-on-Use-of-Ghana-Card-for-all-Financial-Transactions-2.pdf (accessed 10 November 2023).

Bannaseh, M. (2017). 'Police Can't Seize, Search Electronic Gadgets without Warrants – High Court Gives Landmark Order'. https://www.graphic.com.gh/news/general-news/police-can-t-seize-search-electronic-gadgets-without-warrant-high-court-gives-landmark-order.html (accessed 5 November 2023).

Benjakob, O. (2022). 'NSO Ghana Op Exposed: Never-Before-Seen Pegasus Spyware Footage, Workers' Passports', *Haaretz*, 20 January. https://www.haaretz.com/israel-news/tech-news/2022-01-20/ty-article/nso-ghana-op-exposed-never-before-seen-pegasus-spyware-footage-workers-passports/0000017f-f1fb-df98-a5ff-f3ffb9a20000 (accessed 22 November 2022).

Büchi, M., Festic N. and Latzer M. (2022). The Chilling Effects of Digital Dataveillance: A Theoretical Model and an Empirical Research Agenda. *Big Data & Society*. https://doi.org/10.1177/20539517211065368

Business Ghana (2023). 'NIA Opens All District Offices for Free Ghana Card Registration'. 4 September. https://businessghana.com/site/news/General/293186/NIA-opens-all-district-offices-for-free-Ghana-Card-registration (accessed 13 November 2023).

Christian, A. (2020). 'The Ghana Internet Shutdown Conundrum Is Disturbingly Entangled in Press Mis-reportage'. WT, 10 February. https://weetracker.com/2020/02/10/ghana-internet-shutdown-press-misreportage/ (accessed 11 November 2023).

CIPESA (2017). 'The Growing Trend of African Governments' Requests for User Information and Content Removal from Internet and Telecom Companies'. https://cipesa.org/wp-content/files/briefs/The-Growing-Trend-of-African-GovernmentsE28099-Requests-for-User-Information-and-Content-Removal-From-Internet-and-Telecom-Companies.pdf (accessed 20 June 2024).

CIPESA (2021). 'Mapping and Analysis of Privacy Laws in Africa'. https://cipesa.org/wp-content/files/briefs/Mapping-and-Analysis-of-Privacy-Laws-in-Africa-2021.pdf (accessed 5 May 2023).

Cornwall, A. (2002). 'Making Spaces Changing Places: Situating Participation in Development', *IDS Working Paper 170*, Brighton: Institute of Development Studies.

Cornwall, A. and Coehlo, V. S. (2006). 'Introduction', in A. Cornwall (ed.), *Spaces for Change? The Politics of Citizen Participation in New Democratic Arenas*, Brighton: Institute of Development Studies.

Creswell, J. W. and Creswell, J. D. (2018). *Research Design* (5th edn), Los Angeles, CA: SAGE.

Dadoo, S. (2023). 'Is Ghana's Government Using Israeli Kit to Spy on Activists and Dissidents?', *The Africa Report*, 21 July. https://www.theafricareport.com/224982/is-ghanas-government-using-israeli-kit-to-spy-on-activists-and-dissidents/ (accessed 22 November 2022).

Dedman, T. (2011). Agency in UK Hip-hop and Grime Youth Subcultures – Peripherals and Purists'. *Journal of Youth Studies*, 14(5): 507–522.

Dogbevi, E. K. (2022). 'Revealed: Israeli Tech Company NSO's Pegasus Was Used in Ghana – Reports', *Ghana Business News*, 22 January. https://www.ghanabusinessnews.com/2022/01/22/revealed-israeli-tech-company-nsos-pegasus-was-used-in-ghana-reports/ (accessed 10 November 2023).

Eshun, J. S. (2022). 'The Intelligence-led National Security Architecture of Ghana and Its Three Pre-conditions'. https://bura.brunel.ac.uk/bitstream/2438/25898/1/FulltextThesis.pdf (accessed 12 November 2023).

Freedom House (2022). *Freedom in the World 2022: Ghana*. https://freedomhouse.org/country/ghana/freedom-net/2022 (accessed 22 November 2022).

Gaventa, J. (2005). 'Reflections of the Uses of the "Power Cube" Approach for Analyzing the Spaces, Places, and Dynamics of Civic Society Participation and Engagement' (CFP evaluation series No. 4, 2003–6), Brighton: Institute of Development Studies.

Gaventa, J. (2006). 'Finding the Spaces for Change: A Power Analysis', in R. Eyben, C. Harris and J. Pettit (eds), *Exploring Power for Change*, IDS Bulletin 37.6, Brighton: Institute of Development Studies. https://www.taylorfrancis.com/chapters/edit/10.4324/9781351272322-8/applying-power-analysis-using-powercube-explore-forms-levels-spaces-john-gaventa (accessed 9 November 2023).

Gaventa, J. (2019). 'Applying Power Analysis: Using the "Powercube" to Explore Forms, Levels and Spaces', in R. McGee and J. Pettit (eds), *Power, Empowerment and Social Change* (pp. 117–38), London: Routledge.

Ghana Web (2020). 'Election Leaks: Did Cambridge Analytica Play NDC and NPP Ahead of 2016 Polls?', 28 February. https://www.ghanaweb.com/GhanaHomePage/NewsArchive/Election-leaks-Did-Cambridge-Analytica-play-NDC-and-NPP-ahead-of-2016-polls-880060 (accessed 10 November 2023).

Gwagwa, A. and Wilton, A. (2014). 'Protecting the Rights to Privacy in Africa in Digital Age'. https://www.academia.edu/11336932/Protecting_the_right_to_privacy_in_Africa_in_the_digital_age (accessed 10 May 2023).

Hersey, F. (2023). 'Ghana Re-announces Issuance of ID Numbers to Babies, Uganda to Register Citizen School Children'. Biometric Update, 10 March. https://www.biometricupdate.com/202303/ghana-re-announces-issuance-of-id-numbers-to-babies-uganda-to-register-citizen-school-children (accessed 13 November 2023).

Kuuire, J.-A. (2022). 'National Communications Authority Clarifies that the Ghana Card Is Still the Official ID Used for the SIM Re-registration Exercise'. Tech Labari, 6 November. https://techlabari.com/national-communications-authority-clarifies-that-the-ghana-card-is-still-the-official-id-used-for-the-sim-re-registration-exercise/ (accessed 10 November 2023).

Luttrell, C., Bird, K., Byrne, S., Carter, J., and Chakravarti, D. (2007). 'Power Cube Explained'. https://www.shareweb.ch/site/Poverty-Wellbeing/addressingpovertyinpractice/Documents/The%20Power%20Cube%20Explained%20-%20Cecilia%20Luttrell%20November%202007.pdf (accessed 8 November 2023).

McGee, R. (2004). 'Unpacking Policy: Actors, Knowledge and Spaces', in K. Brock, R. McGee and J. Gaventa (eds), *Unpacking Policy: Actors, Knowledge and Spaces in Poverty Reduction*, 1–26, Kampala: Fountain Press.

Media Foundation for West Africa (2021). 'Ghana: MFWA Welcomes High Court Ruling Ordering Government to Stop Collecting Personal Data'. https://mfwa.org/ghana-mfwas-welcome-high-court-ruling-ordering-government-to-stop-collecting-personal-data/ (accessed 28 August 2024).

Nkwanyana, K. (2021). 'China's AI Deployment in Africa Poses Risks to Security and Sovereignty', *The Strategist*, 5 May. https://www.aspistrategist.org.au/chinas-ai-deployment-in-africa-poses-risks-to-security-and-sovereignty/ (accessed 9 January 2023).

Oladapo, O. A. and Appiah-Adjei, G. (2023). 'Ghana Country Report', in Roberts et al. (2023) *Mapping the Supply of Surveillance Technologies to Africa: Case Studies from Nigeria, Ghana, Morocco, Malawi, and Zambia*, Brighton: Institute of Development Studies.

Republic of Ghana (1992). *The 1992 Constitution of Ghana*. https://www.constituteproject.org/constitution/Ghana_1996.pdf?lang=en (accessed 22 July 2016).

Roberts, T., Mohamed Ali, A., Farahat, M., Oloyede, R. and Mutung'u, G. (2021). *Surveillance Law in Africa: A Review of Six Countries*, Brighton: Institute of Development Studies. https://doi.org/10.19088/IDS.2021.059

Roberts, T., Gitahi, J., Allam, P., Oboh, L. Oladapo, O., Appiah-Adjei, G., Galal, A., Kainja, J., Phiri, S., Abraham, K., Klovig Skelton, S. and Sheombar, A. (2023). *Mapping the Supply of Surveillance Technologies to Africa: Case Studies from Nigeria, Ghana, Morocco, Malawi, and Zambia*, Brighton: Institute of Development Studies. https://doi.org/10.19088/IDS.2023.027

Romano, A. (2018). 'The Facebook Data Breach Wasn't a Hack: It Was a Wake-up Call'. *Vox*, 20 March. https://www.vox.com/2018/3/20/17138756/facebook-data-breach-cambridge-analytica-explained (accessed 10 November 2023).

Spencer, G. and Doull, M. (2015). 'Examining Concepts of Power and Agency in Research with Young People', *Journal of Youth Studies*, 18(7): 900–13. https://doi.org/10.1080/13676261.2014.1001827

Stevens, A., Fussey, P., Murray, D., Hove, K., and Saki, O. (2023). 'I Started Seeing Shadows Everywhere: The Diverse Chilling Effects of Surveillance in Zimbabwe', *Big Data & Society*, 10(1): 1–14. https://doi.org/10.1177/20539517231158631

Temin, J. and Smith, D. A. (2002). 'Media Matters: Evaluating the Role of the Media in Ghana's 2000 Elections', *African Affairs*, 101: 585–600.

Tsui, L. and Lee, F. (2019). 'How Journalists Understand the Threats and Opportunities of New Technologies: A Study of Security Mindsets and Its Implications for Press Freedom', *Journalism*, 22(6). First Published May 19, 2019. https://doi.org/10.1177/1464884919849418

Webster, N. and Engberg-Petersen, L. (2002). *In the Name of the Poor: Contesting Political Space for Poverty*, London: Zed Books.

Yin, R. K. (2018). *Case Study Research and Applications: Design and Methods* (6th edn), Los Angeles, CA: SAGE.

# 3

# Phishing, spyware, and smart city tech

## Surveillance in Sisi's Egypt

Afef Abrougui

## Introduction

The Republic of Egypt, located in the northeastern corner of Africa, is the third most populous country (Okafor 2024) and the second largest economy on the continent (Statista 2022b). Internet services in the country were first introduced in 1993 to users in academia before expanding with the development of the local ISP (Internet Service Provider) market (Kamel 1997). Today, an overwhelming majority of the population uses the internet. The internet penetration rate was estimated at 72 per cent in 2024 (DataReportal 2023), well above the Africa average of 43 per cent (Statista June 2022). Egypt has the second largest number of internet users on the continent (76 million) after Nigeria (Statista 2024) and 40 per cent of the population use social media (DataReportal 2023).

Since independence from Britain in 1922, Egypt has gone through a series of tumultuous power struggles, including the struggle against British influence and European colonialism, coups, and wars with Israel (before a 1979 peace treaty). In this climate, surveillance, in its different forms and tactics (such as reliance on human informers, telephone tapping and surveillance cameras), has always been crucial for successive presidents to maintain power and protect their regimes from domestic and foreign threats. With the advent of the digital age, reliance on digital surveillance technologies, first introduced under former president Hosni Mubarak, has steadily increased, although other tactics remain in use.

Over the past decade, Egypt has witnessed an unprecedented rise in authoritarianism after hopes for a successful democratic transition were swept away by a brutal military coup led by Abdelfattah Sisi, the current president, that removed the country's first civilian president, Mohamed Morsi. Since then, the military regime of Sisi has intensified its crackdown on critics, freedom of expression, media freedoms, and the rights to protest, organize, and assembly.

The regime has also continued to deploy surveillance to monitor and spy on the communications and online activities of citizens. It has taken steps to transform the urban space in Egypt by building new cities from scratch equipped with smart city tech and surveillance tech and transforming existing cities into smart ones as well. Surveillance tech is a key component of these cities.

This chapter explores how pervasive surveillance in Egypt is manifesting under Sisi and how it is aiding the political interests of the regime. What new tools and tactics is Egypt deploying under Sisi? How does the development of smart cities fit into the Surveillance State's objectives? What impact does this have on the human rights and agency of citizens?

To explore these questions, the chapter uses secondary research from academic articles, books, and reports by human rights organizations and local civil society groups in Egypt and is guided by concepts of the Surveillance State and pervasive surveillance.

## Background: Surveillance in modern Egypt

Surveillance in Egypt predates not only the digital era but also the modern state. Under Ottoman rule (1517–1798), secret spies, known as Bassassin ('onlookers') served as the watchful eye for those ruling (el-Hamalawy 2023). After the British occupied Egypt in 1882, they modernized that system and called it City Eye, 'an expansive network of informers, or more accurately, common folk reporting any suspicious activities in return for modest rewards; these included beggars, porters, vendors, cab-drivers, telephone operators, and scores of other people' (Kandil 2012: 30). The British colonial authorities established the Interior Ministry in March 1895 and the Special Section tasked with domestic surveillance in 1911 (ibid.). Egypt officially became independent in 1922, with a new constitution establishing a constitutional monarchy. However, Britain maintained troops and a strong influence until after the 1956 Suez Canal Crisis (Jurado 2024), when Britain along with France and Israel invaded Egypt after President Gamal Abd Nasser nationalized the canal (Jurado 2024).

## The new republic of Egypt and the rise of Nasser, 1952–70

In 1952, the Free Officers, a group of nationalist military officers led by Gamal Abdel Nasser, staged a coup against King Farouk, who was forced to abdicate in favour of his infant son with the aim to 'liberate Egypt from foreign occupation and install a reformed civilian regime that would enhance military power and restore its credibility' (Kandil 2012: 24).

On 18 June 1953, the Free Officers established the Republic of Egypt, and one of the movement's leaders, Mohamed Naguib, became the Republic's first president in what later turned out to be a turbulent and short-lived presidency. Nasser, on the other hand, the 'effective leader' of the Free Officers (Kandil 2012: 26), continued to expand his authority and to undermine Naguib, by rooting out potential threats and keeping an eye on them, expanding the surveillance apparatus and the capabilities of different security organs. Following the coup, Nasser assumed the role of Interior Minister, and became Prime Minister in 1954. He created a ministry for censorship and propaganda in 1952, dissolved all political parties and replaced them with the Liberalization Rally, a pro-regime platform, where he appointed himself as Secretary General (Kandil 2012). Naguib was eventually removed from power and Nasser assumed the presidency on 23 June 1956, and ruled until his death in 1970.

Despite the Free Officers promising to abolish the secret police, in October 1953 Nasser enlisted fellow Revolutionary Command Council (RCC) member Zakaria Muhi al-Din to *expand* Egypt's surveillance capabilities (Kandil 2012). The Special Section, established by the British occupation for domestic surveillance, was expanded into a new intelligence body and renamed the General Investigations Directorate (GID). In 1971, this was renamed as the State Security Investigations Sector (SSIS) (ibid.). The Military Intelligence Department (MID) was redirected toward the surveillance of dissidents instead of focusing on external threats. Already, during this period, foreign expertise and intelligence, from Germany, Russia, and the United States were playing a key role in the design and setting of the Egyptian surveillance apparatus. For instance, following the RCC revolution and removal of Farouk, the American embassy provided surveillance and anti-riot equipment after the coup worth a million US dollars (Kandil 2012) and the CIA provided assistance and expertise. Intelligence sharing agreements that included provision of surveillance technologies were signed with the KGB in 1958 and a decade later with Eastern German intelligence, the Stasi (ibid.)

As president, Nasser enlisted the support of the security apparatus for political control and to weaken the political role of the military and its potential threats to his rule. This helped empower security agencies and resulted in a climate of rife surveillance (Kandil 2012). According to Kandil (2012: 66): 'To live in Egypt during this period was to be constantly under the purview of a pervasive surveillance structure: phones, offices, and homes were bugged; mail was regularly checked; neighbours, colleagues, even siblings could not be trusted.' During this period, surveillance continued to rely heavily on humans such as informants and undercover policemen (el-Hamalawy 2023).

## The rise of the police state under Sadat (1970–81)

Nasser started the 'depoliticization' (Kandil 2012: 163) of the military but his successor, Anwar Sadat (1970–81), 'pushed the military to the point of oblivion and downgraded its political influence' (Kandil 2012: 221). Following the October 1973 war, Sadat purged influential military leaders and officers, and embarked on a series of policies that sidelined the military and redirected it to economic development projects, paving the way for the rise of the police state under the Interior Ministry and its intelligence organ, the SSIS (Kandil 2012).

Under Sadat, Egypt's rapprochement with the United States grew significantly, following military and political concessions Sadat made to the United States and Israel after the October 1973 war with Israel, including radically decreasing Egyptian military presence in Sinai before demilitarizing it, ending reliance on Soviet weapons, and in a policy shift that weakened the Arabs' position against the Israeli occupation of territories in Palestine and Syria (the Golan Heights), signing a peace treaty with Israel in 1979. Two years earlier, in a visit to Israel, Sadat promised that the October 1973 war would be the last war between his country and Israel. Security cooperation with the United States also increased, and in return Sadat enjoyed American protection (Kandil 2012). The United States supplied Egypt's security apparatus with training, intelligence sharing, and surveillance tech that helped secure Sadat's regime and allowed 'the Interior Ministry to increase its telephone-tapping capabilities from 1,200 lines in 1971 to 16,000 in 1979' (Kandil 2012: 223). The United States also provided mobile listening posts and surveillance cameras to monitor the streets (ibid.).

With the marginalization of the military and in the wake of the food riots of 18–19 January 1977, the president rapidly grew the police force and its weapons, with support from the United States, which in 1979 alone supplied the paramilitary Central Security Forces with 153,946 tear-gas bombs, 2,419 automatic weapons, and 328,000 rubber bullets. In 1977 the CSD grew from 100,000 to 300,000 troops (Kandil 2012: 245). Repression peaked in 1981 with the Interior Ministry in September of that year detaining 'three thousand of the country's leading intellectuals, journalists, clerics, priests, and members of all opposition groups' (Kandil 2012: 246). Sadat's rule ended with his assassination by military officers during a military parade on 6 October 1981.

## Digital surveillance under Mubarak (1981–2011)

Following Sadat's assassination, his vice president Hosni Mubarak assumed presidential office and stayed in power for thirty years until he was toppled in the January 2011 revolution. Under Mubarak, Egypt completed its transformation into a police state with the interior ministry and its security agencies, in particular the SSIS, being notorious for repression and stamping out dissent. A non-stop state of emergency (under Law No. 162 of 1958) that lasted Mubarak's entire rule (Amnesty 2020b), allowed the government 'a wide margin of control' over the population (Hassanin 2014: 122), including to restrict their freedoms of assembly, protest, and movement, conduct arbitrary detentions, confiscate properties and companies, conduct evictions (Hassanin 2017; Kandil 2012), and ban strikes. The state of emergency also allowed for unchecked surveillance (Hassanin 2017).[1] Under Mubarak, the SSIS grew notoriously, feared for its role in repressing the local population, including arbitrary detentions, torture, and even murder (Amnesty 2020b). The SSIS became exclusively dedicated to domestic surveillance (Kandil 2012).[2]

During the digital age, and as more Egyptians started using digital technologies and the internet, the regime of Mubarak introduced and deployed digital surveillance tech to keep online dissidents, activists, bloggers, and political opponents in check (Hassanin 2017). The regime started to rely increasingly on digital technologies supplied by the private sector. The Mubarak regime bought such tech from companies like the now-defunct Italian firm Hacking Team (Masaar 2022), and US companies BlueCoat and Narus (Privacy International 2019). Egypt received $51 billion in US military aid between 1979 and 2020 (POMED 2020). Egypt is in fact the second largest recipient of Foreign Military Financing (FMF) funds after only Israel (POMED 2020).

## Brief and limited political opening and military re-control (2011–present)

After thirty years in power, Mubarak was ousted after eighteen days of popular mass protests against corruption, repression, and police violence (Teti and Gervasio 2011). Despite the repressive tactics and the murder of hundreds of protesters, his Interior Ministry and police forces were unable to put an end to the protests (Kandil 2012). The military seized this opportunity and intervened, forcing Mubarak to resign and surrender power to the Supreme Council of the Armed Forces (SCAF) (ibid.). SCAF said it would oversee the transitional period and leave politics after an elected authority assumed power. The reforms during this period were superficial and the military, with the Interior Ministry, adopted repressive tactics against demonstrators and activists demanding more radical reforms (ibid.: 332). The SSIS was replaced with a new agency, the National Security Sector, although its old leadership largely remained (ibid.).

## Morsi's brief time in power (2012–13)

Legislative elections were held between the end of 2011 and early 2012, and the Freedom and Justice Party of the Muslim Brotherhood (MB) won 47 per cent of the votes (Carnegie 2012). The country's first competitive presidential elections (Fahmi 2012) were held in May and June 2012. The MB's Mohamed Morsi won, becoming Egypt's first civilian president. Up to this point, all of Egypt's previous former presidents emanated from the military (ibid.). Prior to Morsi's election, the parliament, in which his party had a majority, was dissolved and SCAF reclaimed legislative power (Kandil 2012). After being sworn in as new president on 30 June 2013, Morsi reinstated the parliament, in a move that challenged the military's legislative powers, opening the door for a power struggle between the military and the President (Fahim 2012). Morsi's presidency was short-lived. He was deposed a year later by the military in a bloody coup following mass protests (Hamid 2019).

## The rise of Sisi

Discontent with the Muslim Brotherhood led to mass protests calling for the overthrow of Morsi on 30 June 2013 (El-Shobaki 2013). SCAF responded by issuing an ultimatum to Morsi to meet the demands of protesters, and on 3 July, the then defence minister Abdelfattah al-Sisi, appointed under Morsi, led a military coup that overthrew Morsi (Hoffman 2023). The constitution was suspended, hundreds of anti-coup protesters were killed in a brutal crackdown, and many more were imprisoned (ibid.). Since then, Egyptians have been living under 'unprecedented' repression and military control (Dawn 2021). Under Sisi, the media and civil society are tightly controlled and those who express their opinions and criticize the authorities face persecution. New draconian laws were passed, and are regularly enforced, to restrict freedom of expression and crush any signs of political dissidence. These include a new media law, adopted in 2018, that criminalizes the dissemination of 'fake news' (Barrie and Mahlouly 2024) and a 2017 NGO law that curtails the activities and funding of non-governmental organizations (OHCHR 2017).

Digital surveillance has continued unabated and even intensified under Sisi. In fact, the same year that Mubarak was removed from power, Egypt acquired a monitoring centre and interception management system, equipment necessary for carrying out interception of telecommunications networks (Privacy International 2016a). The authorities also deployed spyware to target human rights defenders and political opponents (Marczak et al. 2021). Coordinated phishing campaigns bearing the hallmarks of the security apparatus and targeting dissidents and NGOs were also documented by human rights groups and security researchers (Amnesty 2019).

## Surveillance landscape

This section reviews the current landscape of digital surveillance in Egypt and is organized into four sections summarizing the use of four categories of digital surveillance technology.

### Internet interception

Deep Packet Inspection (DPI)[3] is used in Egypt to keep a tab on citizens' internet communication online, such as email exchanges, messages, and social media posts and to filter objectionable content – preventing access to entire websites, services, and applications (SMEX 2023). Egypt began deploying such technologies under the Mubarak regime, after it bought them from foreign surveillance tech providers, including US companies Narus and BlueCoat (Privacy International 2016a). Since Sisi's coup and arrival in power, the digital space in Egypt has become even more restricted and tightly controlled with regulations that restrict freedom of expression and what users post, in addition to the blocking of hundreds of websites including those of media outlets and nonprofit organizations. Internet interception tech facilitates Egypt's blocking of websites critical of the government, including those of human rights groups and media outlets, in addition to Virtual Private Networks and Proxy servers, which users use to bypass censorship (SMEX 2023).

For example, technologies provided by US–Canadian company Sandvine facilitate the monitoring and censorship of internet activities (Masaar 2020). In 2017, Sandvine was acquired by private equity firms Francisco Partners and merged with Procera Networks (Gibbs 2017). Procera's PacketLogic solutions were deployed by Vodafone Egypt, and Telecom Egypt are believed to be deploying the same technologies (Masaar 2020).

The use of FinSpy digital surveillance spyware was documented in Egypt by human rights groups and researchers as early as 2015. An investigation by

Citizen Lab (Marczak et al. 2015) documented the deployment of FinSpy in Egypt by a government entity, the Technology Research Department, to conduct a malware campaign. FinSpy was supplied by FinFisher (since dissolved), part of the British–German Gamma Group. The spyware has capabilities to intercept communications, access private data and record video and audio, once it has infected computers and mobile devices without users' knowledge. The link between FinFisher and the Egyptian government was uncovered by protesters in 2011 when they stormed the headquarters of the State Security Investigations Service (McVeigh 2011). One of the documents that the protesters found and disseminated to the public was an offer dated June 2010 from Gamma for the provision of FinSpy to the SSIS for €287,000 (ibid.).

In 2019, Amnesty International revealed a phishing campaign aimed at stealing passwords of civil society groups and human rights defenders and accessing their accounts. Amnesty's (2019) investigation estimated that the number of targeted individuals was 'in the order of several hundreds'. Additional technical investigations by Amnesty's Security Lab later found FinSpy in Egypt, including versions that are used for Windows, Android, Linux, and MacOS (Amnesty 2020a).

## Mobile interception

The Egyptian government also deploys mobile interception technologies to covertly spy on calls, messages, and internet communications. Members of political opposition, civil society, and journalists are often a target of mobile interception.

After former Egyptian MP Ahmed Eltantawy announced his presidential bid for the 2024 election, between May and September 2023, his phone was repeatedly targeted with Cytrox's Predator spyware via links sent on SMS and WhatsApp (Marczak et al. 2023). Researchers at Citizen Lab and Google's Threat Analysis Group discovered that in August and September 2023 Eltantawy's Vodafone Egypt mobile connection was 'persistently' selected for targeting using an iPhone zero-day exploit chain aimed at installing Predator on iOS.

In another example, exiled opposition politician, Ayman Nour, was simultaneously targeted with Cytrox's Predator spyware and NSO's Pegasus in June 2021 (Marczak et al. 2021).

Cytrox is based in Hungary, and was part of Intellexa, a consortium of commercial spyware vendors, based in Greece, founded by former Israeli military officer Tal Dilian (Marczak et al. 2021). In July 2023, the Biden administration blacklisted Cytrox and Intellexa as well as its affiliates in Ireland and Macedonia (AP 2023).

Egyptian authorities also likely deployed International Mobile Subscriber Identity-Catchers or IMSI catchers, which intercept phone calls and messages by pretending to be a cell phone tower. In 2015, the UK government granted licences for the export of IMSI catchers to several countries, including Egypt (Privacy International 2016b).

## Social media monitoring

According to the Association for Freedom of Thought and Expression (AFTE), social media monitoring has been practised for years, but under Sisi it became more regulated (2021a). Monitoring is enabled through different tactics that include sophisticated deep packet inspection tech, hacking of social media accounts, to manual monitoring conducted by government entities.

At the interior ministry, the General Administration of Information Technology and the National Security Agency coordinate to monitor activities on social media (AFTE 2021a). On the other hand, the Supreme Council for Media Regulations (SCMR) has the mandate to monitor personal accounts of more than 5,000 users, and impose fines and blocking orders (Tahrir Institute for Middle East Policy 2019). In 2021, it ordered 212 Facebook accounts, ten Twitter accounts, and five Instagram accounts to be blocked (Freedom House 2022). In 2019, the Public Prosecution established the Communication, Guidance and Social Media Department (CGSMD), with one unit, the Monitoring and Analysis Unit (MAU) dedicated to keeping a tab on social media users by monitoring 'all content in relation to the Public Prosecution', including by analysing news, comments, and opinions (AFTE 2021c). According to AFTE's analysis of the decision that established the unit, by not specifying the scope of content relating to the Prosecution, the MAU 'may monitor everything it considers relating to it [Prosecution] or pertaining to the commission of crimes' (AFTE 2021c). Since its establishment, the MAU has been involved in filing lawsuits against users for their social media posts (ibid.). In 2014, a call for tender by the interior ministry for 'a more sophisticated mass monitoring system' to scan social media was leaked. The system would monitor twenty-six topics that included demonstrations, strikes and sit-ins (Amnesty 2014).

Social media monitoring enables Egyptian authorities to identify and prosecute users who cross red lines. Those targeted do not only include activists, journalists, and opposition politicians, but also those who post entertaining content or content that is not political in nature. Women models and influencers have become a regular target for alleged 'debauchery' and violation of public morals, a trend that skyrocketed under Sisi, and since the adoption of the 2018 cybercrimes law (AFTE 2021b). AFTE documented 300 arrests for social media posts between mid-2013 and the first quarter of 2021 (ibid.).

## Smart City Surveillance

Interest in safe city and smart city tech and its deployment is thriving in Egypt as authorities build new city projects. Sisi's regime has started building a new capital city, known as New Administrative Capital (NAC), in the outskirts of Cairo with an estimated cost of $59 billion (Declan and Yee 2022). The NAC will be fitted with a surveillance system of more than 6,000 surveillance cameras, manufactured by US company Honeywell, feeding into a command and control centre (Thomson Reuters Foundation 2023). According to the company, the command and control centre will run 'sophisticated video analytics to monitor crowds and traffic congestion, detect incidents of theft, observe suspicious people or objects, and trigger automated alarms in emergency situations' (ibid.). Additionally, lamp posts will be fitted with Wifi capabilities and the city's more than 6.5 million residents will access services using one single app (ibid.). According to Enterprise (2018), an Egyptian business news website, quoting the spokesperson of the state-owned company in charge of building the new capital, these systems are worth $31 million; however, a total contract value has not been disclosed.

Such tech is a concern not only when it comes to the future city, but also to Egyptians nowadays. In 2018, the parliament approved a bill forcing restaurants and shop owners to install surveillance cameras under the pretext of countering terrorism (Privacy International 2016a). During COP17, taxis used to transport attendees were fitted with security cameras that recorded both audio and video and connected to a 'security observatory' (Human Rights Watch 2022).

### Biometric digital-ID

The Egyptian National ID Card is machine-readable and contains a unique ID number, a photo, the full name, gender, birthplace, birthdate, address, religion, marital status, parents' names, and signature of the cardholder (Privacy International 2019). It is mandatory for Egyptians aged sixteen and older (ibid.).

In 2014, the Egyptian government contracted Morpho, a French electronics security company and a subsidiary of Safran, to produce the Egyptian national biometric ID cards (EuropaWire 2014). In 2021, Mashable reported that Egypt is planning to integrate finger-vein recognition in its national ID programme, 'the first of its kind initiative by any administration in the world'. Finger vein recognition captures images of the hand's veins using near-infrared light (Dawood 2021). In another initiative Idemia announced in 2020 that it will be working with Egypt Post to build digital identity services (Burt 2020).

SIM card registration with an ID card is compulsory, after the National Telecommunications Regulatory Authority (NTRA), in 2014, required all SIM cards to be registered (Privacy International 2019). The push for the adoption of biometric digital-ID however, has been slow. Linking citizens biometric ID to their mobile SIM cards and to electronic purchases has the potential to further expand the surveillance that Egyptians are subjected to, which raises human rights concerns, given a lack of robust regulations that ensure surveillance is limited and overseen by independent judicial authorities (Roberts et al. 2021).

This section has provided an overview of Egypt's digital surveillance landscape; the next section reviews some concepts that may prove to be useful for framing the analysis that follows.

## Conceptual framework

Surveillance is an expression of power (Lyon 2007) which plays out across unequal power relations between citizens and the state. In a highly surveilled environment, citizens are constantly aware of being watched over and the risks that come with it, leading them to adjust their behaviours. This is Foucault's 'panoptic' model of surveillance where 'an invisible overseer (*surveillant* in French) has a panoptic view of all aspects of prisoners' or workers' life'. In Foucault's account, as a result of knowing they can be constantly observed, those subjected to the panopticon become self-disciplining, 'modifying their behaviour without the need for coercive power' (see introduction to this volume). Surveillance thus aids the shrinking of this civic space and creates a chilling effect, a first-order effect (Roberts and Mohamed Ali 2021). This chapter also explores the second-order effects of digital surveillance (see introduction to this volume) to analyse the political power interests that are served by their deployment of digital surveillance and analyses what effect they have on citizens' rights and power relationships. Under a Surveillance State, citizens' actions, behaviours, and thoughts are closely watched and monitored to maintain control over them. The Surveillance State concept will be used to explore the surveillance of the cyberspace and smart cities in Egypt and its impacts on citizens and their rights.

## Analysis

Throughout its history the modern Egyptian state has deployed surveillance to maintain power over citizens (Kandil 2012). Like other surveillance states across Africa and the rest of the world, the scope of its reach and expansion of methods radically expanded with the digital age and as more Egyptians connect to the internet.

It was digital surveillance, first deployed by the Mubarak regime, that made this surveillance pervasive. As Kandil (2012: 286) writes, 'Egypt's tightly controlled police state was possible only because of the surveillance tools that allowed the SSIS to spy on citizens using their own cell phones, to monitor social communication networks, to trace vehicles via sophisticated satellite technologies, etc.' Pervasive surveillance has a panopticon effect (Foucault 1995), where citizens adjust their behaviours as a result of being watched or the belief that they are constantly being watched.

Since Sisi's takeover in 2013, the military regime has further expanded the country's surveillance machinery to keep a tab on those it considers to be a threat to its power interests. While it has deployed technologies inherited from the Mubarak regime such as FinSpy (Marczak et al. 2015), it has also resorted to the latest state-of-the-art technologies, including Pegasus and Cytrox (Marczak et al. 2021). Shortly after Sisi's military coup, the regime also acquired newer systems, signing a €10 million contract in 2014 with Nexa Technologies (Tesquet 2017), previously known as Amesys, to acquire interception technologies to spy on phone calls and messages (O'Neill 2021). This acquisition was supported by the United Arab Emirates (UAE) (Tesquet 2017), a key geopolitical player in the Arab World that supported Sisi and his coup against the Muslim Brotherhood (Butter 2020).

Additionally, as mentioned above, in November 2019, a unit dictated to monitoring social media users, the Monitoring and Analysis Unit (MAU) at the Communication, Guidance and Social Media Department (CGSMD) was established by the Public Prosecution (AFTE 2021c). The MAU was established following rare anti-government and anti-Sisi protests amid corruption allegations exposed online by a former construction contractor working with the military. Since then, the MAU has filed several cases against social media users (ibid.).

The expansion of the regime's surveillance capabilities unfolded as Egypt witnessed an unprecedented crackdown on human rights (DAWN 2021). The Sisi regime introduced a series of laws restricting civil liberties and freedoms, including freedom of expression and information, press and media freedoms, the right to protest and assembly, leading to a shrinking of civic space (Barrie and Mahlouly 2024; OHCHR 2017; DAWN 2021). Thousands of political prisoners are languishing in jail, independent media and NGOs have been closed, and those that continue to operate face harassment, intimidation, threats, and legal prosecution (Yee et al. 2022). Given that the internet, and social media in particular, was used by protesters and activists to organize and mobilize during the January 2011 uprising that toppled Mubarak, Sisi feels that exercising control over digital civic space is essential to keep any sign of dissent in check, limiting the power of opposition, and maintaining his own hold on political power.

The impacts on citizen's rights and agency have been disastrous. For fear of regime reprisals, citizens resort to self-censoring and avoid taking actions that may fall foul of the regime's many red lines such as taking part in a protest, signing a petition, or voting for the opposition. Those who cross these lines get caught by the surveillance machines of the security and military apparatuses and face reprisals that can lead to imprisonment and even violence. Surveillance is deployed to shrink the civic space and wipe out any form of dissent, including criticism of Sisi, the military, economic management, and security forces.

For Egyptians, it is not only exposing state and military corruption that can trigger the watchful eyes of national security agencies, but also complaining about living conditions. In one case, in September 2021, two members of the same family, Nagy Fawzy Ali Moawad and his nephew Taha Hamdy, were arrested after they posted online a satirical video addressing bad living conditions and rising prices in the country (AFTE 2021b). The State Security Prosecution charged them both with joining a terrorist group, spreading false news, and misusing social media (ibid.).

The military regime's deployment and expansion of surveillance to maintain control is also playing out in public spaces as the Egyptian authorities transform the country's urban landscape in major cities, erase entire neighbourhoods, and build smart cities, including a proposed new capital city. These changes are seen as a 'securitization' of the public space according to critics. Interviewed by el-Hamalawy (el-Hamalawy 2023, n.p.), Egyptian historian Khaled Fahmy said: 'The bridges and highroads that they are building atomize society, which is us, the enemy and source of worry. They also serve to eliminate public space. Where do Egyptians gather and meet? The squares and streets. These are being taken away to deprive us of social unity.'

Smart city tech has been integral in the (re)design and development of urban spaces under Sisi. Thousands of closed circuit surveillance cameras have been linked to a central command-and-control centre (Thomson Reuters Foundation 2023). This isn't the first time that rulers in Egypt took steps to alter and reshape urban and public spaces to serve their security and political interests while marginalizing the freedoms and liberties of citizens (Kandil 2012; el-Hamalawy 2023).

During the 2011 Egyptian uprising that toppled Mubarak, urban spaces were essential to the protest movement. Public squares in Cairo and major cities were occupied and street battles were fought between protesters and security forces (Kandil 2012). Tahrir Square became the epicentre of the uprising, 'determining its trajectory' according to Kandil (2012: 324). In his book *Soldiers, Spies, and Statesmen: Egypt's Road to Revolt* (2012), he reflected on the protestors' choice of Tahrir Square instead of seats of power such as the parliament and government buildings: 'It seems obvious that the only advantage such an expansive and exposed location offered was visibility … For a strategy based on galvanizing domestic and world opinion and daring the regime to shoot civilians in front of hundreds of cameras and news reporters, Tahrir Square (and other central squares throughout Egypt's provincial cities) fit perfectly' (ibid.: 324–5).

It is no wonder then that Sisi is embarking on a plan to build new smart cities, and not just the New Administrative Capital (NAC). As of October 2022, thirty-seven new smart cities are planned while twenty-four cities are being transformed into smart cities (Waisová 2022). Construction for the biggest of these projects, the NAC, is already under way (ibid.).

The government maintains that the new cities are built to ease traffic congestion, address the housing problem and absorb an expanding population, create jobs, and improve the quality of life (Egyptian State Information Service 2018). But critics from urban planners, researchers, and human rights experts argue that this urban transformation, in which surveillance is a fundamental element, is aimed at better controlling the population and maintaining power through 'militarised urban planning' (el-Hamalawy 2023). In fact, the military in Egypt is playing a key role in delivering these massive infrastructure projects, including the NAC (Sayigh 2023).

'SCs combine data and digital technology to make better decisions and improve the quality of life' with different layers working together (Waisová 2022). In the NAC, in addition, 6,000 surveillance cameras connected to a central command centre will also collect data from other sources including mobile phone trackers, digital check points, and digital control gates in public transport stations. Residents will access services, unlock doors, and make complaints and payments using smart cards and apps. This digitization of the urban public space will facilitate more ubiquitous surveillance in real time (Graham and Wood 2003: 228).

This is an epitome of Deleuze's societies of control, where 'The numerical language of control is made of codes that mark access to information, or reject it', arguing that this type of society operates with a type of machine – computers (1992). In smart cities, not only computers but mobile devices, smart cards, digital applications, surveillance cameras, and others all track citizens, their movements, behaviours, and transactions, resulting in a public space of pervasive surveillance and placing citizens in a state of continual uncertainty about who is watching them and why (Lyon 2007). On the other hand, this level of pervasive surveillance, according to Munoriyarwa and Mare (2023), normalizes surveillance to the extent that citizens expect it (Dencik and Cable 2017). As one software engineer who bought an apartment in the NAC told Reuters (Thomson Reuters Foundation 2023): 'What's wrong with having cameras across the city to monitor violations and eliminate crime? I trust the government. The systems will make life much easier for us as residents.'

The result is an erosion of privacy and other fundamental rights that further entrenches the military regime. At the slightest sign of trouble – perceived or real – detected through the constant surveillance, the police, security agencies, and the military can quickly mobilize and prevent civic actions such as protests, strikes, and gatherings from getting out of their control. For Sisi, building smart cities is a matter of exercising and maintaining power over citizens. As el-Hamalawy (2023) writes:

> The motives behind Sisi's plan to build the New Administrative Capital are many. There is little doubt he is driven by megalomania as well as his desire to generate more business opportunities for the military. Yet, the move also reflects an ideological position: Sisi wants to ensure that no revolution ever happens again – that no strikes, roadblocks, or riots bring the government machine to a halt as it did in 2011.

The ruler of Egypt has given up on the old city, and indeed on the entire valley. For him, 'Egypt' has become the New Administrative Capital and the New Alamein – two citadels linked together by a high-speed train. The government claims the new capital is not 'fortified' and will not be walled-off, yet urban planners who viewed the designs paint a different picture. The city will have gates and a surveillance system that will ensure every car and person entering and exiting is monitored and tracked around the clock.

Waisová who researched the NAC as an 'instrument of social and political ordering and exclusion' (Waisová 2022, n.p.) argues that the new city's smart technologies operate 'as an instrument to engineer society to create a "new state"' given the fact that the nature of technologies deployed and planned for the city – predictive policing, surveillance, and crowd management – increase the potential for control. She further describes the city's inhabitants as 'prisoners of the system, with less freedom than any other citizens of the country' despite benefiting from better services and modern infrastructure:

> The smart technologies are not used for civic participation, protection of civil liberties or crime prevention. They are rather used for data-driven policing and deep control. The inhabitants of the NAC have only a limited possibility of living authentically and experiencing a natural and organic development of society. The NAC has become an instrument of segregation, exclusion and a source of social, political and economic inequality.

## Resistance

During the January 2011 uprising, protesters stormed the headquarters of the notorious and feared SSIS and leaked documents about the agency's dealings with providers of surveillance software (McVeigh 2011). In this act of resistance, Egyptians turned the tables and reversed the gaze on a once feared agency, notorious for its surveillance and repression tactics. Now citizens exercise their agency by spying on the spies in the Surveillance State, in what Mann (Mann et al. 2003) termed *sousveillance*: literally 'watching from below'.

While under Sisi, the Surveillance State has become even more pervasive, Egyptian civil society groups have continued to engage in sousveillance exposing the surveillance apparatus and the entities and companies complicit in such practices through research, investigations, policy analysis, and leaks (Masaar 2020; AFTE 2021a, b, c). This form of resistance is essential to current and future accountability efforts and for raising awareness to educate the public, particularly vulnerable groups, so that they can take precautions.

Another key form of resistance for activists, human rights defenders, opposition politicians, and civil society actors is through the adoption of tools, apps, and features that enhance the security and protection of their personal information such as messages, emails, photos, and contacts. This includes the use of encrypted messaging apps and VPNs.

Strategic litigation was also previously deployed to rein in surveillance, although with no major positive impact. In February 2017, a citizen went to a court to suspend a tender by the Interior Ministry for a social media security risk monitoring software system (Farahat 2021). The case was dismissed for procedural errors.

Civil society has also engaged in strategic litigation against providers of surveillance technologies. For instance, the Cairo Institute for Human Rights Studies supported litigation action taken by FIDH and the LDH against Nexa Technologies for selling surveillance tech to the Sisi regime (FIDH 2017).

## Recommendations

Arising from the above analysis the following recommendations arise for policy, practice, and further research.

**Egyptian legislators** need to adopt regulations that reign in government surveillance and protect the personal information of citizens and residents from the watchful eyes of security and military agencies. Independent judicial oversight of government surveillance should also be enshrined in law.

**The Egyptian government** should be more transparent about its use of surveillance tech, including in the smart cities it is building, and should provide citizens with mechanisms to address harms arising from its use and deployment of such technologies.

**Providers of surveillance technologies** should refrain from doing business with the Sisi regime until after reforms have been established and proper human rights impact assessments have been conducted. Foreign governments and policymakers should regulate the export of surveillance technologies to prevent companies in their jurisdictions from selling such technologies to governments that are likely going to abuse them.

**Researchers and civil society** should pay close attention to the smart cities Egypt is building to understand the surveillance technologies being used and their potential impacts on the rights and lives of their inhabitants.

## Conclusion

Digital surveillance in Egypt was first deployed under the Mubarak regime as more and more Egyptians connected to the internet and used digital technologies. Despite Mubarak's repressive police state and his security agencies' deployment of surveillance tech, popular mass protests that were in part coordinated using digital technologies, succeeded in toppling his rule. Wary of a repeat scenario, Sisi, who rose to power after leading a bloody military coup against the Muslim Brotherhood in 2013, has been imposing an unprecedented crackdown on civil and political rights in the country. Digital surveillance is a key instrument deployed by his regime to exercise control over citizens and maintain political power. Two key developments characterize surveillance under Sisi: first, he not only inherited digital surveillance tactics used under Mubarak but also entrenched them through the deployment of new and state-of-the-art technologies like Cytrox and NSO and through the establishment of newer entities dedicated to monitoring the activities of users on social media such as the SCMR and the MAU.

Second, an urban transformation, where smart city tech will keep a tab on inhabitants is under way. In fact, the country is planning thirty-seven smart cities, thirteen of which, including the New Administrative Capital (NAC), are completely new. As explained in the analysis, the technologies planned and being deployed as part of these cities signal an aim to control their inhabitants.

By exercising control over cyberspace and expanding control over urban spaces through smart city tech, the Sisi regime is seeking to decimate the public sphere, the civic space where citizens can come together to communicate, discuss, and form public opinions (Habermas 1991), and thus erode citizen agency. Given that the media is already tightly controlled in Egypt, this will help insulate the regime from potential threats to its existence and potential downfall. The question remains as to what extent this will be successful.

## Notes

1    The state of emergency was lifted after the 25 January revolution, before it was reinstated again in April 2017. In October 2021, Sisi terminated the state of emergency, but only after many aspects of it were permanently codified into law. See: Freedom House's Freedom on the Net 2023 edition, Egypt report.

2    SSIS was dissolved after the revolution before it was immediately replaced by the National Security Agency (NSA).

3    Deep Packet Inspection (DPI) is a type of network packet filtering where
network packets are evaluated as they pass a given checkpoint. A real-time
decision is then made, depending on what a packet contains and based on rules
assigned by an enterprise, an internet service provider, or a network manager.
DPI could be used to remove spam, viruses, intrusions and any other defined
criteria to block the packet from passing through the inspection point. DPI
could also be used to decide if a particular packet is redirected to another
destination.

# Bibliography

AFTE (2021a). 'Internet without Surveillance. How Can the Egyptian Government
End the Policy of Mass Surveillance?' https://afteegypt.org/en/research-en/policy-
papers-en/2021/06/03/22766-afteegypt.html#_ftn10 (accessed 8 June 2024).

AFTE (2021b). 'Ongoing Violations'. The Third Quarterly Report on the State of
Freedom of Expression in Egypt (1 July–30 September 2021). https://afteegypt.
org/en/research-en/monitoring-reports-en/2021/11/07/25715-afteegypt.html
(accessed 8 June 2024).

AFTE (2021c). 'Public Prosecution and Digital Transformation: An Introduction to
Mass Surveillance of the Internet'. https://afteegypt.org/en/research-en/policy-
papers-en/2021/08/08/24363-afteegypt.html (accessed 8 June 2024).

Amnesty (2014). 'Egypt's Plan for Mass Surveillance of Social Media an Attack
on Internet Privacy and Freedom of Expression'. https://www.amnesty.org/en/
latest/news/2014/06/egypt-s-attack-internet-privacy-tightens-noose-freedom-
expression/ (accessed 8 June 2024).

Amnesty (2019). 'Phishing Attacks Using Third-Party Applications against Egyptian
Civil Society Organizations'. https://www.amnesty.org/en/latest/research/2019/03/
phishing-attacks-using-third-party-applications-against-egyptian-civil-society-
organizations/ (accessed 8 June 2024).

Amnesty (2020a). 'German-made FinSpy Spyware Found in Egypt, and Mac and
Linux Versions Revealed'. https://www.amnesty.org/en/latest/research/2020/09/
german-made-finspy-spyware-found-in-egypt-and-mac-and-linux-versions-
revealed/ (accessed 8 June 2024).

Amnesty (2020b). 'Hosni Mubarak: A Living Legacy of Mass Torture and Arbitrary
Detention'. https://www.amnesty.org/en/latest/news/2020/02/hosni-mubarak-
legacy-of-mass-torture/ (accessed 8 June 2024).

AP News (2023). 'Two European Spyware Firms Added to US Export Blacklist'. https://apnews.com/article/spyware-cytrox-intellexa-blacklist-exports-surveillance-technology-6dfd45c27f48f71b8e662326073003c8 (accessed 8 June 2024).

Barrie, C. and Mahlouly, D. (2024). 'In Sisi's Egypt "Laws Aimed at Curbing Disinformation Are Instruments of Political Repression"', *African Arguments*. https://africanarguments.org/2024/03/in-sisis-egypt-laws-aimed-at-curbing-disinformation-are-instruments-of-political-repression/ (accessed 8 June 2024).

Burt, C. (2020). 'Idemia to Build Biometrics-backed Digital Identity Service in Egypt, Supply TSA Trials, Joins Kantara', Biometric Update. https://www.biometricupdate.com/202003/idemia-to-build-biometrics-backed-digital-identity-service-in-egypt-supply-tsa-trials-joins-kantara (accessed 8 June 2024).

Butter, D. (2020). 'Egypt and the Gulf', Chatham House. https://www.chathamhouse.org/2020/04/egypt-and-gulf/sisis-debt-his-gulf-arab-backers (accessed 8 June 2024).

Carnegie Endowment for International Peace (2012). '2012 Egyptian Parliamentary Elections'. https://carnegieendowment.org/posts/2015/01/2012-egyptian-parliamentary-elections (accessed 8 June 2024).

DataReportal (2023). 'Digital 2023: Egypt'. https://datareportal.com/reports/digital-2023-egypt (accessed 1 July 2024).

DAWN (2021). 'Analysis – Eight Broken Promises: Eight Years after the Coup, al-Sisi Has Failed the Egyptian People'. https://dawnmena.org/analysis-eight-broken-promises-eight-years-after-the-coup-al-sisi-has-failed-the-egyptian-people/ (accessed 8 June 2024).

Dawood, A. (2021). 'Egypt to Unlock Futuristic ID Verification with Finger-Vein Recognition Tech'. Mashable. https://me.mashable.com/tech/12805/egypt-to-unlock-futuristic-id-verification-with-finger-vein-recognition-tech (accessed 8 June 2024).

Declan, W. and Yee, V. (2022). 'A New Capital Worthy of the Pharaohs Rises in Egypt, but at What Price?' *The New York Times*. https://www.nytimes.com/2022/10/08/world/middleeast/egypt-new-administrative-capital.html (accessed 8 June 2024).

Deleuze, G. (1992). 'Postscript on the Societies of Control', *October*, 59: 3–7.

Dencik, L. and Cable, J. (2017). 'The Advent of Surveillance Realism: Public Opinion and Activist Responses to the Snowden Leaks', *International Journal of Communication*, 11: 763–81.

Egyptian State Information Service (2018). 'Fourth Generation Cities: Smart Communities in Egypt'. https://invest-gate.me/features/4th-generation-cities-egypts-urbanization-dream-towards-achieving-sustainable-development/ (accessed 8 June 2024).

El-Hamalawy, H. (2023). 'Cairo's Panopticon 2.0. The History and Present of State Surveillance in Egypt', Rosa Luxemburg Stiftung. https://rosaluxna. org/publications/cairos-panopticon-2-0-the-history-and-present-of-state-surveillance-in-egypt/ (accessed 8 June 2024).

El-Shobaki, A. M. (2013). 'The End of Muslim Brotherhood Rule in Egypt', Carnegie Endowment for International Peace. https://carnegieendowment. org/research/2013/08/the-end-of-muslim-brotherhood-rule-in-egypt?lang=en&er=middle-east (accessed 8 June 2024).

Enterprise (2018). 'Honeywell to Develop USD 31 Mn-worth of Security Systems in Egypt's New Capital'. https://enterprise.news/egypt/en/news/story/606581d6-1c49-498c-9d84-2ba1fdd59f2e/honeywell-to-develop-usd-31-mn-worth-of-security-systems-in-egypt%E2%80%99s-new-capital (accessed 8 June 2024).

EuropaWire (2014). 'Morpho (Safran) Signs Multi-year Contract with Arab Organisation for Industrialisation Electronics to Produce the Egyptian National eID Card'. https://news.europawire.eu/morpho-safran-signs-multi-year-contract-with-arab-organisation-for-industrialisation-electronics-to-produce-the-egyptian-national-eid-card-0654321234567890/eu-press-relea se/2014/12/03/21/16/51/30386/ (accessed 8 June 2024).

Fahim, K. (2012). 'Egypt's Military and President Escalate Their Power Struggle', *The New York Times*. https://www.nytimes.com/2012/07/10/world/middleeast/egypt-tension-after-order-to-reconvene-parliament.html?_r=1&pagewanted=all (accessed 8 June 2024).

Fahmi, G. (2012). 'Egypt Presidential Election 2012: The Survival of the July 1952 Regime', Arab Reform Initiative. https://www.arab-reform.net/publication/egypt-presidential-election-2012-the-survival-of-the-july-1952-regime/ (accessed 8 June 2024).

Farahat, M. (2021). 'Egypt Country Report', in Roberts et al. (2021), *Surveillance Law in Africa: A Review of Six Countries*, Brighton: Institute of Development Studies. https://opendocs.ids.ac.uk/opendocs/bitstream/handle/20.500.12413/16893/Egypt%20Country%20Report.pdf?sequence=5&isAllowed=y (accessed 8 June 2024).

FIDH (2017). 'Sale of Surveillance Equipment to Egypt: Paris Prosecutor Opens a Judicial Investigation'. https://www.fidh.org/en/region/north-africa-middle-east/egypt/sale-of-surveillance-equipment-to-egypt-paris-prosecutor-opens-a (accessed 8 June 2024).

Foucault, M. (1995). *Discipline and Punish: The Birth of the Prison*, New York: Vintage Books.

Freedom House (2022). 'Freedom on the Net 2022: Egypt'. https://freedomhouse.org/country/egypt/freedom-net/2022 (accessed 31 August 2024).

Gibbs, C. (2017). 'Sandvine to Be Combined with Procera in $444M Deal'. *Fierce Wireless*. https://www.fierce-network.com/wireless/sandvine-to-be-combined-procera-444m-deal#:~:text=The%20cash%20deal%20marks%20a,Francisco%20Partners%2C%20in%20the%20announcement (accessed 8 June 2024).

Graham, S. and Wood, D. M. (2003). 'Digitizing Surveillance: Categorization, Space, Inequality', *Acoustics, Speech, and Signal Processing Newsletter, IEEE*, 23(2): 227–48.

Habermas, J. (1991). *The Structural Transformation of the Public Sphere*, Cambridge, MA: The MIT Press.

Hamid, S. (2019). 'The Tragedy of Egypt's Mohamed Morsi'. https://www.brookings.edu/articles/the-tragedy-of-egypts-mohamed-morsi/ (accessed 31 August 2024).

Hassanin, L. (2014). 'Egypt's Internet Surveillance: A Case of Increasing Emergency', in *Global Information Society Watch 2014: Communications Surveillance in the Digital Age*. https://www.giswatch.org/sites/default/files/egypts_internet_surveillance.pdf (accessed 31 August 2024).

Hoffman, J. (2023). 'Ten Years After Coup, the U.S. Still Supports Tyranny in Egypt', Cato Institute. https://www.cato.org/commentary/ten-years-after-coup-us-still-supports-tyranny-egypt (accessed 8 June 2024).

Human Rights Watch (2022). 'Egypt: Arrests, Curbs on Protests as COP27 Nears'. https://www.hrw.org/news/2022/11/06/egypt-arrests-curbs-protests-cop27-nears (accessed 8 June 2024).

Jurado, N. (2024). 'Navigating Crisis: A Brief History of the Suez Canal Crisis'. https://www.researchgate.net/publication/378010887_Navigating_Crisis_A_Brief_History_of_the_Suez_Canal_Crisis (accessed 8 June 2024).

Kamel, T. (1997). 'The Internet Commercialization in Egypt: Challenges and Opportunities', ISOC. https://web.archive.org/web/20160103081314/http://www.isoc.org/inet97/ans97/tarek.htm (accessed 8 June 2024).

Kandil, H. (2012). *Soldiers, Spies, and Statesmen: Egypt's Road to Revolt*, London and New York: Verso Books.

Lyon, D. (2007). 'Surveillance, Power, and Everyday Life', in Chrisanthi Avgerou et al. (eds), *The Oxford Handbook of Information and Communication Technologies*. https://doi.org/10.1093/oxfordhb/9780199548798.003.0019 (accessed 31 August 2024).

Mann, S., Jason, N. and Wellman, B. (2003). 'Sousveillance: Inventing and Using Wearable Computing Devices for Data Collection in Surveillance Environments', *Surveillance & Society*, 1(3): 331–55.

Marczak, B., Scott-Railton, J., Senft, A., Poetranto, I. and McKune, S. (2015). 'Pay No Attention to the Server Behind the Proxy: Mapping FinFisher's Continuing

Proliferation', Citizen Lab. https://citizenlab.ca/2015/10/mapping-finfishers-continuing-proliferation/ (accessed 8 June 2024).

Marczak, B., Scott-Railton, J., Razzak, B. A., Al-Jizawi, N., Anstis, S., Berdan, K. and Dibert, R. (2021). 'Pegasus vs. Predator: Dissident's Doubly-Infected iPhone Reveals Cytrox Mercenary Spyware', Citizen Lab. https://citizenlab.ca/2021/12/pegasus-vs-predator-dissidents-doubly-infected-iphone-reveals-cytrox-mercenary-spyware/ (accessed 8 June 2024).

Marczak, B., Scott-Railton, J., Roethlisberger, D. J., Razzak, B. A., Anstis, S. and Dibert, R. (2023). 'Predator in the Wires: Ahmed Eltantawy Targeted with Predator Spyware After Announcing Presidential Ambitions', Citizen Lab. https://citizenlab.ca/2023/09/predator-in-the-wires-ahmed-eltantawy-targeted-with-predator-spyware-after-announcing-presidential-ambitions/ (accessed 8 June 2024).

Masaar (2020). 'Sandvine ... The Surveillance Octopus in the Arab Region'. https://masaar.net/en/sandvine-the-surveillance-octopus-in-the-arab-region/ (accessed 8 June 2024).

Masaar (2022). 'Hacking Team'. https://masaar.net/en/hacking-team-surveillance-companies-in-the-mena-region/ (accessed 8 June 2024).

McVeigh, K. (2011). 'British Firm Offered Spying Software to Egyptian Regime – Documents', *The Guardian*. https://www.theguardian.com/technology/2011/apr/28/egypt-spying-software-gamma-finfisher (accessed 8 June 2024).

Munoriyarwa, A. and Mare, A. (2023) *Digital Surveillance in Southern Africa*, London: Palgrave Macmillan. https://doi.org/10.1007/978-3-031-16636-5_1

OHCHR (2017). 'Repressive New NGO Law Deeply Damaging for Human Rights in Egypt, Zeid'. https://www.ohchr.org/en/press-releases/2017/05/repressive-new-ngo-law-deeply-damaging-human-rights-egypt-zeid#:~:text=Law%2070%20of%202017%2C%20which,development%20and%20social%20welfare%20plans (accessed 8 June 2024).

Okafor, C. (2024). '10 African Countries with the Highest Population at the Start of 2024', Business Insider Africa. https://africa.businessinsider.com/local/lifestyle/10-african-countries-with-the-highest-population-at-the-start-of-2024/jb1dytw (accessed 8 June 2024).

O'Neill, P. H. (2021). 'French Spyware Bosses Indicted for Their Role in the Torture of Dissidents', *MIT Technology Review*. https://www.technologyreview.com/2021/06/22/1026777/france-spyware-amesys-nexa-crimes-against-humanity-libya-egypt/ (accessed 8 June 2024).

POMED (2020). 'U.S Military Assistance to Egypt: Separating Fact from Fiction'. https://mideastdc.org/wp-content/uploads/2018/01/Egypt-FMF-2.pdf (accessed 8 June 2024).

Privacy International (2016a). 'The President's Men'. https://privacyinternational.org/sites/default/files/2018-02/egypt_reportEnglish_0.pdf (accessed 8 June 2024).

Privacy International (2016b). 'With New Spying Powers on Horizon, Surveillance Companies Descend on UK'. https://privacyinternational.org/news-analysis/641/new-spying-powers-horizon-surveillance-companies-descend-uk (accessed 8 June 2024).

Privacy International (2019). 'State of Privacy Egypt'. https://privacyinternational.org/state-privacy/1001/state-privacy-egypt#:~:text=Under%20President%20Mubarak%27s%20administration%2C%20Egypt,were%20used%20on%20Etisalat%20networks (accessed 8 June 2024).

Roberts, T. and Mohamed Ali, A. (2021). 'Opening and Closing Online Civic Space in Africa: An Introduction to the Ten Digital Rights Landscape Reports', in T. Roberts (ed.), *Digital Rights in Closing Civic Space: Lessons from Ten African Countries*, Brighton: Institute of Development Studies. https://opendocs.ids.ac.uk/opendocs/handle/20.500.12413/15964 (accessed 8 June 2024).

Roberts, T., Mohamed Ali, A., Farahat, M., Oloyede, R., and Mutung'u, G. (2021). *Surveillance Law in Africa: A Review of Six Countries*, Brighton: Institute of Development Studies. https://doi.org/10.19088/IDS.2021.059

Sayigh, Y. (2023). 'Assessing Egypt's State Ownership Policy: Challenges and Requirements', Carnegie Endowment for International Peace. https://carnegieendowment.org/research/2023/05/assessing-egypts-state-ownership-policy-challenges-and-requirements?lang=en (accessed 8 June 2024).

SMEX (2023). 'What Is DPI Technology, and Why Is Egypt Abusing It?' https://smex.org/what-is-dpi-technology-and-why-is-egypt-abusing-it-2/ (accessed 8 June 2024).

Statista (2022a). 'Internet Penetration Rate in Africa as of June 2022, Compared to the Global Average'. https://www.statista.com/statistics/1176654/internet-penetration-rate-africa-compared-to-global-average/ (accessed 8 June 2024).

Statista (2022b). 'African Countries with the Highest Gross Domestic Product (GDP) in 2022'. https://www.statista.com/statistics/1120999/gdp-of-african-countries-by-country/ (accessed 8 June 2024).

Statista (2024). 'Internet Usage in Africa – Statistics & Facts'. https://www.statista.com/topics/9813/internet-usage-in-africa/#topicOverview (accessed 8 June 2024).

Tahrir Institute for Middle East Policy (2019). 'The Law Regulating the Press, Media, and the Supreme Council for Media Regulation'. https://timep.org/wp-content/uploads/2018/12/SCMR-Law-5-15-2019-1.pdf (accessed 31 August 2024).

Tesquet, O. (2017). *Amesys: Egyptian Trials and Tribulations of a French Digital Arms Dealer*. https://www.telerama.fr/monde/amesys-egyptian-trials-and-tribulations-of-a-french-digital-arms-dealer,160452.php (accessed 8 June 2024).

Teti, A. and Gervasio, G. (2011). 'Egypt's Second January Uprising: Causes and Consequences of a Would-be Revolution', European Institute of the Mediterranean. https://www.iemed.org/publication/egypts-second-january-uprising-causes-and-consequences-of-a-would-be-revolution/ (accessed 8 June 2024).

Thomson Reuters Foundation (2023). 'FEATURE-CCTV Cameras Will Watch over Egyptians in New High-Tech Capital'. https://www.reuters.com/article/egypt-tech-surveillance-idAFL8N33I0DO/ (accessed 8 June 2024).

Waisová, Š. (2022). 'The Tragedy of Smart Cities in Egypt. How the Smart City Is Used towards Political and Social Ordering and Exclusion', *Applied Cybersecurity & Internet Governance*, 1(1): 1–10. https://doi.org/10.5604/01.3001.0016.0985

Yee, V. et al. (2022). 'Egypt's Revolving Jailhouse Door: One Pretrial Detention After Another', *The New York Times*. https://www.nytimes.com/interactive/2022/07/16/world/middleeast/egypt-prisoners.html

# 4

# State surveillance and digital rights in Zambia

Sam Phiri and Kiss Abraham

## Introduction

This chapter interrogates the nexus between state surveillance and digital rights in Zambia. It takes both a historical and a contemporary view of that relationship. Thus, it traces the origins of surveillance from the foundation of the Zambian nation, dominated by an imperial British private business entity, to the modern era where the country is ruled by Africans themselves. The basic assumption here is that the Zambian state has been 'spying' on its citizens throughout its history as a strategy for maintaining power and political privileges for the ruling elite.

What is different is that, unlike other non-democratic states, where power is openly in the hands of the few and retained by a limited elite, Zambia prides itself on being an open democracy where people have human rights which, in some instances, translate into digital rights. However, instead of Zambia opening up digital spaces, what we have observed is the opposite. There has been an increase in the closing of those online spaces and the acquisition of sophisticated equipment by the Zambian government, costing millions in US dollars, from countries like China, Britain, and Israel. Among other things, this equipment enables the Zambian state to monitor the country's digital space closely, to exercise control over its citizens, and to snoop into their private affairs without the people's knowledge.

On a broader level, the chapter notes that, although the political system may have changed hands and governance style over the past sixty-plus years, and citizen surveillance practices may have shifted stances, the snooping intentions to ensure state control over citizens have remained largely the same.

The chapter tracks those changes and teases out how post-independence governments have used surveillance systems to spy on their people, repress citizens' agency, and suppress their human rights, as the state has worked to promote the power interests and dominance of the political elite.

This chapter addresses the following questions:

- How has the state been surveilling its citizens over the years?
- Has the practice of spying on citizens changed with the changing political orientation of its leadership?
- How have citizens responded to this kind of prying into their privacy?

In addressing these issues, we first offer some background to locate surveillance in Zambia within a historical and political context. Then, we review some theoretical concepts to frame our analysis of the surveillance phenomenon more broadly. Thereafter, we highlight the views and experiences of a selected group of citizens, who are direct victims of state surveillance. These experiences are accompanied by the ripostes from human rights groups who are outraged by the existence of this form of rights violations. Finally, using the conceptual and theoretical framework referred to above, we analyse the interview evidence, using focus group debates with groups of conscientious rights violations objectors, to answer the research questions and recommend areas for further action.

## Background: A history of surveillance

In response to the first question, the following section gives an overview of, and deals with, the evolution of surveillance systems in Zambia since independence in 1964. It highlights both the internal and international dynamics which contributed to the existence, growth, and breadth of surveillance systems in Zambia.

From geographical maps, we see that Zambia is centrally located within the environs of Southern Africa. It shares borders with the Democratic Republic of the Congo (DRC) and Tanzania in the North, Malawi and Mozambique in the East and South-East, Zimbabwe, Botswana, and Namibia in the South, and Angola in the West.

At the political level, the Zambian constitution states that the country is a unitary, indivisible, multi-ethnic, multiracial, multireligious, multicultural and multiparty democratic state (Zambia 2016). It was founded as Northern Rhodesia in 1890 under the control of the British South Africa Company (BSAC), and then turned into a Protectorate under the British Colonial office from 1924 to 1963. The British introduced state surveillance in Zambia in the shape of the Special Branch Police, whose job it was to spy on those considered to be threats to colonial power interests.

In 1964, the country became an independent state, named Zambia, under indigenous black people's rule (Phiri 2006: 1). The Zambia Police is established under the law of the new Republic (Government of Zambia 1966). Zambia's history has been immensely influenced by political and economic events in all the neighbouring countries since 1964. This involvement included Zambia's support for anti-colonialist liberation wars then taking place in most neighbouring countries. Such support was offered both diplomatically and while training rebel anti-colonial armies which prompted investment in surveillance activities, as a way of fighting against espionage, anarchy, and treason.

The political party that brought Zambia to independence was the United National Independence Party (UNIP) under Kenneth Kaunda. After liberation, UNIP retained the surveillance function of the Special Branch but redirected its focus to perceived threats to the power of the newly independent nation.

From 1964 to 1972, Zambia practised multipartyism, although under long-standing state of emergency regulations under the Emergency Powers Act (National Assembly of Zambia 1964). The Act empowered the President to make emergency regulations whenever an emergency proclamation is in force with surveillance in effect and increased restrictions on civic space (Mwape 2017). With the Emergency Powers in place, the elections, which were held regularly, were characterized by violations of human rights, including the detention of Kaunda's political opponents (Mwanakatwe 1994: 90).

Thereafter, and up to 1991, the country was a legislated one-party state with Kaunda and his UNIP in control. Moreover, the country was also faced with surveillance activities (Hitchcock 1973). For instance, in the 1970s, a number of people were detained by the Zambian government accused of being associates of Adamson Mushala and his anti-government rebels then operating in the northwestern rural parts of Zambia between 1972 and 1973. After some surveillance and investigations, the accused were brought to court and said to have been trained by the then ruling Portuguese in Angola and South African soldiers in South West Africa (now Namibia) to sabotage and eventually overthrow the Zambia government (Zambia Lii 2023).

At the same time, the government was closely monitoring the activities of the black liberation movement based in Lusaka, Zambia. To do so, the government established what was called the Liberation Centre in Lusaka, where all such movements were instructed to open offices. Overseeing their operations, the Centre was initially placed under the intelligence wing in the President's office, and later transferred to the Zambia Army Special Duties Unit, which assumed the 'task of controlling the liberation movements' in Zambia (Chisala 1994: 132).

This was at a time when many people were detained on mere suspicion. As one court judgement states, people were detained when there was 'insufficient evidence to secure a conviction; or it may not be possible to secure a conviction without disclosing sources of information which it would be contrary to the national interest to disclose; or the information available may raise no more than a suspicion, but one which someone charged with the security of the nation dare not ignore' (Zambia Lii 2023).

That aside, Chisala (1994: 154), a former Zambian State House aide and intelligence officer, states every country has an intelligence system whose purposes are to protect the country from subversive activities and to detect threats of espionage. But in Zambia, the system evolved into 'an organ of terror' which ensured that people lived in 'a state of pathological fear and suspicion of each other' as no one knew who could be trusted.

According to Chisala (1994: 155), government spies numbered in the thousands and included 'informers who are planted in all institutions and places of work'. Various offices were opened across the country and instructors came from the United States, Britain, West Germany, and Romania. Chisala (1994: 156) argues that, during Kaunda's presidency, Zambia's intelligence system was 'probably one of the most sophisticated and atrocious systems' in Africa. The agents of the intelligence system also 'bugged' telephone lines and 'followed' some people 24 hours a day (Chisala 1994: 159).

For example, a South Africa-based white journalist who wanted to interview President Kaunda was watched and followed 'round the clock … by two black gentlemen with tough features and big feet' for three days before being allowed to meet Kaunda (Hitchcock 1973: 15).

Further, Chisala (1994: 50–2) narrates how an American, Marshall Sogoian, installed 'the most powerful and elaborate communication network in Africa' in Zambia. This connected every office and the houses of government and governing party officials to Kaunda's State House. Sogoian, in 1969, also provided devices that ensured that 'all the telephone lines in the country were bugged'. This equipment was flown into the country from the United States by Zambia's future president, Rupiah Banda, 'under the blanket of diplomatic immunity'. The whole surveillance system, which connected the police, army, and senior government officials in all parts of the country, was controlled from a communication centre built at State House.

Perhaps the creation of this elaborate surveillance system is understandable, because at about the same time, white South Africa, Rhodesia (now Zimbabwe), and British military intelligence agents were active in Zambia, while China and Russia were a part of the undercover scene in Zambia providing technical strategic assistance to regional African liberation movements which were housed in Zambia. All these countries were spying on each other and on Zambia, to an extent that Lusaka, the capital, became 'the most vital, stamping ground in southern Africa for professional spies from both the East and West' (Hitchcock 1973: 58–9). As Sardanis (2007: 1) argues, with regard to Africa, 'everybody has been meddling … and everybody has a formula for its [Africa's] salvation'. For instance, the British had a top-level 'insider' in the Zambian government who ended up as Kaunda's principal secretary to the cabinet. This was Valentine Musakanya who, according to Sardanis (2003), was among the first ranked Zambian civil servants to be recruited by the British Intelligence agency, MI6, who from 1963 were monitoring the civil war situation in neighbouring Congo.

That was the situation in Zambia. For many years, its capital, Lusaka, was a hive of activities involving various intelligence agents from different countries, prompting Kaunda to establish what Sardanis (2014: 89) calls a 'very extensive State Security Department', which was 'ubiquitous' and oppressive.

Overall, surveillance was institutionalized in the psyche of future Zambian politicians by the British administration with the introduction of an intelligence collection wing, the Special Branch, within the colonial police force. The Special Branch was established, among other reasons, to protect colonial power by spying on liberation activists in Zambia. However, that political surveillance function was retained after liberation to spy on those people considered to be threats to the power of the post-colonial administration, which was authoritative, patrimonial, and an almost imperial presidency that has maintained tight control over opposition and journalists. The opposition and dissenting voices were proscribed and repressed under successive administrations, and at times forced underground. That formed the political context in which surveillance grew in Zambia in total violation of citizens' rights. It was also a means of self-preservation by the incumbent power interests which have governed Zambia over the past sixty years.

From the above discussion, it may be clear that, as a strategy for maintaining power and political privileges, UNIP, like other post-independence governing parties, continued or even upgraded, colonial surveillance systems in Zambia. For example, UNIP created and sustained a special civilian enforcement agency consisting of youths who spied on and controlled several sectors of society. These were all members of the UNIP Youth League, also known as 'UNIP Vigilantes.'

For instance, a former member of this much feared wing of the ruling party, Charles Chisala (2018), who later became a journalist, writes of that era:

> Besides its core role of mass political mobilisation, the UNIP Youth League had been turned into the defacto civilian unit of the Zambia Police Force (ZP). A vestige of the repressive colonial Northern Rhodesia Police then, the force was stretched to the limit as a result of widespread public discontent. It therefore heavily relied on the UNIP vigilantes to supplement its efforts in maintaining law and order. To be honest the youths were a militia in every sense of the word. The police had unofficially extended or ceded some of their powers to the feared vigilantes.

He further comments:

> We used to meet the District Intelligence Officer (DIO) under the Special Branch of the then dreaded Office of the President (OP) at the big,

well-maintained house hidden by a high concrete fence. It also served as a transient centre for captured subversive elements, enemies of the State or unpatriotic citizens. Once we captured such people in well-planned and executed raids we took them to the house, where the DIO would interrogate them before deciding where to take them ... The house also served as a secret indoctrination school where vigilantes used to receive political lessons on patriotism, national security and rudimentary skills in intelligence gathering.

(Chisala 2018)

This narration demonstrates that there was a significant section of the community that was recruited as surveillance operatives. These were also imparted with rudimentary surveillance skills. This is not too far removed from McGregor's (2013) observations, in Zimbabwe, with regard to the role of surveillance in post-colonial Africa. McGregor argues that surveillance is 'close observation, especially of a suspected spy or criminal', so as to achieve control in a manner that is distinct from coercion through force and threats. McGregor notes that academic debates around African government surveillance activities have primarily focused on 'physical watching rather than technology' and are centred in countries with highly centralized, authoritarian governments with extensive state reach, and dense administrative bureaucracies that closely intersect with militarized ruling party hierarchies, as was the case with Chisala's UNIP Youth League in Zambia. The aim is to reduce the need for overt violence, and to discipline populations by 'generating self-restraint' (Lavoie 2014: 33).

However, with the global winds of political systems' change, blowing eastwards, across the world in the late 1980s, leading to the collapse of the Soviet Union, the Iron Curtain in Eastern Europe, and the downfall of Apartheid in South Africa, Zambia was bound to change its governance and surveillance systems.

Thus, Kaunda under pressure, after twenty-seven years in office, scrapped the law barring the existence of alternative political parties. Barely two years later, in 1991, UNIP lost to a new party, the Movement for Multiparty Democracy (MMD) under Frederick Chiluba. The UNIP Youth League members who, as shown above, acted as surveillance operatives for the outgoing governing party, were dispersed. However, the new sheriffs in town, MMD, exercised political power using similar surveillance methods as those of the UNIP era. It created its own youth security wing which continued to spy on people, or enforced the will of the governing party. This practice was unremitting through three different MMD presidents and administrations, until ten years later, in 2011, when MMD lost to a new party, Patriotic Front (PF), led by MMD's former strongman, Secretary-General Michael Sata, a former police constable. A more overt and uniformed militia referred to as 'party cadres' with their own commanders, was subsequently formed and sent to Sudan for further training (*Lusaka Times* 2013). These were the surveillance operatives of the PF. However, in 2013, Sata died in office. He was replaced by the then little-known Edgar Lungu, who strengthened the youth surveillance activities even further. Lungu went ahead with purchasing digital spying equipment from China, Israel, and other countries (Phiri and Abraham 2023). However, after seven years in office, in 2021, Lungu lost to an eighteen-year-old opposition party, the United Party for National Development (UPND) led by Hakainde Hichilema, who completed the building of the multi-million-dollar Chinese-funded national surveillance centre in Lusaka (ZNBC 2022).

Until then, Hichilema had neither worked in, nor for, government. His arrival therefore, brought some hope of the possibilities of a less repressive environment, the further opening-up of Zambia's political sphere and civil society spaces, social reforms, and greater democratic practices. Three years down the line (at the time of writing in 2024), little seemingly has changed. What we see, therefore, on scanning Zambia's political history, is that the more things appear to change, the more they remain the same, especially with regard to the practice of state surveillance of Zambian communities. Besides the fact that the country has gone through four political dispensations: the colonial era, multiparty democracy, one-party dictatorial rule, and then back into multiparty democracy, there has remained one constant – that is, the state's surveillance of citizens. The style in which this was conducted, or its focus, may have altered within changed political systems, but incidents of political violence and infringements on civic space across the country remain unchanged (Phiri and Abraham 2023; CCMG 2024). If anything, it has become more sophisticated and erudite, as we demonstrate below.

During the colonial period relatively crude surveillance methods were used, such as physically following political activists. Colonial surveillance operations were small in scale. Initially, the operatives fell directly under the crime intelligence unit within the colonial police force (Zambia Laws). Things changed soon after independence. The governing party, UNIP, under Kaunda faced a number of challenges, both internal and external. In response, an intelligence collection organization was established outside the Zambia Police and placed directly under the office of the president.

Internally, Kaunda's opponents coalesced around various mushrooming political parties which contested the leadership of the country – they were soon either banned, or their leaders were incarcerated under state of emergency regulations which were carried over from the colonial period and never revoked (Sakala 2016). In 1972 the repressive environment was formalized with the introduction, by legislation, of the one-party state in which only Kaunda's UNIP was allowed to operate.

Externally, Kaunda's Zambia faced various challenges from what was then called the 'White South'. This referred to countries south of Zambia which were still under white minority rule, such as Angola, Mozambique, Rhodesia (now Zimbabwe), South West Africa (now Namibia), and apartheid South Africa.

Surveillance and intelligence collection during the one-party state thus focused on Kaunda's political opponents. As Sardanis (2014: 89) argues, Kaunda set up a 'very extensive State Security Department', which was 'ubiquitous' and oppressive: 'in hotels, bars and restaurants, one would often notice a "waiter" milling around one's table without doing anything in particular, except eavesdropping'. Further, Kaunda built the massive intelligence infrastructure, including its then state-of-the-art headquarters in Lusaka, the so-called 'Red Brick' building, reportedly with the support of either Nicolai Ceausescu's Romania or President Josip Broz Tito's Yugoslavia. This was the nerve centre of a massive collection of information and analysis about citizens' political, economic, and other activities and views by the then much feared and variously named 'Special Branch', or 'intelligence'.

The continued existence of such a system of spying on citizens today has led to opposition leader Fred M'membe accusing the current government of using surveillance intelligence to intimidate the governing party's opponents. M'membe states that President Hichilema has resorted to 'despotic actions', including deploying officers 'who I have personally confronted following me' (*Lusaka Times* 2022).

Surveillance in Zambia previously included photographing opponents, tapping telephone calls, or just opening up political rivals' postal mail. Now, such human intelligence may have largely been set aside for a more technology-based brand of spying, i.e. signals intelligence. For examples of these new forms of digital surveillance refer to this book's introductory chapter.

This chapter's discussions acknowledge the various changes that may have taken place within the secretive Zambian state surveillance systems over the years, with a detailed historical view, in order to understand the surveillance background of Zambia in light of emerging new technologies – how people have responded to spying, the impact that surveillance systems have had on human rights, as well as on social power balances as a consequence.

This chapter is not centrally about what happened in the past, during the colonial era, or immediately after independence, nor does it intend to provide a comprehensive history of foreign intelligence interests and operations in Zambia. However, these aspects are the necessary context for understanding what is happening now. The discussion is about now. It is about how the Zambian government may have used surveillance systems to repress people's agency and human rights, and to promote the power interests of political elites. This chapter is about how surveillance technologies have recently been deployed, with the support of foreign powers, to service the interests of the nation's power elites.

## Conceptual framework

This section defines and reviews the concepts of digital rights, power interest, and human agency that this chapter later uses to frame its analysis of digital surveillance in Zambia. The starting point is the acknowledgement that Zambia, like any other nation, is now within what may be termed the digital society. A digital society is one 'affected by digitally networked communication tools and platforms, such as the internet and social media' (Lindgren 2017: 4). With the emergence of such a society there have necessarily developed digital rights, which are existing human rights in online or digital contexts.

## Digital rights

Digital rights are universal human rights in digital spaces (Roberts et al. 2021). They include, but are not limited to, the right to privacy, freedom from violence, freedom of political opinion, freedom of expression, and freedom of association (Phiri and Abraham 2021b). Moreover, the right to privacy is explicitly recognized in international human rights law, including the Universal Declaration on Human Rights (UN 1948), the International Covenant on Civil and Political Rights (UN 1976), and the Declaration of Principles of Freedom of Expression and Access to Information in Africa (African Commission 2019). Without access to privacy, it can be unsafe to dissent from dominant narratives or protest injustice, impossible to compete commercially, to develop policy alternatives, or relax in one's home (Roberts 2023).

It is important to note that Information Communication Technology (ICT) is socially constructed as an artefact of a particular environment created by particular stakeholders for particular purposes (Buskens and Webb 2009), within the context of surveillance of citizens. According to the Association of Progressive Communications (APC 2020), digital rights are a set of 'universal human rights that ensure everybody ... has equal access to an open Internet that is governed in an inclusive, accountable, and transparent manner to ensure peoples' fundamental freedoms and rights'. In that regard, digital rights are human rights. Further, these rights deal with a variety of concerns, which include freedom of expression, invasions of privacy, data surveillance, and other political and commercial activities that impede on citizens' rights and undermine democracy (Calzada 2021).

## Power

In this chapter, we limit our discussions to conceptions of panoptic power, which is, according to Foucault, social control in which individuals begin to police themselves due to constant surveillance, shaping disciplined, docile, and productive behaviour (Raine 2024; see also the review of power concepts in Chapter 1, the introduction to this volume). We relate this concept to analysis of the ability of the Zambian surveillance state to spy on its citizens in order to serve and preserve the political interests of the ruling elites by shrinking the capacity of citizens to express themselves and move freely.

As an exercise of power, surveillance doesn't only act as indirect coercion, a form of structural violence, but is also an expression of pervasive power; opaque or invisible power; and a channel for the population's conformity and self-control (Holloway 2019). As Prior (2015: 43) adds, modern democracies are surveillance societies where visibility is an essential component and privacy has become increasingly obsolete. In the United States, surveillance technologies and activities have reached an 'apogee' where they are politically and legally justified as necessary for national security. Similarly, in Zambia, such control devices and systems have been justified and placed under the re-Christened Ministry of Home Affairs and Internal Security with little citizen participation.

Application of state power to surveil citizens is a self-preservation mechanism by the incumbent power interests that have governed Zambia over the past sixty years. Looking at the Zambian case through the lens of Foucault 'panopticism' to analyse the power of the state, it can be argued that states spy on their citizens to perpetuate the elite's control over them. We see that power interests may be opposed to the establishment of freedom of expression, which protects against despotism (Lavoie 2014). The incumbent UPND government is at odds with its very own electoral promises of increased freedoms, signalling a desire to consolidate and perpetuate its own control by diminishing opposition. This is illustrated by the administration's commissioning of the Smart City Project, Zambia's single greatest digital surveillance investment yet, despite having condemned it while in opposition (Phiri and Abraham 2023).

The use of surveillance on citizens is an expression of state power, making the Zambian President's rhetoric about freedoms at odds with state practices such as restricting public gatherings and the arrest of citizens for insulting the president. Gaventa (2006) contrasts 'visible power', which focuses on who participates in observable decision making and 'hidden power' which focuses on how out-of-sight manoeuvering 'backstage' determines who gets a seat at the decision-making tables and what issues are (not) discussed. Gaventa refers to a 'mobilisation of bias' through rules of the game which favours certain power interests over others. 'Invisible power' focuses on how the internalization of dominant ideologies, norms, and values leads to social acceptance of an unjust status quo and self-censorship on certain contentious issues (Gaventa 2021).

## Human agency

Agency refers to the thoughts and actions taken by people that express their individual power (Cole et al. 2019). Human agency is what Bandura (1989: 1175) refers to as a people's belief about their capabilities 'to exercise control over events that affect their lives' and the 'exercise of self-influence'. Within the context of panoptic power, agency emerges when individuals resist or subvert the panopticon's control mechanisms and, in order to reach this extent of agency against the panopticon, citizens would recognize the existence of a restrictive panoptic power, resist and challenge norms, engage in organized collective action, and ultimately navigate pervasive surveillance, challenge restrictive norms, and promote awareness (Gaventa 2021).

Amartya Sen in his 'capabilities approach' maintains that to exercise agency, people require capabilities, i.e. freedom of choice and the ability to act in pursuit of their goals and values. A person's capabilities can be constrained 'through inadequate processes (such as the violation of voting or other political or civil rights)' (Sen 1999: 3). Panoptic social control in which individuals begin to police themselves due to constant surveillance, shaping disciplined, docile, and productive behaviour is thus disempowering and averse to agency.

Here we see that the mere existence of the knowledge that the state has the ability to snoop into the public and private affairs of citizens, limits the people's ability to act freely on social issues. In fact, we see that 'social discipline' is facilitated and maintained in society through the state's coercive power. As Roberts and Mare state in the introduction to this volume, the presence of such ubiquitous 'disciplinary mechanisms ... lead[s] to citizens self-monitoring and modifying their behaviour'. This chapter therefore seeks to see what these disciplinary mechanisms are, how citizens respond to them and subsequently, how people may, or may not modify their approach to asserting their civic and digital rights.

## Zambia's digital landscape

According to DataReportal (2024), Zambia had a population of 20.85 million in January 2024 and 6.5 million internet users. At that point, internet penetration stood at 31.2 per cent and there were 3.5 million social media users, which equates to 17 per cent of the total population. A total of 16.4 million cellular mobile connections were active in Zambia in early 2024, with this figure equivalent to 78.7 per cent of the total population (DataReportal 2024).

The marked growth of the ICT sector in the last decade is evidence of an ever-growing population of Zambian citizens using digital tools and online spaces. Digital spaces are connecting citizens, transcending the limitations of physical spaces. In physical space Zambian citizens still require a police permit for a public assembly of more than twenty people. Social media has increased opportunities for self-expression, and the development of digital communities, which have established a vibrant digital citizenship in Zambia. The expansion of political expression online by Zambian citizens has been interpreted by the state as a threat to its power, due to the way it has swiftly responded by investing in digital surveillance technologies and implementing new laws to control online freedoms.

## State surveillance

Surveillance within this context refers to any listening, observing, monitoring, or recording by agents of the state of citizens' conversations, correspondence, or communications without due regard for privacy of citizens. Phiri and Abraham (2023) conducted research into interception technologies procured and implemented by the Zambian state in recent times and identified five main forms of interception technologies: internet interception, mobile interception, social media surveillance, safe city technologies, and biometrics identification technologies.

### Internet interception

In September 2021, Member of Parliament for Nalolo Constituency, Hon. Imanga Wamunyima, asked the Minister of Technology and Science, Felix Mutati, whether the government was aware that citizens' phones, WhatsApp, Skype calls and Short Message Service (SMS) were tapped by the Financial Intelligence Centre (FIC). Wamunyima also wanted to know whether such snooping was an infringement of citizens' right to privacy as enshrined in the Constitution and whether there were any measures taken to ensure that citizens' rights to privacy were protected (National Assembly of Zambia

2022). The background to this question was a procurement by the Zambian government, through its Financial Intelligence Centre (FIC), of $10 million worth of surveillance technology from the Israeli company Cyberbit in 2017 (*Daily Nation Zambia* 2021). The FIC is the Financial Intelligence Unit (FIU) of the government and was established in November 2010 by the Financial Intelligence Centre Act, No. 46 of 2010.

Minister Mutati responded that the government was not aware of any citizen's phone, WhatsApp, Skype calls, and SMS's being tapped by FIC, adding that FIC operates within the confines of the law. The Centre is the sole designated National Agency mandated to receive, request, analyse, disseminate, and disclose information about money laundering (ML), terrorist financing (TF) and other serious offences to competent authorities for investigation.

### Mobile interception

There is a recorded use of Circles surveillance technology in Zambia in 2018. Circles is an Israeli surveillance firm whose surveillance technology system enables governments to exploit weaknesses to snoop on calls, texts, and the location of phones around the globe. Circles is affiliated with the Israeli NSO Group, which develops the oft-abused Pegasus spyware. Circles, whose products work without hacking the phone itself, says they sell their technologies only to nation-states.

According to leaked documents, Circles customers can purchase systems that connect to local telecommunications companies' infrastructure or can use another separate system called the 'Circles Cloud'. This interconnects with telecommunications companies around the world. 'We identified what appears to be a single Circles system in Zambia, operated by an unknown agency', states a report by University of Toronto's Citizen Lab Report (Bill Marczak et al. 2020). But it is yet to be established whether the Circles technology deployed is state-sponsored mobile phone surveillance of citizens.

### Social media surveillance

As for social media, in 2020, the ICT regulator, the Zambia Information Communication Technologies Authority (ZICTA), revealed that the police had the capability of tracking down social media abusers (Lwizi 2020). ZICTA Director-General, Patrick Mutimushi, later confirmed that there were indeed circumstances that permit ZICTA to intercept people's communication (Sakala 2020).

### Safe city technologies

In 2022 the Zambian government under the Chinese government supported the Safe City project and completed the construction of a national surveillance command centre, thirty-six communication towers, radio communication, and video surveillance systems costing some $210 million. These funds were obtained from Chinese banks and paid to a Chinese technology firm, ZTE. The infrastructure is fashioned on the Safe City initiatives implemented by Huawei and ZTE across Africa and in other regions.

Seemingly, to augment the deployment of the Safe City programme, the government has a framework for developing state capacity to implement biometric data systems through the Smart Zambia project which will integrate biometric data into the national registration citizenship system, the electoral system, and the healthcare system. The system, known as the Integrated National Registration Information System (INRIS), will be implemented at an approximate cost of US$55 million (National Assembly of Zambia 2022).

Stakeholders have already raised concerns about the national mobile phone SIM-card registration requirement, which compulsorily collects biometric data of users. Such a system is considered as a way of silencing and targeting potential dissent (Chiumbu 2021). Additionally, citizens' free speech is threatened on platforms like social media networks, with arrests for basic offences such as bringing the name of the President into disrepute (*Lusaka Times* 2022).

### Biometric identification technologies

Zambia is seeking to implement citizens' biometric identification systems. Internal Security Minister Jack Mwiimbu told Parliament that the country would invest K1,069,366,200 in biometrics ($55 million). According to Mwiimbu, this would ensure enhanced security systems through proper identification of citizens (*Lusaka Times* 2022). The biometric system would be under the umbrella of the Integrated National Registration Information System

(INRIS) which would be the national and civil registration management system affecting all citizens. Thus, Zambians would have biometric-enabled National Registration Cards (NRCs), birth and death certificates, passport, and citizenship registrations (National Assembly of Zambia 2022).

This new venture would replace the current system whereby Zambians get hardcopy national registration cards which they use to access various public and social services. Mwiimbu averred that when the new system was in place, citizens could not easily change their identity, especially for repeat offenders. Mwiimbu further claimed that the new system would contribute towards the promotion of good governance, strengthen and broaden tax administration and national health insurance, reduce cost of voter registration, minimize wasteful expenditure by ministries, provinces, and other state spending agencies, and contribute towards financial inclusion among the unbanked population.

Meanwhile, the Electoral Commission of Zambia (ECZ) has also implemented a biometric voter registration system at a cost of US$16 million, based on Smartmatic equipment supplied by the United Kingdom. The biometric voter registration and verification system primes a digital reconciliation process, as well as ensuring fast processing of voters.

## ICT regulations

Legislation to regulate citizens' use of digital platforms and potentially enable the state to undertake surveillance on its citizens has raised concerns about accountability of authorities' ability to pry into the activities of private citizens (Phiri and Abraham 2023). In tandem with the institution of legislation, there has been a massive investment in technology and infrastructure for state surveillance.

In 2021 alone, the country instituted the Cyber Crimes Act No. 2 of 2021 (the 'Cyber Act'), following the repeal of the Electronic Communications and Transactions Act of 2009, the Data Protection Act, the e-Government Act, and the Electronic Communications and Transactions Act. Further, the African Union Convention on Cybersecurity and Personal Data Protection (Malabo Convention) was ratified in November 2021 and the National Cyber

Policy, Media Development Policy, and Postal and Courier Services Policies were passed, while the Postal and Courier Services bill was drafted alongside a revised National ICT policy and National Digital Transformation strategy in 2021 and 2022. All this was done within a span of months.

The speed at which this was done raised some concerns. Ahead of enactment of the Cyber Security and Cyber Crime law in 2021, the Civil Society Constitution Agenda (CiSCA) expressed concern about the violations of freedoms embedded within it: 'we are aware that there are several provisions in The Cyber Security and Cyber Crimes Bill, 2021 which pose a threat to our human rights. The inalienability and inherency of human rights are not subordinate to laws especially inimical provisions contained in the law', said Chairperson of CiSCA, Ms Judith Mulenga (Mulenga 2021).

Upon the enactment of the Act, a group of non-governmental organizations alleged, among other issues, the unconstitutionality of certain provisions of the Act and the lack of consultation during the drafting and enactment process of the Act, and filed a petition against the Attorney-General and the Director of Public Prosecutions. The petitioners expressed concern over several provisions of the Act that alleged to threaten the right to protection from deprivation of property guaranteed by Article 16, the right to privacy guaranteed by Article 17, the right to protection of the law guaranteed by Article 19, the freedom of expression guaranteed by Article 20 (1), and the freedom of the press guaranteed by Article 20 (2) of the Constitution of the Republic of Zambia. Due to the magnitude of the changes proposed by stakeholders that needed to be made to the Act, it was decided to draft a Bill to repeal and replace the Cyber Security and Cyber Crime Act, prompting a review of the Act by the Zambia Law Development Commission, which made sweeping recommendations (ZLDC 2024).

Relatedly, Sheombar and Skelton (2023) observe that there are six discernible motives for state surveillance from the perspectives of African governments and the surveillance equipment suppliers. These are: surveillance as legitimacy for state security; surveillance for political gain; surveillance as diplomacy; surveillance as a tool for development; surveillance as neocolonialism; and surveillance as a business opportunity. This discussion, in keeping with observations and concerns of Zambian civil society on growing state power and reducing tolerance for freedom of movement and freedom of expression, focuses only on surveillance for state security and as an activity for political gain as a means to shed more light on the extent to which digital rights are at odds with a rising panoptic power enabled by state-of-the-art surveillance technologies in Zambia.

## Methodology

Our research adopted a hybrid of classical qualitative content analysis of the existing scholarly materials on Zambia's political history, surveillance practices, and concepts of power, agency, and digital rights; and interviews with respondents who included journalists and other citizens who have been subjected to surveillance by the state. Their testimonies express their experience with state surveillance.

## On being watched: Lived experience of the surveillant gaze

In this section, we focus on the experiences of some citizens who have suffered state surveillance and thereafter highlight the views of civil rights activists who are subject to the state's panoptic gaze.

Despite a context in Zambia where criticism of the state is repressed, there have been cases where courageous individuals have come out strongly against the state's surveillance activities. One such person is Thomas Zg'ambo who was associated with the independent online website Zambian Watchdog. The Watchdog website and Facebook have been banned several times by administrations before the assumption of power of the UPND, with claims that the Watchdog was inciting violence in the country through false and unprofessional reports in support of the UPND when it was in opposition. When the UPND party was elected in 2021, replacing the PF, Zg'ambo established the *Zambian Whistleblower*, an investigative online paper. Since then, Zg'ambo has had running battles with the state and internet providers in courts, the media, and state-sponsored detention centres. His former colleague at the Watchdog, Clayson Hamasaka, is ensconced in the comfort of State House. At the time of writing, Zg'ambo was in custody, accused of sedition for writing that his death would be the responsibility of President Hichilema. Previously, he had taken to court an international mobile phone service provider, accusing the company of being used by the state to spy on him.

Zg'ambo wrote that 'a multinational corporation participated in an illegal interception of private phone communication. It is in the interest of every Zambian citizen to have this matter concluded for the sake of protection of our inalienable right to Freedom of Expression' (Zambian Whistleblower 2023). A few weeks later, Zg'ambo was re-detained for sedition. In an interview with the authors, Zg'ambo said that he was certain of surveillance attempts on his communications.

Another person who had a run-in with the state is Wilson Pondamali in 2023; Pondamali was detained by the Sata regime, while working for Zambian Watchdog. In an interview for this chapter, Pondamali said he wasn't too sure if his detention was an outcome of the surveillance activities of the state. 'I am not too sure that we were being followed. We don't have facts that they were following us when using digital space. We had secured the space. Perhaps that is why they fabricated charges against us,' he said. Pondamali was referring to the digital platform on which his *Zambian Whistleblower* online paper is published. He added that he expected little difference from the UPND government as the governing party does not recognize freedom of the media, as a principle.

Zg'ambo, Pondamali, and Clayson Hamasaka have all had run-ins with the state for their investigative reporting. Less so for Hamasaka, who has now joined the state as a presidential spokesperson. For Zg'ambo and Pondamali, being outside the state system means that their problems have continued. They are joined by a few more citizens who have been under surveillance since the UPND came into office in 2021.

The challenges faced by the above-mentioned journalists provide sufficient example to citizens that they should not speak critically of the government. Panoptic power finds utility in inhibiting dissent or deviance from the government line. Zambians internalize the invisible power of social norms against claiming rights or holding government to account. The result is a controlled society based on fear through the example of reprimand for 'errant' citizens.

## Civil society responses

The issue, therefore, arises about how Zambians have responded to such surveillance activities. The fact is that state actions have caused an uproar among civil society organizations. For example, the Council of Churches in Zambia (CCZ), which groups together all Protestant churches, accused the government of creating an 'unhealthy political and social environment' that could lead to governance challenges. The CCZ said: 'this is not the Zambia we want' (Chikoya 2023).

A few days later, a group of opposition political parties issued a statement read by the former leader of the Catholic Church in Zambia, in which the group accused the government of 'emerging authoritarian tendencies of the New Dawn government' (Mpundu 2023). The parties argued that the governing UPND was threatening freedom in Zambia. Previously, the Evangelical Fellowship of Zambia (EFZ), which brings together evangelicals, Law Association of Zambia (LAZ), and the Zambia Institute of Independent Media Association (ZIIMA) had added their objections to the perceived violations of human and digital rights by the UPND government.

While surveillance in digital spaces aims to watch and restrict the freedom of association and speech of citizens, it is important to note that these digital spaces themselves enable the critical agency of citizens by providing them with a space to organize and coordinate actions across geographic distance and in limitless numbers pushing back against the very power systems that govern their restricted physical communities.

From the above discussion, it can be recognized that Zambian state surveillance is exercised through internet interception, mobile surveillance, social media monitoring, and citizens' biometric registration (Phiri and Abraham 2023); and that the motivations for those who sell surveillance equipment, software, and technologies to Zambia and other African countries go beyond commercial interests. For some, the technologies serve a legitimate state security interest: they are used to further political interest; they are tools used to further diplomatic interests; and can just as easily be apparatuses for development as channels for neocolonialism.

It is clear in the case of Zambia that surveillance has been practised not only to protect national security, but as a means to exercise power over citizens, especially critical voices and political rivals. The use of surveillance to serve incumbent power interests can be traced through Zambian politics from the days of British colonialism to the present governing regime of President Hichilema. The implication of this is that, historically, surveillance has been used by the state to exert power that overrides constitutionally protected human rights and limits human agency.

The Constitution guarantees citizens' rights to private communication and correspondence. This is the 'freedom to impart and communicate ideas and information without interference, whether the communication be to the public generally or to any person … and freedom from interference with correspondence'. The Zambian Constitution also states that 'except with his own consent, no person shall be subjected to the search of his person or his property or the entry by others on his premises' (Zambia 2016). These protections clearly include a person's digital property and online communication and information relating to a person's family, health status, or private life. Although the above freedoms are guaranteed by Zambia's national constitution, these freedoms are being violated by the surveillance systems, which are a direct challenge to digital rights.

## Resistance

Millions of Zambian citizens have adopted digital technologies and become users of online spaces including social media. This has been aided by massive investment in internet and cellular infrastructure by the private sector, enabling a knowledge-based economy (ZICTA 2023). The rapid implementation of laws and regulations of digital space has stimulated a fledgling digital rights community in Zambia civil society. Small budgets and limited human capacity have been inhibiting the development of agenda-setting for digital rights advocacy (Phiri and Abraham 2021).

While the surveillance state grows, Zambian civil society has often failed to sustain pressure on government to secure lasting changes in the form of constitutional reform in the wake of presidential powers. It has not helped that donor funding for civil society has declined at a time when key civil society actors have been co-opted into political parties (Hinfelaar, Rakner, and Walle 2022).

Gaventa suggests that new spaces of power present new opportunities, moments, and channels for citizens to challenge and change policies, discourses, decisions, and relationships that affect their lives and interests. This chapter has documented the changing Zambia digital surveillance landscape in search of such opportunities. One place where this is clearly apparent is the way in which citizens are using digital spaces for campaigns and organizing to raise social awareness by sidestepping established institutionalized structures that serve to reinforce incumbent power. There is a growing resistance by Zambian civil society against state surveillance excesses (*Lusaka Times* 2021). This research has explored these activities by seeking out activists and learning from them what their perspectives are on the Zambian surveillance state. In many instances, highlighted above, the response has been expressions of resistance against the state's encroachment of their private spaces.

## Conclusion

This chapter examined the nexus between state surveillance and digital rights in Zambia through a historical and contemporary view of that relationship, from pre-colonial to post-independence times. In seeking to answer the questions, this chapter addressed the following questions: How has the state been surveilling its citizens over the years, has the practice of spying on citizens changed with the changing political orientation of its leadership … and how have citizens responded to this kind of prying into their privacy? We observed that, although the political systems may have changed over time, forms of surveillance remained, although the styles differed. To some extent, the characteristics of the surveillance system may have reflected the political, historical, economic, and technological transformations taking place in the different eras. Ultimately, though, national surveillance systems tended to serve the political class, while citizens either resorted to conformity or resistance. The right to online privacy should be protected and promoted as should freedom of expression, information, assembly, and association online in order to have citizenry able to live fulfilled, emancipated lives in democratic society.

It is therefore recommended that, to address some of these issues, there is a need for more enhanced advocacy for digital rights consciousness among citizens, for the promotion of human agency in fighting for those rights, and increased research in understanding new forms of state surveillance and its impact on freedom and civil society operations in constitutional states.

# Bibliography

African Commission (2019). *Declaration of Principles on Freedom of Expression and Access to Information in Africa 2019*. https://achpr.au.int/en/node/902#:~:text=The%20Declaration%20establishes%20or%20affirms,to%20express%20and%20disseminate%20information (accessed 4 September 2024).

APC (2020). 'What Are Digital Rights?' www.apc.org/en/news/coconet-what-are-digital-rights (accessed 18 January 2022).

Bandura, A. (1989). 'Human Agency in Social Cognitive Theory', *American Psychologist*, 44(9): 1175–84. https://doi.org/10.1037/0003-066X.44.9.1175

Buskens, I. and Webb, A. (2009) African Women and ICTs: *Investigating Technology, Gender, and Empowerment*, New York: Zed Books.

Calzada, I. (2021). 'The Right to Have Digital Rights in Smart Cities', *Sustainability*, 13(20). https://www.researchgate.net/publication/356109773_Digital_Rights (accessed 23 August 2023).

Chikoya, E. (2023, 21 November). 'Smart Eagles'. https://web.facebook.com/SmartEaglesZambia/videos/council-of-churches-in-zambia-voices-out-strong-concerns-over-governance-of-the-/356025923748959/?_rdc=1&_rdr (accessed 1 January 2024).

Chisala, B. (1994). *The Downfall of President Kaunda*, Lusaka: Co-op Printing.

Chisala, C. (2018). 'A Day in the Life of a UNIP Vigilante', *Daily Mail*. http://www.daily-mail.co.zm/day-in-the-life-of-a-unip-vigilante/ (accessed 24 September 2023).

Chiumbu, S. (2021). 'Chinese Digital Infrastructure, Smart Cities and Surveillance in Zambia', Johannesburg: Media Policy and Democracy Project (accessed 21 September 2022). https://www.mediaanddemocracy.com/uploads/1/6/5/7/16577624/zambia_report.pdfj

Christian Churches Monitoring Group (CCMG) (2024, 24 May). 'CCMG Deeply Concerned About the Increasing Incidents of Political and Civic Space Infringements'. CCMG Zambia. https://ccmgzambia.org/2024/05/24 (accessed 9 June 2024).

Cole, R., Brockhaus, M., Wong, G. Y., Kallio, M. H., and Moeliono, M. (2019, August). 'Local Agency in Development, Market, and Forest Conservation

Interventions in Lao PDR's Northern Uplands', *Southeast Asian Studies*, 8(2): 172–202. https://doi.org/10.20495/seas.8.2_173

*Daily Nation Zambia* (2021, 23 September). 'Financial Intelligence Centre (FIC) $18m Scandal Deepens'. https://dailynationzambia.com/2021/09/financial-intelligence-centre-fic-18m-scandal-deepens/?fbclid=IwY2xjawFCcdlleHRuA2FlbQIxMAA BHWa6doORwQQwlTTrB_J5oG45kXuj1Yyijmk6c9aR8C0b3XyBUc83ZlFCEA_ aem_UXPuPM1h4StZFwf0GEpMOw (accessed 2 September 2024).

DataReportal (2024). 'Digital Zambia 2024'. https://datareportal.com/reports/digital-2024-zambia (accessed 1 July 2024).

Gaventa, J. (2006). 'Finding the Spaces for Change: A Power Analysis', in R. Eyben, C. Harris and J. Pettit (eds), *Exploring Power for Change, IDS Bulletin*, 37(6): 23–33.

Gaventa, J. (2021, 10 February). 'Linking the Prepositions: Using Power Analysis to Inform Strategies for Social Action', *Journal of Political Power*, 14(1): 109–30. https://doi.org/10.1080/2158379X.2021.1878409

Government of Zambia (1966). *Zambia Police Act* (Vol. 8). Lusaka, Zambia: National Assembly Zambia. https://www.parliament.gov.zm/node/844 (accessed 4 September 2024).

Hinfelaar, M., Rakner, L. and Walle, N. v. (2022). 'Democratic Backsliding in Africa? Autocratization, Resilience, and Contention', in L. R. Arriola, L. Rakner and N. v. Walle (eds), *Zambia: Backsliding in a Presidential Regime*, Oxford: Oxford University Press. https://doi.org/10.1093/oso/9780192867322.003.0008

Hitchcock, B. (1973). *Bwana – Go Home*, Cape Town: Howard Timms.

Holloway, D. (2019). 'Surveillance Capitalism and Children's Data: The Internet of Toys and Things for Children'. *Media International Australia*, 170(1): 27–36. https://doi.org/10.1177/1329878X19828205

Lavoie, C. (2014). 'Institutional Racism and Individual Agency: A Case Study using Foucault's Disciplinary Power', *Critical Social Work*, 15(1): 30–40. https://doi.org/10.22329/csw.v15i1.5906

Lindgren, S. (2017). *Digital Media & Society*, London: Sage.

*Lusaka Times* (2013, 12 November). 'Violence Has Vindicated Me When I Said PF Sent Youths for Militia Training in Sudan-HH'. https://lusakatimes.com/2013/11/12/violence-vindicated-said-pf-sent-youths-militia-training-sudan-hh/ (accessed 24 September 2023).

*Lusaka Times* (2021, 25 February). 'Cyber Laws Pose a Threat to Our Human Rights – CiSCA'. https://www.lusakatimes.com/2021/02/25/cyber-laws-pose-a-threat-to-our-human-rights-cisca/#:~:text=The%20Zambian%20Constitution%20in%20 Article%2017%20provides%20for,or%20the%20entry%20by%20others%20on%20 his%20premises.%E2%80%99 (accessed 1 October 2023).

*Lusaka Times* (2022). 'HH Abusing Intelligence and Security Wings to Spy on Opposition'. https://www.lusakatimes.com/2022/10/29/hh-abusing-intelligence-and-security-wings-to-spy-on-opposition/ (accessed 1 October 2023).

Lwizi, G. (2020, 14 March). 'Social Media Abuse Suspects Can Now Be Tracked Down – Police', *Zambia Business Times*. https://zambianbusinesstimes.com/social-media-abuse-suspects-can-now-be-tracked-down-police/ (accessed 4 September 2024).

Marczak, B., Scott-Railton, J., Prakash Rao, S., Anstis, S., and Deibert, R. (2020, 1 December). 'Running in Circles, Uncovering the Clients of Cyberespionage Firm Circles'. Citizen Lab. https://citizenlab.ca/2020/12/running-in-circles-uncovering-the-clients-of-cyberespionage-firm-circles/ (accessed 4 September 2024).

McGregor, J. (2013). 'Surveillance and the City: Patronage, Power-Sharing and the Politics of Urban Control in Zimbabwe', *Journal of Southern African Studies*, 39(4): 783–805. https://doi.org/10.1080/03057070.2013.858541

Mpundu, T. (2023, 20 October). 'Emeritus Archbishop Telesphore Mpundu Accuses UPND of Authoritarianism'. *Lusaka Times*. https://www.lusakatimes.com/2023/10/20/emeritus-archbishop-telesphore-mpundu-accuses-upnd-of-authoritarianism/ (accessed 1 October 2023).

Mulenga, J. (2021, 25 February). 'Cyber Laws Pose a Threat to Our Human Rights – CiSCA'. *Lusaka Times*. https://www.lusakatimes.com/2021/02/25/cyber-laws-pose-a-threat-to-our-human-rights-cisca/ (accessed 4 September 2024).

Mwanakatwe, J. M. (1994). *End of Kaunda Era*, Lusaka: Multimedia.

Mwape, L. (2017, 25 July). 'Zambia: State of Emergency Signifies Worrying Signs for Civic Space'. CIVICUS. https://civicus.org/index.php/media-resources/media-releases/2901-zambia-state-of-emergency-signifies-worrying-signs-for-civic-space (accessed 9 June 2024).

National Assembly of Zambia (1964, 24 October). *Emergency Powers Act*. https://www.parliament.gov.zm/sites/default/files/documents/acts/Emergency%20Powers%20Act.pdf (accessed 9 June 2023).

National Assembly of Zambia (2022, 30 March). 'Question for Oral Answer, Street Cameras Safe City Project'. https://www.parliament.gov.zm/node/10140 (accessed 19 September 2022).

Phiri, B. J. (2006). *A Political History of Zambia*, Trenton: Africa World Press.

Phiri, S. and Abraham, K. (2021a). *Digital Rights in Closing Civic Space: Lessons from Ten African Countries* (T. Roberts, Ed.). London: Bloomsbury Publishers.

Phiri, S. and Abraham, K. (2021b). *Zambia Digital Rights Landscape Report*, Africa Digital Rights Network. https://opendocs.ids.ac.uk/opendocs/bitstream/handle/20.500.12413/15964/Zambia_Report.pdf?sequence=7&isAllowed=y (accessed 1 October 2023).

Phiri, S. and Abraham, K. (2023). 'Zambia Report', in T. Roberts (ed.), *Mapping the Supply of Surveillance Technologies in Africa: Case Studies from Nigeria, Ghana, Morocco, Malawi, and Zambia* (pp. 120–35), Brighton: Institute of Development Studies. https://doi.org/10.19088/IDS.2023.027

Prior, H. R. (2015). 'Democracy Is Watching You: From Panopticism to the Security State', *Teoris da Communicacao*, 22(1): 33–58.

Raine, S. (2024, 7 May). 'What Is Panopticism?' Perlego. https://www.perlego.com/knowledge/study-guides/what-is-panopticism/ (accessed 9 June 2024).

Roberts, T. (2023). *Mapping the Supply of Surveillance Technologies to Africa: Case Studies from Nigeria, Ghana, Morocco, Malawi, and Zambia* (T. Roberts, ed.), Brighton: Institute of Development Studies. https://doi.org/10.19088/IDS.2023.027

Roberts, T., Mohamed Ali, A., Farahat, M., Oloyede, R. and Mutung'u, G. (2021). *Surveillance Law in Africa: A Review of Six Countries*, Brighton: Institute of Development Studies. https://opendocs.ids.ac.uk/opendocs/handle/20.500.12413/16893

Sakala, N. (2020). 'We Don't Pry into People's Phones but There's Lawful Interception – ZICTA', *News Diggers*, 4 February. https://diggers.news/local/2020/02/04/we-dont-pry-into-peoples-phones-but-theres-lawful-interception-zicta/ (accessed 28 April 2023).

Sakala, R. S. (2016). 'Zambia's Political History: From Colonialism to the Third Republic', in R. Mukwena and F. Sumaili (eds), *Zambia at Fifty Years* (pp. 1–28), Bloomington, IN: Partridge.

Sardanis, A. (2003). *Africa: Another Side of the Coin*, London: IB Taurus.

Sardanis, A. (2007). *A Venture in Africa: The Challenges of African Business*, London: IB Taurus.

Sardanis, A. (2014). *Zambia: The First 50 Years*, London: IB Taurus.

Sen, A. (1999). *Development as Freedom*, London: Oxford University Press.

Sheombar, A. and Skelton, S. K. (2023). 'Follow the Surveillance: A Breadcrumb Trail of Surveillance Technology Exports to Africa', in *After Latour: Globalisation, Inequity and Climate Change*, New York: Springer. https://doi.org/10.1007/978-3-031-50154-8_19

United Nations (1948, 10 December). *Universal Declaration of Human Rights*. https://www.un.org/sites/un2.un.org/files/2021/03/udhr.pdf (accessed 2 September 2024).

United Nations (1976, 10 December). *Universal Declaration of Human Rights*. https://treaties.un.org/doc/treaties/1976/03/19760323%2006-17%20am/ch_iv_04.pdf (accessed 2 September 2024).

Zambia (2016). *Constitution of the Republic of Zambia Amendment Act of 2016*, Lusaka: Republic of Zambia.

Zambia LII (2023). *Munalula and Others v Attorney-General* (S.C.Z. Judgment 2 of 1979) ZMSC 2 (2 January 1979). https://zambialii.org/akn/zm/judgment/zmsc/1979/2/eng@1979-01-02 (accessed 9 December 2023).

Zambian Whistleblower on Facebook (2023). https://www.facebook.com/story.php/?story_fbid=837254741742646&id=100063743840552&_rdr

ZICTA (2023, 7 March). 'The ICT Sector Recorded Positive Growth in 2022', ZICTA. https://www.zicta.zm/storage/posts/attachments/IfCnl5CiPfRDCjjWk45SnMyFGRRekZBZbsB0L9mV.pdf (accessed 1 October 2023).

ZLDC (2024, 2 May). 'Report on the Review of the Cyber Security and Cyber Crimes Bill, 2024', Zambia Law Development Commission. https://www.zambialawdevelopment.org/download/report-on-the-review-of-the-review-of-the-cyber-security-and-cyber-crimes-bill-2024/ (accessed 6 June 2024).

ZNBC Today (2022, 30 August). 'Home Affairs and Internal Security Minister Jack Mwiimbu Says Government Has Prioritized Public Security and Will Invest More in Making the Country Safe'. https://www.facebook.com/znbctoday/videos/home-affairs-and-internal-security-minister-jack-mwiimbu-says-government-has-pri/3380683542175085/ (accessed 9 June 2024).

# 5

# State surveillance in Malawi

## Changes and continuities

Jimmy Kainja

## Introduction

In the last decade, the Malawi government has spent tens of millions of dollars on a programme of mass identification and centralized data collection, raising fears that Malawians could be sleepwalking into a surveillance state. This chapter provides a critical evaluation of digital surveillance systems in Malawi and addresses the questions of what form or shape of digital surveillance is being practised in Malawi; what are the human rights implications of expanding surveillance; how does it affect power relationships; and what forms of citizen agency and resistance does it provoke?

The data collection and centralization programmes, implemented since 2017, include the national identification programme issuing biometric national identity (ID) cards for everyone over sixteen years of age, coupled with the mandatory registration of mobile phone SIM cards. Since 2010, Malawi has spent at least $28 million on mobile interception and biometric ID technology (Kainja 2023b). The biometric ID has replaced all previously siloed forms of identity for all public transactions, accessing social welfare benefits, healthcare, voter registration, and travel document applications. The ID is also required to open a bank or mobile money account. These programmes aid the government's digital surveillance at the expense of citizens' right to privacy, protected under section 21 of the Constitution of Malawi and several international human rights instruments to which Malawi is a signatory.

However, digital surveillance is hardly public discourse in Malawi. The government has implemented surveillance technologies under the pretext of national security while ignoring the human rights implications. Munoriyarwa and Mare (2023) observed that the development of communication technologies, from the telegraph to the internet, can be a blessing and a curse for human rights. On the one hand, digital technologies have given human beings more convenient and flexible means of communication. On the other hand, it has made surveillance technologies more sophisticated than ever before – making it easier for governments to surveil citizens. Thus, the implementation of surveillance technologies should be evaluated for any potential human rights violations. This chapter conducts a rights-based analysis of digital surveillance in Malawi; it draws on theories of power, particularly Jeremy Bentham's panopticon, as theorized by Michel Foucault. It also assesses individual and collective agency as it manifests as resistance to state surveillance.

The remainder of this chapter is organized as follows: the next section outlines the methodological approach before providing political context for readers unfamiliar with Malawi. It then discusses Malawi's historical context to surveillance. The next section provides a literature review. The final two sections offer an analysis of state surveillance and citizen resistance before outlining conclusions and recommendations.

## Methodology

The study employed a qualitative research design, utilizing the interpretative approach. According to Putnam and Banghart (2017), the interpretive qualitative approach encompasses social theories and perspectives that embrace a view of reality as socially constructed or made meaningful through actors' understanding of events. This design allows the researcher to acquire rich data from subjective experiences (Creswell et al. 2007). The researcher draws conclusions based on content analysis of secondary data, research papers, and historical accounts of Malawi. These include a study of five categories of digital surveillance in Malawi (see Roberts et al. 2023), papers on surveillance in Malawi and the region, and a theoretical analysis of surveillance.

# Historical context of surveillance in Malawi

State surveillance was introduced in Malawi under colonialism but retained as a state function after independence. The British Special Branch spied on internal opposition to colonial power; after liberation, the surveillance function of the Special Branch was retrained on those perceived as a threat to the power of the independence leaders – the Malawi Police Service introduced its version of the Special Branch. Malawi gained independence in 1964, becoming a republic in 1966, with Hastings Kamuzu Banda as its founding president. After independence, Malawi retained most of its colonial architecture, including its legal and policy framework.

In his book *Political Prisoner 3/75* (Mpasu 2014), Mpasu, a former political prisoner under Kamuzu Banda's rule, narrates how the Malawi Congress Party (MCP), through its youth wing, the League of Malawi Youth, the Malawi Young Pioneers, and the Malawi Police's Special Branch, oversaw a physical surveillance network. Informers were used to eavesdrop on people's conversation and report to the authorities what people were saying about the State President, Kamuzu Banda, in power from 1964 to 1994, and his Malawi Congress Party, the only political party allowed in Malawi during this period. The surveillance network also monitored compliance with MCP's four cornerstones: *Unity, Loyalty, Discipline,* and *Obedience*. Mpasu's account also shows that reports from informants were taken seriously, and people were arrested on unverified information. A simple informant report on someone disregarding the four cornerstones, 'insulting' Kamuzu Banda or the MCP, was enough to get someone arrested. Ordinary citizens were empowered to monitor one another – anyone could be a spy at the time. The League of Malawi Youth and the Malawi Young Pioneers were not just spy networks but also reporting hubs for informants.

The communication surveillance and heavy censorship during Kamuzu Banda's reign (1964–94) affected the growth of the country's information communication and technology (ICT) sector. By the time Kamuzu Banda lost power in the 1990s, Malawi's ICT sector had one of the lowest ICT penetration rates in the region (Clarke et al. 2003). Although the industry has grown steadily since the political changes, the country still has one of Africa's lowest rates of ICT use. According to DataReportal (2023), Malawi has only

24.4 per cent internet users; however, this is an increase of 2.6 per cent from 2022. Internet growth in the county has been steadily growing, and the digital surveillance landscape, discussed in the next section, has also been increasing.

## Malawi's digital surveillance landscape

This section draws on a report mapping the supply of surveillance technologies to Nigeria, Ghana, Morocco, Malawi, and Zambia (Roberts et al. 2023). The report documents which companies, from which countries, are supplying which digital surveillance technologies to which African countries. It organizes its analysis around five categories of digital surveillance technologies: internet interception technologies, mobile interception technologies, social media monitoring tools, safe city/smart city systems, and biometric digital-ID systems (ibid.).

Digital surveillance involves 'monitoring of online activity, location tracking via Bluetooth or Global Positioning System (GPS), tracking financial transactions, video surveillance, facial scans, and the collection of biometric data' (Eck and Hatz 2020: 604). According to Miles (2014), surveillance violates privacy and has a chilling effect on citizens; it causes public distrust and feelings of vulnerability, and it is a potential source of discrimination and unjust domination and, therefore, a threat to democracy and the integrity of the public sphere (Königs 2022: 8).

The following sections draw on Kainja's (2023) more extensive analysis documenting evidence of the Malawi government's procurement of digital surveillance technologies.

### Internet interception technologies

While there is no evidence of internet interception in Malawi, there is evidence of covert surveillance of internet messages. People have been arrested for their posts on WhatsApp groups, an encrypted instant messaging service. This indicates state surveillance or monitoring of citizens' communication. Screenshots are used by the police as evidence in court (see Kainja 2022). Covert surveillance implies gathering information about groups or individuals without their knowledge. The process 'may require watching, following and listening to people without them being aware that they are under police surveillance' (Dahl 2022: 1). Dahl calls covert surveillance 'chameleonizing', akin to a chameleon changing its colours so it is not identified. Security agents in Malawi use vague provisions in the Electronic Transactions and Cyber Security Act of 2016, prohibiting 'cyber harassment' (section 86) and 'offensive communication' (section 87), to arrest the victims of covert surveillance.

## Mobile interception surveillance

Although 'the history of surveillance is as long as human history' (Lauer 2011: 571), suspicions of digital surveillance in Malawi date back to 2010 when the country's telecommunication regulator, the Malawi Communications Regulatory Authority (MACRA), procured a Consolidated ICT Regulatory Management System (CIRMS) from a US firm, Agilis International, for $6 million. A further $20 million was spent on CIRMS software updates after its initial purchase (Priezkalns 2022), to aid MACRA verify the service quality and revenue in the telecom sector (Chitsulo 2020). However, a court order stopped the implementation of CIRMS following a petition from private citizens, arguing that MACRA could use the technology for surveillance, contravening section 21 of the constitution, which protects privacy (Kainja 2021b). A subsequent court order allowed MACRA to implement CIRMS. However, the ruling came a year after MACRA had terminated its contract with Agilis (Chimjeka 2016).

In 2017, Malawi implemented mandatory mobile phone SIM card registration following the enactment of Communications Act 34 of 2016. Compulsory registration means all mobile phone SIM cards must be registered on a central database, and all unregistered SIM cards must be deactivated (Sangala 2018). Although the policy is that SIM cards can be registered using identification documents such as a passport or driver's licence,[1] most agents only accept the national digital-ID card in practice. Implementing mandatory SIM card registration contradicts the Human Rights Council's (2015) recommendation that countries refrain from identifying users as a condition for access to digital communications and online services and requiring SIM card registration for mobile users. Wanyama (2018) asserts that it is essential that governments should carefully reconcile the state's interests, personal data, and privacy rights.

## Safe-city surveillance

In July 2022, the government of Malawi commissioned a data centre in partnership with Huawei (Huaxia 2022). The specifications of the agreement are private. However, in Zambia and South Africa, Munoriyawa, and Mare (2023) found that, although these projects are promoted as developmental, they benefit a small clique of political elites and political parties in power against legitimate political opposition. In addition, *The Wall Street Journal* reported that Huawei employees embedded in cyber security forces helped ruling parties in Zambia and Uganda intercept encrypted communications and used cell data to track political opponents (Parkinson et al. 2019). This concern adds to the fears that Malawi lacks adequate safeguards for data abuse, exposing citizens to cybercrime. Manda (2011) noted a general lack of interest in Malawi's cybersecurity capacity. He observes, 'Malawi still has a long way to go regarding the development of the necessary legal frameworks, standards, and capacity to enhance cybersecurity and keep cybercrime in check' (Manda 2011: 5).

## Biometric digital-ID

In 2016, the government of Malawi hired a French company specializing in scratch cards, SELP (SELP Group n.d.), for $1.3 million to supply, deliver, install, and commission training for National Registration Bureau (NRB) staff to implement a biometric digital-ID programme. SELP is also active in Senegal, Spain, France, the United Arab Emirates, and India. The Malawi National Registration Act No. 13 of 2010 governs the NRB programme (World Bank 2017). The total cost of the national biometric-ID is not publicly known. However, the Malawi government contributed 40 per cent of the project's total cost. The remaining 60 per cent was funded by the United Kingdom's now-defunct Department for Internal Development, the European Union, Irish Aid, the Government of Norway, the United States Agency for International Development, and the United Nations Development Programme (Malik 2020). National ID registration targets those who are sixteen years old and over (GSMA 2019).

The National Registration Bureau uses the National Registration and Identification System, which is also used by several government agencies, replacing previously siloed ID programs within a brief period (Malik 2020). Since 2019, the Malawi Electoral Commission has used the national ID as the only acceptable identification to register voters. The Malawi Revenue Authority uses it to record taxpayers; it is used to pay public and civil servants, and the immigration department uses it to verify applicants for travel documents. The finance ministry also uses digital-ID to consider households for inclusion in social protection programmes. Government ministries, departments, and agencies have integrated digital-ID into financial development and inclusion programmes, farm subsidies, healthcare, and other social protection services (Malik 2020).

This means that, through the national digital-ID system, the government has created a centralized database of personal data with no robust legal framework in place to protect citizens' data. In 2022, the Malawi government partnered with the Chinese telecommunication firm Huawei to launch its first national data centre. Huawei has invested over $300 million in Africa's data centre and cybersecurity market (Garowe Online 2023). As observed by Munoriyarwa and Mare (2023), companies that provide data centres, like Huawei, are private profit-seeking, and their partnership with governments could easily pave the way for unwarranted and extra-legal surveillance, as is already the case in Zambia. Because data centres rely on private technology companies, this raises serious questions about surveillance, privacy, and security. For instance, what kind of trade-offs between governments and private companies exist in smart-city technologies, which of these are known to the public, and what type of oversight mechanisms exist to protect inalienable human rights? (Munoriyarwa and Mare 2023). The same pertinent questions hover around Malawi's data centre project, which the data collection programmes, including the national ID, have hitherto supplemented.

## Theoretical literature

The panopticon theory is standard in the framing and analysis of surveillance (Galič et al. 2016). Panopticon is a Greek term that translates as *all-seeing*.

As noted by Goodman (2014), Jeremy Bentham proposed the panopticon as an architectural design for a prison, which would have twenty-four-hour monitoring of the prison's inmates. McMullan (2015, paragraph 5) simplified Bentham's panopticon as follows:

> There is a central tower surrounded by cells. In the central tower is the watchman. In the cells are prisoners – or workers, or children, depending on the use of the building. The tower shines bright light so the watchman can see everyone in the cells. However, the people in the cells cannot see the watchman and therefore have to assume that they are always under observation.

In popular culture, a panopticon is akin to the reality television show *Big Brother*, in which housemates are put in one house and monitored by cameras that are visible to television viewers twenty-four hours a day.

In the academic literature, the panopticon concept was popularized by Michel Foucault in his thesis, *Discipline and Punish* (1977), where he used it as a metaphor for pervasive surveillance in modern institutional practices and the 'disciplinary effect' in making people self-regulating. The panopticon created a situation whereby the inmates perceived themselves under constant surveillance, as they were inescapably visible to the correctional officers, even when the guards were not watching. According to Foucault, the 'disciplinary effect' of panoptic surveillance is to make people conform to behaviours they think are expected of them when they are being monitored.

Strub (1989) notices that Bentham's panopticon, as an original conceptualization for the technology of power, had been almost wholly overlooked until Foucault examined it in *Discipline and Punish: The Birth of the Prison* (1977). Through this work, 'Foucault analysed how the panopticon's design refined the exercise of power by reducing the number of those who exercise it while increasing the number of those upon whom it is used' (Strub 1989: 43). Foucault believed that the panopticon is a technology of power and control that has significant implications on human subjectivity, primarily regarding how thought and behaviour are regulated in modern societies (Goodman 2014). Thus, Foucault believed the panopticon is about disciplinary power to regulate behaviour and control populations.

Fox (1989: 724) observes that Foucault's work is crucial as it demonstrates that the key behind the panopticon theory is 'one-way looking, in which those doing the looking constitutes those being looked at as objects'. He says those being looked at can be prisoners, workers, poor people, the insane, the ill, children, or managers. In this case, the constitution is, at the same time, the exercise of power. Fox argues that the panopticon functions today in ways that we all take for granted, following the rise of bureaucracy in public and private sectors. Key to the panopticon is that people who believe they are being surveilled conform to behaviours they think are expected of them and become self-disciplining, which connects to Gaventa's (2006) concept of invisible power.

Gaventa used the term 'invisible power' to refer to the conscious and unconscious internalization of social norms and values. According to Gaventa (2006), invisible power shapes the psychological and ideological boundaries of people's participation in public affairs – it influences how individuals think about their place in the world and what they feel unable to do. Invisible power 'shapes people's beliefs, sense of self and acceptance of the status quo – even their superiority or inferiority' (Gaventa 2006: 29).

Gaventa's perspectives on power enable a substantial analysis of modern societies, mainly, how a few influential persons and groups maintain control of the majority without resistance. It is akin to what Chomsky (1997) calls 'manufacturing consent', a form of ideological power capable of fending off any opposing view about how things should be.

Foucualt's panoptic theory and Gaventa's invisible power inform this chapter's analysis, and the critical questions about digital surveillance in Malawi as an exercise of power are addressed in the following section.

## Analysis

The analysis is divided into three sections: the first will discuss panoptic power, the second will analyse digital rights, and the final will discuss agency and resistance.

### Panoptic power

Communication surveillance, while often justified on grounds of national security and crime prevention, poses significant dangers that can impact individual privacy, civil liberties, and democratic processes. Whereas the panopticon involves external surveillance – the ever-watchful eye of the state over the rest – panopticism indicates the internalization of surveillance in which the watcher gains control, where the prisoner becomes their own guard (Foucault 1991). Thus, panopticon leads to panopticism, in which citizens are stripped of their agency by the oppressive system and conditioned to accept the status quo.

For Malawi, this is akin to what Dencik and Cable (2017) call surveillance realism, which is the normalization of surveillance and practices that serve the state's interests and violate citizens' rights. Surveillance realism nurtured the colonial and dictatorship eras. The lack of public discourse about digital surveillance amid surveillance technologies is a testimony to surveillance realism in Malawi.

Thus, the panopticon is problematic because it limits people's freedom. Constant surveillance has a 'chilling effect' where people suppress their own expression due to fear of legal or social sanctions, discouraging individuals from exercising their right to free speech. This has broader societal implications because self-censorship stifles freedom of expression, as people may refrain from speaking or acting freely due to the potential repercussions of their actions being monitored.

Free speech is a necessary precondition for the enjoyment of other rights, such as the right to vote, free assembly, and freedom of association, and it is essential to ensure press freedom (Howie 2017). Press freedom is necessary because the press is a means to an end; it enables people to access information, which is crucial to democratic governance; it allows citizens to hold governments and public officials accountable. This enhances transparency, which reduces corruption and fosters trust in public institutions; citizens must be informed about policies, laws, and governmental actions, enabling them to make informed decisions during elections and participate meaningfully in public discourse.

If future governments were to link biometric-ID, social media, mobile phones, and mobile banking data using the national data centre, then that potential exists. It is essential that the government implement legislation that civil society groups actively promote regulation and avoid surveillance creep, and that more research be conducted to evaluate the emerging practices of digital surveillance and citizen resistance in Malawi.

## Digital rights

Surveillance technology poses a serious threat to digital rights in Malawi.

Digital rights, also known as internet or online rights, refer to individuals' existing rights and freedoms in the digital world. These rights are an extension of fundamental human rights and are applicable in the context of digital technologies, particularly the internet. In Malawi, the government tends to pay more attention to security concerns and national development at the expense of digital rights, as if these issues are incompatible. Thus, the government of Malawi has invested heavily in surveillance technologies, which, unfortunately, have been implemented without resistance from the Malawian population, believing that the investment serves public interests.

The government's disregard for digital rights is also apparent as people are arrested for online activities, especially on social media platforms, including WhatsApp, which has an end-to-end encryption service. As one of the countries with the lowest ICT penetration in the world, there is an urgent need to catch up with trends elsewhere, and in the process, the Malawi government has been overlooking critical safeguards in its adoption and implementation of technologies. Hersey (2020) observed how Malawi established its digital-ID system at 'breakneck speed', arguing that Malawi was the only country in its region without a national identification system. Its leading implementing partner, the United Nations Development Programme (UNDP), said the national ID would enable Malawians to 'prove their identity and benefit from their rights' (UNDP 2022). Malik (2020), who worked on the project as a UNDP consultant, said the ID was critical in enhancing transparency, for example, during elections, ensuring 'one person, one identity, one vote'. It is a tool for combating electoral fraud. Clearly surveillance technologies, mandatory SIM card registration, national biometric-ID, and the national data centre have been implemented for the public interest. After all, Duncan (2019) observes that no country that considers itself a democracy would want to be caught covertly spying on its unsuspecting citizens.

Despite the implementation of surveillance technologies, surveillance is not part of everyday discourse in Malawi because surveillance has been naturalized and normalized decades after its implementation in the name of public interest and national security. Justification for surveillance has become entrenched to the point that it is now 'common sense' that the state has to monitor its citizens' movements for the citizens' good. According to Gaventa (2006), citizens' compliance with their oppression is achieved through 'invisible power'. 'Invisible power involves the internalised, often unconscious acceptance of dominant norms, institutions, languages and behaviours as natural and normal, often desirable, even if they appear to be against the interests of the actors involved' (Scott-Villiers and Oosterom 2016: 2). Chomsky (1997) identifies this as the process of manufacturing consent, which is a process of overcoming the fact that, in democratic societies, people have different opinions on how things should work. By manufacturing consent, governments can structure and control people's views so that people will always do what their governments tell them.

This explains why people in Malawi are arrested for their social media activities, using draconian legal provisions; but there is a backlash against such abuse of the law. Kainja (2022) has observed that people arrested using these vague laws have offended influential people or large institutions, such as the state president, members of parliament, and banks. This means the laws serve to protect powerful people against the powerless. It shields influential people from accountability. Thus, manufacturing consent is a successful political and social control tool; it is manipulative, cynical, and undemocratic. It is a form of control and begets conformity, similar to the coercive powers of the panopticon in which the majority conforms to the coercive power of a few influential individuals.

Manufacturing consent draws on hegemonic powers – a different side of the same tool. The concept of hegemony indicates a society in which, despite oppression and exploitation, there is a high degree of consensus and a considerable measure of social stability (Storey 2015). All these have traces of invisible power, which, according to Gaventa, not only keeps people from the decision-making table, but also the minds and consciousnesses of the different players involved, even those directly affected by the problem.

## Resistance

In Southern Africa, Munoriyawa and Mare (2023) observe that there is a mixed bag of resistance to surveillance. Resistance to surveillance has followed a continuum, mainly from individual efforts to encourage people to use safe digital practices that leave little to no digital footprints in which surveillance thrives. Surveillance on social media platforms is being countered by encryption services, especially on WhatsApp, which has end-to-end encryption. Munoriyarwa (2021) observes that literature on resistance to surveillance remains scant in the Global South, although people have resisted surveillance for centuries in the countries of the Global North. Munoriyarwa notices that Parisians opposed the city's plan to install fixed streetlights, arguing that this was an unacceptable form of surveillance and that early American welfare programmes were resisted as they were ways of gathering private data by the state.

Kainja (2022) noticed that while the implementation of the CIRMS ICT management system faced resistance, mandatory SIM card registration did not face notable objections, although MACRA is the regulatory authority of both policies. There are two possible reasons for this. First, citizens were content with the justifications for SIM card registration implementation. Second, citizens failed to see and articulate how it could lead to a violation of human rights. This is reminiscent of Gaventa's (2006) invisible power, in which citizens unconsciously accept dominant norms, institutions, languages, and behaviours as natural and normal, even if it appears to be against their interests. This includes the country's civil society organizations, which did not articulate or oppose the possibility of human rights violations.

However, there are signs that, with a growing number of surveillance technologies and covert surveillance in the country, Malawian citizens are not entirely passive in the face of these emerging digital surveillance practices, and the Digital Rights Coalition, a coalition of like-minded activists, researchers, and academics from different institutions in Malawi, was formed. The emergence of the coalition is evidence that resistance is also emergent. 'The formation of a new digital rights network provides an opportunity to put human rights-sensitive legislation in place before surveillance creep begins' (Roberts et al. 2023: 27).

The Digital Rights Coalition should be encouraged because the country's judiciary is independent and pro-human rights when called upon. For instance, the courts blocked the country's telecommunication regulator from implementing the Consolidated ICT Regulatory Management System (CIRMS), agreeing with concerns that CIRMS would undermine personal privacy, contrary to section 21 of the Constitution of Malawi.

## Recommendations

Drawing on the analysis in this chapter, the following recommendations arise for policy, practice, and further research. They are organized by actor:

**Government:** Like all governments, Malawi must monitor its citizens for efficient welfare distribution and mitigating public health emergencies. However, the Malawi government has implemented surveillance programmes without legal safeguards, undermining the privacy of its citizens, which is ironic as the programmes were meant to benefit the citizens. The government should implement the human rights approach in programmes that expose people to privacy breaches.

**Civil society organizations:** The formation of the Digital Rights Coalition (discussed in the previous section) should be commended. However, Malawi's civil society has been inactive regarding surveillance and privacy issues. This has paved the way for the government to implement surveillance technologies without debate. Surveillance even affects the work of civil society by allowing the state and non-state actors to target civil society groups, dissidents, journalists, and political opposition – closing civic space and open debate – and crushing the fabric of a democratic society.

**Academia:** Academia is critical in researching and creating knowledge and solutions about societal issues. Although the issue of surveillance is not a public discourse in Malawi, academics can create one by raising awareness and producing evidence and knowledge. Discussions about surveillance can be polarizing, but academics can facilitate a nuanced and balanced discussion, leading to objective conclusions.

# Conclusion

This chapter examined the emerging digital surveillance practices in Malawi. It addressed the following questions: What are the human rights implications of expanding surveillance? How does it affect power relationships? What forms of citizen agency and resistance does it provoke? These questions have power, rights, and agency embedded in them. Addressing these questions naturally led to the conceptual framing of the chapter.

The simplest way to characterize the emerging digital surveillance in Malawi is Gaventa's (2006) invisible power in which citizens subconsciously submit to their domination. Surveillance of different forms has been a reality in Malawi since the colonial days, from 1891. In the last six years, the Malawi government has invested heavily in the following surveillance technologies: mandatory SIM card registration, national biometric-IDs, and national data centres. Although there is no admissible evidence that these technologies are being used for surveillance, the investment is worrying because they have been implemented without the necessary legal frameworks to protect citizens from possible abuse of the technology. The country's digital surveillance space is characterized by an invisible power, which Gaventa (2006) describes as citizens' compliance with their oppression.

Digital surveillance exposes citizens to violation of privacy, which is protected under section 21 of the Malawi constitution. Also, the lack of evidence that the technology is currently being used for surveillance does not mean it is not being used or that a future government will not use it. Furthermore, the chapter has found covert surveillance in Malawi, especially on social media platforms, including WhatsApp, a private network with end-to-end encryption. Security agents use draconian legal provisions in the Electronic Transactions and Cyber Security Act of 2016 to arrest people who have offended influential individuals and corporate institutions. In this case, the work of invisible power allows covert surveillance. It protects influential people from accountability, as people are afraid to use digital platforms to hold their leaders to account.

The chapter has found encouraging cases of emerging resistance against digital surveillance in the country, particularly the establishment of the Digital Rights Coalition, which has the potential to put the discussion of emerging digital surveillance in the country on a public agenda. The emergence of this grouping should take advantage of the growing visibility of digital rights networks and organizations on the continent to leverage their knowledge and experience. The chapter has identified the government as a critical stakeholder in adopting a human rights approach to implementing surveillance technology. It has also implored civil society to be vigilant in guarding the civic space against surveillance, and it has requested that the academia do more research in this area and facilitate a sober discussion about the emerging digital surveillance in the country.

## Note

1    https://macra.mw/frequently-asked-questions-2/

## Bibliography

Chimjeka, R. (2016). 'MACRA to Terminate CIRMS Supplier Deal', Nation Publications Limited. https://mwnation.com/macra-to-terminate-cirms-supplier-deal (accessed 28 August 2024).

Chitsulo, L. (2020). 'MACRA Speaks on CIRMS', Nation Publications Limited. https://mwnation.com/macra-speaks-on-cirms/ (accessed 28 August 2024).

Chomsky, N. (1997). 'What Makes Mainstream Media Mainstream?' *Z Magazine*. https://chomsky.info/199710__/ (accessed 28 August 2024).

Clarke, G., Gebreab, F. and Mgombelo, H. (2003). 'Telecommunications Reform in Malawi', *Policy Research Working Papers*. The World Bank. https://documents1. worldbank.org/curated/zh/946981468776800237/107507322_20041117182014/ additional/multi0page.pdf (accessed 28 August 2024).

Creswell, J. W., Hanson, W. E., Clark Plano, V. L. and Morales, A. (2007). 'Qualitative Research Designs, Selection, and Implementation', *The Counseling Psychologist*, 35(2): 236–64.

Dahl, J. Y. (2022). 'Chameleonising: A Microsociological Study of Covert Physical Surveillance', *European Journal of Criminology*, 19(2): 220–36. https://doi. org/10.1177/1477370819896204

DataReportal (2023). 'Digital 2023 Malawi'. https://datareportal.com/reports/digital-2023-malawi (accessed 28 August 2024).

Dencik, L. and Cable, J. (2017). 'The Advent of Surveillance Realism: Public Opinion and Activists Responses to the Snowden Leaks', *International Journal of Communication*, 11: 763–81.

Duncan, J. (2019). 'Bulk Communication Surveillance in South Africa – Fix or Nix it', *Daily Maverick*. https://www.dailymaverick.co.za/article/2019-09-30-bulk-communication-surveillance-in-south-africa-fix-it-or-nix-it/ (accessed 3 September 2023).

Eck, K. and Hatz, S. (2020). 'State Surveillance and the COVID-19 Crisis', *Journal of Human Rights*, 19(5): 603–12.

Foucault, M. (1977). *Discipline and Punish: The Birth of the Prison*, New York: Pantheon Books.

Foucault, M. (1991). *Discipline and Punishment: The Birth of the Prison* (trans. A. Sheridan), Harmondsworth: Penguin Books.

Fox, S. (1989). 'The Panopticon: From Bentham's Obsession to the Revolution in Management Learning', *Human Relations*, 42(8): 717–39.

Galič, M., Timan, T. and Koops, B. J. (2016). 'Bentham, Deleuze and Beyond: An Overview of Surveillance Theories from the Panopticon to Participation', *Philosophy & Technology*, 30(1): 9–37. Article 1. https://doi.org/10.1007/s13347-016-0219-1

Garowe Online (2023). 'Chinese Tech Giant to Invest Over $300 Million in Africa/s Data Centre and Cyber Security Market'. https://www.garoweonline.com/en/featured/business-n/chinese-tech-giant-to-invest-over-300-million-in-africa-s-date-center-and-cyber-security-market (accessed 28 August 2024).

Gaventa, J. (2006). 'Finding the Spaces for Change: A Power Analysis', *IDS Bulletin*, 37(6): 23–33. https://doi.org/10.1111/j.1759-5436.2006.tb00320.x

Goodman, D. (2014). 'Panopticon', in T. Teo (ed.), *Encyclopedia of Critical Psychology*, New York: Springer.

GSMA (2019). 'Digital Identity Country Report: Malawi', GSMA. https://www.gsma.com/solutions-and-impact/connectivity-for-good/mobile-for-development/wp-content/uploads/2019/02/Digital-Identity-Country-Report.pdf (accessed 6 June 2024).

Hersey, F. (2020). 'How Malawi Established a Biometric National ID System at Break-neck Speed'. https://www.biometricupdate.com/202010/how-malawi-established-a-biometric-national-id-system-at-breakneck-speed (accessed 28 August 2024).

Howie, E. (2017). 'Protecting the Human Right to Freedom of Expression in International Law', *International Journal of Speech–Language Pathology*, 20(1): 12–15.

Huaxia (2022). 'Malawi Government, Huawei Commission National Data Centre', Xinhua. https://english.news.cn/20220722/0e891dbd59d84d42821a122f057d5e75/c.html (accessed 24 July 2023).

Human Rights Council (2015). 'Report of the Special Rapporteur on Promoting and Protecting the Right to Freedom of Opinion and Expression', David Kaye. https://www.ohchr.org/en/HRBodies/HRC/RegularSessions/Session29/Documents/A.HRC.29.32_AEV.doc (accessed 28 August 2024).

Kainja, J. (2021a). 'Malawi Telcos Further Reduce Data Prices, but Affordability Concerns Remain', CIPESA. https://cipesa.org/2021/05/malawi-telcos-further-reduce-data-prices-but-affordability-concerns-remain/ (accessed 24 July 2023).

Kainja, J. (2021b). 'Mapping Digital Surveillance and Privacy Concerns in Malawi', The Media Policy and Democracy Project. https://www.mediaanddemocracy.com/uploads/1/6/5/7/16577624/malawi_report.pdf (accessed 28 August 2024).

Kainja, J. (2022). 'Arrests Mar Malawi's Digital Rights Landscape', in *Digital Rights in Southern Africa*. https://africaninternetrights.org/en/node/2587 (accessed 28 August 2024).

Kainja, J. (2023a). 'Legal and Policy Gaps Affecting Digital Rights in Malawi', *Journal of Humanities*, 31(1). https://doi.org/10.4314/jh.v31i1.1

Kainja, J. (2023b). 'Malawi Country Report', in T. Roberts, J. Gitahi, P. Allam, L. Oboh, O. Oladapo, G. Appiah-Adjei, A. Galal, J. Kainja, S. Phiri, K. Abraham, S. Klovig Skelton and A. Sheombar (eds), *Mapping the Supply of Surveillance Technologies to Africa: Case Studies from Nigeria, Ghana, Morocco, Malawi, and Zambia*, Brighton: Institute of Development Studies. https://opendocs.ids.ac.uk/opendocs/bitstream/handle/20.500.12413/18120/ADRN_Surveillance_Supply_Chain_Report_Malawi_Country_Report.pdf?sequence=6&isAllowed=y (accessed 28 August 2024).

Königs, P. (2022). 'Government Surveillance, Privacy, and Legitimacy', *Philosophy & Technology*, 35(8). https://doi.org/10.1007/s13347-022-00503-9

Lauer, J. (2011). 'Surveillance History and the History of New Media: An Evidential Paradigm', *New Media & Society*, 14(4): 566–82.

Malik, T. (2020). 'Malawi's Journey Towards Transformation'. Centre for Global Development. https://www.cgdev.org/sites/default/files/malawi-journey-towards-transformation.pdf (accessed 28 August 2024).

Manda, D. T. (2011). 'Maturity of Cybersecurity Initiatives in Malawi: A Comparison with the Drive for Fast and Ubiquitous Internet Connectivity'. DiPLO. https://www.diplomacy.edu/wp-content/uploads/2021/06/IGCBP2010_2011_Manda.pdf (accessed 24 July 2023).

McMullan, T. (2015). 'What Does the Panopticon Mean in the Age of Digital Surveillance?' *The Guardian*. https://www.theguardian.com/technology/2015/

jul/23/panopticon-digital-surveillance-jeremy-bentham (accessed 2 September 2023).

Miles, K. (2014). 'Glenn Greenwald on Why Privacy Is Vital, Even If You "Have Nothing to Hide"'. *Huffington Post*. https://www.huffpost.com/entry/glenn-greenwald-privacy_n_5509704 (accessed 28 August 2024).

Mpasu, S. (2014). *Political Prisoner 3/75: A True Story by Sam Mpasu*, Balaka: Montfort Media.

Munoriyarwa, A. (2021). 'When Watchdogs Fight Back: Resisting State Surveillance in Everyday Investigative Reporting Practices Among Zimbabwean Journalists', *Journal of Eastern African Studies*, 15(3): 421–41. https://doi.org/10.1080/17531055.2021.1949

Munoriyarwa, A. and Mare, A. (2023). *Digital Surveillance in Southern Africa: Policies, Politics and Practices*, Cham: Palgrave Macmillan.

Parkinson, J., Bariyo, N.and Chin, J. (2019). 'Huawei Technicians Helped African Governments Spy on Political Opponents', *The Wall Street Journal*. https://www.wsj.com/articles/huawei-technicians-helped-african-governments-spy-on-political-opponents-11565793017 (accessed 28 August 2024).

Priezkalns, E. (2022). 'Anti-Corruption Bureau Halts Purchase of National Revenue Assurance System in Malawi', Comms Risk. https://commsrisk.com/anti-corruption-bureau-halts-purchase-of-national-revenue-assurance-system-in-malawi/ (accessed 28 August 2024).

Putnam, L. L. and Banghart, S. (2017). 'Interpretive Approaches', in *The International Encyclopedia of Organizational Communication*, 1–17, New York: John Wiley & Sons. https://doi.org/10.1002/9781118955567.wbieoc118 (accessed 28 August 2024).

Roberts, T., Gitahi, J., Allam, P., Oboh, L. Oladapo, O., Appiah-Adjei, G., Galal, A., Kainja, J., Phiri, S., Abraham, K., Klovig Skelton, S. and Sheombar, A. (2023). *Mapping the Supply of Surveillance Technologies to Africa: Case Studies from Nigeria, Ghana, Morocco, Malawi, and Zambia*, Brighton: Institute of Development Studies. https://doi.org/10.19088/IDS.2023.027

Sangala, T. (2018). 'MACRA Sets New SIM Card Registration Deadlines', *Times Media Group*. https://times.mw/macra-sets-new-sim-card-registration-deadlines/ (accessed 28 August 2024).

Scott-Villiers, P. and Oosterom, M. (2016). 'Power, Poverty and Inequality', *IDS Bulletin*, 47(5). https://archive.ids.ac.uk/eldis/document/A102112.html (accessed 28 August 2024).

SELP Group (n.d.). 'About Us'. https://www.selp.fr/en/selp-group-en (accessed 28 August 2024).

Storey, J. (2015). *Cultural Theory and Popular Culture: An Introduction* (7th ed.). London: Routledge. https://doi.org/10.4324/9781315744148

Strub, H. (1989). 'The Theory of Panoptical control: Bentham's *Panopticon* and Orwell's *Nineteen Eighty-Four*', *Journal of the History of the Behavioral Sciences*, 25(1): 40–59.

UNDP (2022). 'Malawi's Foundational Legal Identity System Sets the Stage for a More Efficient and Responsible Digital Future'. https://www.undp.org/digital/ stories/malawi%E2%80%99s-foundational-legal-identity-system-sets-stage-more-efficient-and-responsible-digital-future (accessed 28 August 2024).

Wanyama, E. (2018). 'The Stampede for SIM Card Registration: A Major Question for Africa', CIPESA. https://cipesa.org/2018/04/the-stampede-for-sim-card-registration-a-major-question-for-africa/ (accessed 28 August 2024).

World Bank (2017). 'The State of Identification Systems in Africa: Country Briefs', World Bank Group. https://openknowledge.worldbank.org/bitstream/ handle/10986/28310/119065-WP-ID4D-country-profiles-report-final-PUBLIC. pdf?sequence=1&isAllowed=y (accessed 28 August 2024).

# 6

# Panoptic real-time surveillance in Kenya

Judy Gitahi and Muthuri Kathure

## Introduction

The advent of the digital age has transformed the global landscape, including the ways in which surveillance is conducted, and human rights are upheld. In Kenya, there has been a rapid acquisition of surveillance technologies. The challenges posed by this rapid acquisition of mass surveillance technologies are multifaceted and demand urgent attention since acquisitions often lack transparent justification, casting a shadow on the motives behind their deployment. Moreover, there are no legal frameworks governing the acquisition of surveillance technologies. The threat of terror attacks is often used to legitimize these acquisitions and raises ethical and legal concerns.

In this chapter, we explore state acquisitions of five categories of technology, namely mobile interception, internet interception, social media monitoring, safe city/smart city surveillance, and biometric digital-ID. When the five methods of surveillance are integrated, they make it possible to conduct mass surveillance that violates citizens' human rights, which are protected in the constitution. This chapter begins by tracing surveillance in Kenya from its introduction by the British to monitor the resistance of the anti-colonial Mau Mau movement. After national liberation, the post-colonial government retained this political surveillance capability, which has evolved into the technology-enabled surveillance landscape we have in Kenya today. Using the concept of panoptic power (Gravett 2021), we analyse how surveillance technology acquisition in Kenya provides the government with the power to conduct mass surveillance of citizens in ways that violate rights and could lead to citizens self-limiting their behaviour.

The main research questions we aim to answer are: (1) How does the acquisition of digital technologies enhance the panoptic power of different actors in Kenya's surveillance system? and (2) How could this panoptic power lead to citizens limiting their behaviour, and why is this important for human rights?

We draw from various sources including secondary literature, media reports, peer-reviewed analysis, online blogs, and reports by organizations researching human rights violations. This chapter contributes to the literature by providing an analysis that is framed using the concepts of panoptic power to assess digital surveillance technology acquisitions in Kenya. This is the first comprehensive mapping of surveillance technologies across the five categories in Kenya, and we hope that this provides a foundation for thinking about the human rights implications of expanding surveillance acquisitions.

The rest of the chapter will be structured as follows: the next section provides an historical and political background of surveillance in Kenya. We then outline the country case study and surveillance landscape of Kenya, detailing which surveillance technologies are being used by whom, for what purpose, and with what consequences for human rights. The subsequent section then presents the contextual literature to review for the reader what we already know and what gaps in knowledge exist before briefly summarizing the conceptual literature related to power analysis and a description of the framework chosen to analyse digital surveillance in Kenya. We then analyse Kenya's surveillance technology landscape using the panopticon framework. The final sections outline forms of resistance to surveillance before offering recommendations and conclusions.

# Background

In order to understand current digital surveillance practices in Kenya, we begin by tracing institutionalized surveillance from its origins in pre-independence Kenya. Kenya was a British colony until 1963, during which time physical surveillance through the Home Guard was popularized and used to control the actions of Kenyans in the system (Ocobock 2012). The Home Guard was a government paramilitary force in Kenya from early 1953 until January 1955 and formed in response to insurgent attacks during the Mau Mau uprising. The Special Branch was a branch of the British police force established to spy on internal opposition to the ruling elite in the United Kingdom. The Special Branch was later exported to the colonies to spy on opposition to colonial rule, including in Kenya to spy on the Mau Mau (Shaffer 2019). The physical surveillance provided power to the colonists, enabling them to maintain their authority despite being a minority. This section summarizes the history of Kenya's surveillance systems in three broad historical periods: Mau Mau surveillance (before 1963), post-independence surveillance (1963–2002), and digital surveillance (post-2002).

## Mau Mau surveillance (before 1963)

The Mau Mau uprising was an important anti-colonial uprising between 1952 and 1960. It was mainly led by the Kikuyu ethnic group, who opposed the expropriation of their land by British troops. The British colonial government responded to the uprising with harsh measures, including the establishment of concentration camps (Anderson 2005).

The British colonial government also used Kikuyu Home Guard, also known as the 'Loyal Guards', who were a majority Kikuyu paramilitary force used to put down the Mau Mau uprising. According to Ogema and Otika (2013), the Kikuyu Home Guard played a complex role in the surveillance scene. They were responsible for identifying Mau Mau sympathizers in their communities and providing intelligence to the colonial authorities. This created a climate of suspicion and mistrust within the Kikuyu community, as individuals feared being accused by their own people of collaborating with the colonial regime or being viewed as traitors by their own people. This use of surveillance during colonization eroded trust within communities, and the trauma experienced by those who suffered in the harsh conditions of the concentration camps has persisted for generations (Ogema and Otika 2013).

## Surveillance post-independence (1963–2002)

The use of surveillance in colonial Kenya shaped the country's post-independence politics, as the memory of colonial surveillance influenced the country's efforts to establish its own security apparatus (Anderson 2015). After gaining independence in 1963, Kenya inherited many institutions and structures established during the colonial period, including the security and intelligence apparatus. The Special Branch, a colonial-era intelligence agency, continued to exist and became an integral part of Kenya's security apparatus after independence, and was responsible for monitoring and suppressing dissent, maintaining control, and ensuring the stability of the new nation (Ogara and Odhiambo-Otieno 2003). Kenya was under authoritarian rule under its first two presidents: Jomo Kenyatta and Daniel Arap Moi. Under both presidents, mechanisms of surveillance and control were enhanced, often borrowing from colonial-era models to suppress dissent and maintain political power. Jomo Kenyatta's presidency (1963–78) suppressed political dissent to weaken opposition and retain power. The Special Branch, which operated under the auspices of the police force, played an important role in surveillance and intelligence gathering. The government used a combination of legal and extra-legal means to silence dissent. The Law on Police Protection and the Public Order Act were used to arrest and detain suspected opponents without trial. The Kenyatta regime's surveillance methods were based on a colonial model, using informants, spies, and secret agents to infiltrate and monitor political organizations and gatherings (Omolo Ochilo 2013).

The presidency of Daniel Arap Moi (1978–2002) continued the authoritarian practices of the Kenyatta era. The Special Branch became the Directorate of Security Intelligence (DSI), whose role was to suppress internal political opposition. Moi's government expanded its surveillance capabilities, with a particular focus on monitoring academics, journalists, and human rights activists (Human Rights Watch 1991). Tactics such as arbitrary arrest, torture, and intimidation were used to silence critics. The government also used informant networks to gather intelligence on opposition groups. The torture chambers of the Nyayo House in Nairobi became known for their brutal treatment of political detainees, reflecting the dark history of the colonial concentration camps (Anaïs 2017).

The persistence of post-independence surveillance activities reinforced a culture of fear and self-censorship. People were hesitant to express their dissenting views because of the risk of surveillance, arrest, and torture, causing a 'chilling effect' that stifles free speech, impedes political discourse, and contributes to the consolidation of power among ruling elites. The surveillance techniques used during the post-independence period were not only based on colonial models but expanded upon them, adapting to the changing political landscape while maintaining the control objectives of the colonialists. The legacy of this era has had a lasting impact on Kenya's political and social dynamics, shaping the relationship between the state and its people.

## Digital surveillance (post-2002)

Kenya faces threats from extremist groups such as Al-Shabaab[1] due to its proximity to Somalia. Surveillance technology has begun to play an important role in detecting potential threats and preventing terrorist activity. To curb terrorism and prevent attacks from groups like Al-Shabaab, the Kenyan government has launched initiatives like the Usalama Watch, which involves increased surveillance in Somali neighbourhoods to identify potential terrorists or sympathizers.

Kenya also applies financial surveillance as part of its efforts to combat money laundering and terrorist financing. The Financial Reporting Center (FRC) was established to monitor financial transactions and identify suspicious activity that may be related to terrorist financing.

Although digital technology has become an important part of surveillance efforts, physical monitoring methods are still used. Security forces employ tactics such as tracking and monitoring the movements of individuals or groups suspected of engaging in criminal or subversive activities (Maundu 2021). Following the post-election violence in Kenya in 2007–8, there was awareness of the role that hate speech and incitement played in fuelling the violence. This has led to closer surveillance of communications, both online and via text messaging, to identify and address hate speech and incitement. The National Coherence and Integration Commission (NCIC) and the Communications Commission of Kenya (CCK) were involved in regulating and monitoring these communications.

Overall, since 2002, Kenya has experienced an expansion of digital surveillance technologies and practices, particularly in response to terrorist threats. According to Land et al. (2012), government efforts to monitor financial transactions, use spyware, and use physical and digital surveillance methods have raised concerns about privacy and civil liberties. The push for digitization, including initiatives such as the Huduma number[2] and mandatory mobile phone SIM-card registration, which requires capturing of personal identification information, has further aligned digital technology and surveillance within the country's security and governance strategy.

## Kenya's surveillance landscape

The Kenyan surveillance landscape comprises multiple actors, each with different powers to acquire and use technologies. This section summarizes the main actors in the surveillance landscape and their roles. We then provide a contextual literature review that explores the main digital surveillance technology acquisitions across five categories, which are chosen and validated based on the most common surveillance technology types across African countries.

### Main actors in the surveillance landscape

The National Intelligence Services (NIS) and the police are the main intelligence organizations and are in charge of gathering and evaluating intelligence pertaining to national security. The NIS has the authority to intercept communications for national security reasons alongside the police and has direct access to communication networks across the country, sometimes without the knowledge of telecom companies (Privacy International 2017). This ability is governed by the Regulation of Interception of Communications Act (RICA), which specifies the conditions and methods for such interception. RICA also aims to protect citizens by deterring SIM card fraud and aiding in criminal investigations to reduce illegal access to personal information stored on phones.

The Communications Authority of Kenya (CAK) is an independent agency established by the Kenyan government to regulate the telecom sector and oversee the country's communications network. The CAK is responsible for increasing access to communication services, ensuring fair competition, and defending the rights of consumers. It has the power to assign spectrum resources, license and regulate communication service providers, and enforce adherence to communication laws and regulations.

The Cybersecurity Steering Committee formulates and implements national cybersecurity frameworks, strategies, and policies by bringing together numerous government ministries, departments, and agencies in a common forum.

The ICT Authority is in charge of all information and communication technology policies and sets standards related to network security and data management practices.

The final key players are telecommunications companies (e.g., Safaricom), who frequently work with law enforcement organizations, supplying information and technological support for the legal interception of communications as allowed by laws. Telecommunications companies play a crucial role in facilitating communication surveillance while balancing the customers' right to privacy.

## Acquisition of surveillance technologies

This section summarizes some of the known acquisitions and amounts spent by the Kenyan government in each of the five categories of digital surveillance technologies: internet interception, mobile interception, social media monitoring, safe/smart city surveillance, and biometric digital-ID. While some acquisitions and amounts are public, we note that limited data was available on the value of some acquisitions and the companies providing these technologies. This is not intended to be a comprehensive listing of all acquisitions but rather to provide an overview of Kenya's surveillance landscape and an indication of its dimensions.

### Internet interception

An investigation by Citizen Lab of the University of Toronto identified the installation of Blue Coat PacketShaper surveillance technologies in Kenya

(Marquis-Boire et al. 2013a). This 'deep packet inspection' technology enables the monitoring and surveillance of citizens' internet messaging, including Facebook, Gmail, Skype, and Twitter, among others. However, no evidence of specific use cases in Kenya has become public. In 2017, the country's largest telecommunication company, Safaricom, reportedly installed a 'middlebox' in its cellular network. Such middleboxes are 'dual use' as they can be used for legitimate purposes like protecting the network from malicious programs; however, they also provide the state with the power to surveil, censor, and manipulate internet traffic (CIPIT 2017).

## Mobile interception

The National Intelligence Service (NIS) is known to have intercepted mobile phones since 2007 (Privacy International 2017). The NIS may have an 'IMSI catcher' or a similar device which pretends to be a cell-phone tower, in order to intercept private mobile phone communications and surveil voice calls and phone messages, as well as reveal the location of the phone (Privacy International 2017). In 2023, the Communications Authority of Kenya (CAK) received Kenya's Supreme Court approval to install a Device Management System (DMS) on mobile phone networks to detect counterfeit phones (Kiplagat 2023). This system would allow the CAK to access all mobile subscriber phones across the country.

Pegasus, a mobile phone spyware technology provided by Israeli-based company NSO group, has also been reported as having been used in Kenya (Marczak et al. 2018). Kenya is also listed as a likely customer of Circles, which is also an NSO affiliated firm that exploits weaknesses in the mobile phone system to snoop on calls, texts, and location of phones (Marczak et al. 2020).

The role of private companies in mobile interception has also been documented, although not as widely. Breckenridge (2018) discusses the monopoly power that Safaricom has as the largest telecom company in Kenya and the technical potential of using this data in surveillance systems. Privacy International (2017) has claimed that the NIS has direct access to communication networks, with network operators having little knowledge of the interception of communications occurring on its network.

## Social media monitoring

Cambridge Analytica (CA), a British political consulting firm, was involved in the 2013 and 2017 elections in Kenya. The company is said to have leveraged algorithms that prioritize polarizing content to influence public opinion and potentially influence the election process (Crabtree 2018). While the specific technologies used by CA remain unknown, the Jubilee Party, a political party, paid $6 million for the contract in exchange for these services in 2017 (Nyabola 2019). During the 2017 elections, the Communications Authority also reported that it would be acquiring a system to enable monitoring of social media activity, and indicated having spent $5.8 million (Ksh 600 million) on a social media monitoring system (*The East African* 2020).

## Safe city/Smart city technologies

Huawei, a large Chinese telecom company, is building a data centre in Konza through a concessional loan from China worth Ksh 17.5 billion ($172 million) (Moss 2019). This data centre is linked to China's Safe City Initiative, which is an urban planning initiative that uses thousands of CCTV cameras to surveil citizens and cars, using facial recognition technology driven by artificial intelligence and car licence plate recognition. Analysing these real-time data feeds in a central data centre can dramatically increase the visibility of citizens to the state. Some analysts have claimed that the Safe City programme is a means for China to export not just its digital technologies but also its own form of digital authoritarianism by providing the infrastructure for governments to surveil, repress, and manipulate populations (Bradford 2023). Huawei has countered accusations of digital authoritarianism by claiming that the installation of safe city infrastructure in Kenya has led to reduced rates of crime in Nairobi and Mombasa (Wangari 2024). However, Huawei later retracted these claims and the national police unit reported smaller reductions in crime in Nairobi and an increase in crime in Mombasa since the smart city installations (Wangari 2024).

Hikvision, a Chinese company, has supplied surveillance cameras to Nairobi's central business district (Jili 2022a). While there is no clear indication that these cameras provide Chinese actors with access to data, cybersecurity vulnerabilities have been identified that allow hackers to remotely control cameras or infect them with malware (Jili 2022a). SenseTime, a Hong Kong-based company, has also introduced surveillance technologies to Kenyan airports through a Japanese-funded initiative, whose amount is unknown (Burt 2019).

China is a key player in spreading smart city technologies and part of its strategy has been to expand its geopolitical footprint in African countries through Foreign Direct Investment (FDI) (Jili 2022a; 2022b). By funding acquisitions of surveillance technologies, the expansion of its geopolitical footprint often comes at the expense of citizens' human rights, as the technologies introduced by foreign powers pay little attention to the human rights implications and more to the state actor and equipping them with power. China's role has also been described as a form of digital neocolonialism, with the potential for China to use technologies to apply political and economic pressure on countries like Kenya (Gravett 2021).

## Biometric digital-ID

In 2013, Kenya launched a biometric digital-ID scheme intended to make every citizen machine readable. The system was popularly known as the Huduma number and was based on the government's National Integrated Identity Management System (NIMS). The Huduma system issued a unique number to every citizen verified with biometric data, which would then be needed to access all government services. However, it raised concerns about data security since a significant amount of personal data was being collected with no clear legal framework of data privacy protections (Privacy International 2022). By requiring an additional registration process, the Huduma number was also argued as creating further exclusion for Kenyans who already lack documentation such as birth certificates (Open Society Justice Initiative n.d.). Further, the harmonization and interlinking of databases in NIIMS was argued to carry a high risk for privacy violations that would allow the government to conduct mass surveillance through searching aggregated data on individuals (ibid.). These concerns were raised before a high court by the Nubian Rights Forum (NRF), the Kenya Human Rights Commission (KHRC), and the Kenya National Commission on Human

Rights (KNCHR) in February 2019, and a ruling was made halting the rollout of Huduma numbers in October 2021 (Privacy International 2022). It is reported that the government spent over Ksh10 billion ($78 million) on the Huduma number registration exercise (Hersey 2023), with support from the Estonian government (UN Kenya 2021). The government is currently exploring an alternative Unique Personal Identifier (UPI) system, which will be issued to register children in primary and secondary school and become their national identity number once they turn eighteen (Kombo 2023). To roll out this system, the government claimed to have set aside 1 billion Kenyan Shillings ($6 million) (Cheruiyot 2023).

## Conceptual literature review

Having mapped out the main actors and acquisitions of surveillance technologies in Kenya, this section reviews the concepts of panoptic power, digital rights, and agency, which we use to assess how technology enables some actors to expand their surveillance power.

### Panoptic power

The term 'panopticon', coined by Jeremy Bentham and subsequently studied by Michel Foucault, refers to a type of institutional structure intended to facilitate continuous monitoring (Foucault 1995). Foucault (1995) defines panoptic power as the coercive power of states to cause citizens to change their behaviour since they feel they are being watched. The concept of the panopticon revolves around the psychological effects of observation and is a shift from coercive power and physical punishment to more subtle population control. Foucault argued that being aware of potential surveillance at all times can cause those being surveilled to self-censor and conform to the demands of people in positions of power. Digital surveillance technologies enable actors to gain access to thousands of data points on every call, text, message, search, purchase, like, or follow. Such pervasive, constant monitoring of individuals can manipulate them into acting differently. This panoptic surveillance environment where individuals are conscious of being constantly monitored, can lead to a 'chilling effect' on dissent and a pre-emptive self-censorship of behaviour. The constant possibility that you are being watched thus becomes the primary mechanism of control.

## Digital human rights

If digital surveillance provides panoptic power to monitor individuals, misuse of this power could lead to violation of fundamental human and digital rights. The United Nations defines digital rights as principles and practices that aim to protect and promote fundamental human rights in the digital environment, building on established human rights instruments (United Nations n.d.). Digital rights include the right to privacy, ensuring control over personal data, and protection from unwarranted surveillance. A digital rights framework enables us to see conflicts between fundamental freedoms like privacy and freedom of expression and the panoptic power to digitally surveil the everyday lives of citizens.

## Agency

In response to the use of panoptic power and violation of digital rights, citizens may resist by organizing and protesting against those who wield power. This chapter thus also utilizes the concept of agency, which has multiple definitions. Sen (1999) defines agency as the ability to act in pursuit of one's goals or values. Individuals with agency are free to pursue their valued goals and function effectively within their societies, but this 'agency freedom' is limited by repressive social structures that limit the ability of an individual to exercise their agency. Alkire (2008b) also explores the concept of agency as the ability to act on your values and achieve your goals. Exercising agency, like achieving goals or developing skills, can lead to social or economic power, while power in the form of resources or influence empowers individuals to pursue their goals more effectively. Agency and power are thus closely interlinked. This chapter uses the definition of agency as the ability to act on values to achieve a goal or to resist an unfreedom – in this case, the repressive power of the state's expansion of panoptic digital surveillance.

# Methodological approach

This chapter conducts an analysis of secondary research sources. The main secondary sources we use are peer-reviewed articles, publications by human rights organizations and groups like Privacy International, media articles, and publicly available government records. We then use the theory of panoptic power to guide our analysis of secondary data collected on Kenya's digital surveillance practices to answer our research questions. We adopt a thematic analysis approach, where we identify the main themes in the known surveillance technology acquisitions and analyse them against the conceptual framework (Clarke et al. 2015).

# Analysis

Based on this literature review and description of the concepts of panoptic power, digital rights, and agency, this section answers the research questions: How does the acquisition of digital technologies enhance the panoptic power of different actors in Kenya's surveillance system? How could this panoptic power lead to citizens amending their behaviour, and why is this important for human rights?

## Panoptic power and citizen behaviour

Surveillance technology can create a pervasive sense of being watched, even in the absence of a direct observer, thus fostering panoptic power. This may lead to individuals self-regulating their behaviour as there is a threat that their activities are being monitored online through mobile interception or social media monitoring tools or offline through cameras installed in public places. Whereas some of the effects of panoptic power could be positive, for instance, reduced crime as a result of increased cameras in public areas, some panoptic power may cause a chilling effect where individuals' free speech is limited by the threat of punishment. In this section, we discuss how this panoptic power could emerge or has already emerged, from each of the known acquisitions of surveillance technology in Kenya.

### Internet interception

By making it possible to monitor and spy on online activity, internet interception technologies like Blue Coat PacketShaper increase panoptic power (Marquis-Boire et al. 2013a). State authorities are able to monitor and examine digital conduct, and citizens – fearing their browsing history, communication, and online interactions are being scrutinized – may self-censor, limiting what they post online. This stifles free expression, hindering open discourse. Furthermore, internet interception can be used to restrict access to information deemed controversial, limiting our ability to freely seek and receive knowledge. This self-censorship has been seen in Kenya, during the 2017 election, where interviewed journalists cited avoiding reporting on certain stories, as they were likely to receive threats, intimidation, harassment, and online and phone surveillance (Namwaya 2017). This threat arose from the intimidation of journalists in 2015 who had reported on parliamentary proceedings about irregular payments by the cabinet secretary for interior and national coordination. While it is unclear the extent to which internet interception technology was used to monitor journalists in this period, self-censorship in response to the perceived threat of constant visibility is evident.

### Mobile interception

Mobile interception technology like IMSI catchers makes it possible to intercept mobile communications in real-time, which leads to self-censorship, as people hesitate to express themselves freely or access information on their phones for fear of being monitored. This panoptic power is exemplified by the National Intelligence Service (NIS) who are claimed to have direct access to telecommunications networks like Safaricom, the leading telecom in Kenya (Privacy International 2017). Similarly, the Communications Authority of Kenya (CAK), has panoptic power through a Device Management System that grants access to all mobile phones across the country. CAK has claimed that this system enables them to catch users of counterfeit phones, but the petition claims that the system exposes Kenyans to indiscriminate monitoring (*Law Society of Kenya v CAK* 2023). The perceived threat of panoptic power is seen in media reports following initial reports of this acquisition. A leading newspaper, *Nation*, described it as Big Brother, referencing the Orwellian concept of an unseen authoritarian leader watching over you (*Nation* 2017). Another leading newspaper, *The Standard*, published an article on why citizens should be worried about the CAK's device management system (*The Standard* 2017).

The impact of this panoptic power has been documented in the case of Human Rights Defenders (HRDs). Kenyan HRDs raised concerns about their mobile phones being tapped and their communication intercepted, feeling that the threat of their phones being monitored limited the exercise of their rights and freedoms of expression, association, and assembly (Defenders Coalition 2020).

### Social media monitoring

Panoptic power could also be gained through social media monitoring and used to modify individual behaviour to fit the state interests, as seen in the example of Cambridge Analytica. By accessing large amounts of Facebook user data, CA was able to create psychological profiles on voters and then design personalized messages to voters on social media to influence their voting behaviour in the 2013 elections (Crabtree 2018). Some of these messages included negative framings of the key opponent as violent, corrupt, and dangerous. The access to Facebook data gives CA panoptic power, from which they gain insights on voters and tailor advertisements that shape the behaviour and voting decisions of social media users. While there is no documented evidence of changing behaviour following the CA scandal, it is likely that behaviour on social media changed to make people more aware and critical of the ads they see.

### Safe city/Smart city technologies

Safe city technologies allow the government to evaluate public behaviour, establishing a panoptic environment in which people are aware that they are being watched. Safe city technologies make use of CCTV cameras that use facial recognition and number plate recognition to collect and track information. This data can be accumulated and used to track individuals across places. CCTV cameras, for instance, could lead to less theft since people are aware that they are under surveillance, thus amending negative behaviour to fit social norms. Smart city technology thus provides panoptic power, which can have positive outcomes on crime, but if misused, could be used to track and collect data on people perceived as threats to the state. In the case of smart city technology in Kenya, initial reports by Huawei showed reduced crime, which, if true, can be viewed as a positive impact of panoptic power on behaviour (Wangari 2024). However, smart city technologies also give panoptic power to states, providing them the ability to surveil citizens constantly. The threat of panoptic power being used to surveil citizens is also increased by the dominance of China as a sponsor for these projects, a country known to use surveillance extensively to monitor dissent (The Markup 2022). The constant visibility by surveillance cameras is likely to create feelings of safety among people, with people feeling safer in areas where cameras have been installed. In Nairobi, CCTV cameras are claimed to have reduced crime, although to a smaller rate than initially claimed by Huawei, while the police claim they have also improved traffic control (Wangari 2024). Others claim that crime has actually steadily increased (Uhuru 2023). CCTV cameras provide panoptic power to the police, but behaviour change could be determined by perceptions of whether the state is able to act on the power they have to surveil. Crime could thus initially reduce based on the perceived threat of panoptic power and later increase upon realization that the state will not act to try crimes documented on CCTV.

### Biometric-ID

Biometric-IDs provide panoptic power by creating a system that assigns each person a unique identification and gathering a large amount of personal identification information that is verifiably linked to one person using their biometrics, i.e. facial recognition and fingerprints data. A Huduma number would consolidate a citizen's passport, national identification, driver's licence, and social-security card into a single credential to streamline access to public services (Jill 2022b). The Huduma number would thus provide the Kenyan government with panoptic power to track and identify registered persons using their personal information, making citizens constantly visible to the government. Some Kenyans rushed to register to meet the deadline, while others refused to register, either because of concerns over privacy and data security or to protest the government's coercion and threats to register before a deadline (Mungai 2019). This refusal to register within the deadline can be seen as a change in behaviour resulting from the threat of panoptic power and the constant surveillance that would result from enrolling for a Huduma number.

## Panoptic power and digital human rights

Kenya's rapid expansion of digital surveillance technologies, if integrated, provides the potential for real-time panoptic surveillance. This potential has created concern among human rights organizations alert to the potential violations of fundamental rights to privacy, association, and expression. This section describes the rights violations that could arise, or have already arisen, from the integration of the digital technologies described in this chapter.

### *The right to privacy*

Panoptic surveillance threatens the right to privacy, which is a fundamental right enshrined in the Constitution of Kenya 2010 under Article 31. The DMS system acquired by the Communications Authority of Kenya has been argued to infringe the right of privacy. Before its implementation was approved by the Supreme Court, the High Court had ruled that the DMS infringed the right to privacy and consumer rights and did not involve affected citizens in the decision-making process implementation (Gathirwa 2023). Since the extent to which the CAK uses the DMS is unclear, it is difficult to assess which, if any, violations of privacy have occurred since the implementation of the system. The right to privacy was also violated in the rollout of the Huduma number, where the court cited issues arising from the collection and processing of personal data and sensitive personal data without clear data protection procedures (Privacy International 2022).

The right to privacy could also be violated by the ability of state actors to collect and access data on mobile phone users. Although Kenyan law requires judicial approval for the interception of communications when matters of national security are concerned, there is no independent oversight body to supervise surveillance practice (Roberts et al. 2021). The Data Protection Act 2019 also allows the government to access private data if it is for national security reasons.

### Freedom of speech

One of the main effects of panoptic surveillance is the chilling effect it causes among people who suppress their free speech or expression due to the fear of negative consequences. Panoptic surveillance thus infringes the freedom of speech, by limiting people's ability to speak freely. The limit on the freedom of speech is seen in the example of journalists following the 2017 election, who mention avoiding reporting on certain stories, fearing repercussions from the government (Namwaya 2017).

## Agency and resistance

Digital rights organizations have used their individual and collective agency to resist the use of panoptic surveillance, using strategic litigation, advocacy, and public awareness raising to positive effect. This section discusses two ways agency in the face of panoptic surveillance is exercised in Kenya: the legal system and through advocacy groups.

Agency exercised through the legal system is exemplified by the landmark ruling that the Huduma rollout was unconstitutional. A similar petition has been brought forward to the High Court by the Haki na Sheria Initiative (HSI), who argue that the new ID system violates the rights and freedoms of marginalized communities in Kenya (KICTA 2023). In a different ruling, the High Court has ruled that installation of CCTV cameras in a residential area is a violation of a person's constitutional right to privacy (*Ondieki v Maeda* (Petition E153 of 2022)). By providing a framework for holding authorities accountable and ensuring their actions comply with the law, the legal system empowers individuals to challenge surveillance practices through the court system.

Second, agency has been exercised through the formation of advocacy and activist groups, both online and offline, to champion the rights of citizens. Such groups have been formed to champion specific groups; for instance, the Defenders Coalition, which has championed for the rights of human rights defenders violated by online surveillance (Defenders Coalition 2020), or the Nubian Rights Forum, a key petitioner against the Huduma number, citing its impact on the already marginalized Nubian community (Petition 56 of

2019; Open Society Justice Initiative n.d.). Activists have also raised concerns about the safe city initiatives and the surveillance power they provide to often authoritarian governments (Woodhams 2022).

These activists and advocacy groups use their agency and access to resources or influence to champion the rights of individuals who may otherwise lack the individual agency to voice their concerns. Alkire (2008) describes exercising agency as requiring one to have some power, which individual marginalized communities may lack. Activists and advocacy groups such as the NRF and KHRC thus utilize their power as organizations with financial resources and influence to bring litigation to court as a way of championing the rights of those who lack the power and thus agency to do so themselves. Exercising agency can also lead to gaining social or economic power (Alkire 2008), which is seen in the case of agency that is exercised through the legal system or advocacy groups, eventually leading to court rulings that uphold citizen rights, for instance, the Huduma number ruling.

## Recommendations and conclusion

This chapter set out to address the questions: (1) How does the acquisition of digital technologies enhance the panoptic power of different actors in Kenya's surveillance system? and (2) How could this panoptic power lead to citizens amending their behaviour, and why is this important for human rights? To analyse these questions, we used a conceptual framework of panoptic power, digital rights, and agency. We find that all known acquisition of surveillance technology enables panoptic surveillance of everyday citizen behaviour. These technologies provide panoptic power by providing access to large amounts of data on citizens, who, due to the threat of surveillance, may change their behaviour. These changes in behaviour could be positive, for instance, reduced crime due to the presence of CCTV cameras, or negative, in the case of journalists feeling inhibited from reporting on certain stories because they fear they are constantly being watched. We then analysed the implications of panoptic surveillance on digital human rights, where we highlighted the threats to the right to privacy and freedom of speech, which are rights provided for in the Kenyan constitution. Additionally, we find that the lack of clear laws in surveillance makes it easy for actors to misuse their panoptic power to infringe the rights of citizens. Finally, we discuss how agency, the ability to act on your values, has been exercised through the legal system and advocacy groups to oppose the state's misuse of panoptic power.

Based on this analysis and findings, we make the following recommendations. First, the establishment of an independent watchdog to scrutinize the uses of surveillance technologies by state actors. This would protect against abuses of power, maintain ethical standards, and limit possible rights violations. Relatedly, we recommend further revision of the existing data protection framework to fill gaps that enable state actors to collect, store, and use information unlawfully. Finally, we recommend public participation during the acquisition of surveillance technologies to ensure that citizens are fully aware of their right to privacy. All of the surveillance technologies discussed in this chapter have been acquired with no involvement of the public. However, we note that some surveillance technologies may be beneficial in maintaining national security, and in such cases, citizens need to be notified when their privacy is breached for security reasons.

## Notes

1   Al-Shabaab is an Islamist insurgent group based in Somalia who are known for complex bombings, ambushes, and attacks on civilians in Somalia, Kenya, and Uganda.
2   The Huduma number is a unique and permanent personal identification number randomly assigned to every resident individual at birth or upon registration/ enrolment and only expires or is retired upon the death of the individual. The rollout was halted in December 2023 for non-compliance with Data Protection Regulation.

## Bibliography

Alkire, S. (2008). Concepts and Measures of Agency, Working Paper 9. Oxford, Oxford Poverty and Human Development Initiative (OPHI).

Anaïs, A. (2017). 'Jomo Kenyatta and the Repression of the "Last" Mau Mau Leaders, 1961–1965', *Journal of Eastern African Studies*, 11(3): 442–59. https://doi.org/10.10 80/17531055.2017.1354521

Anderson, D. (2005). *Histories of the Hanged: The Dirty War in Kenya and the End of Empire*, New York: W. W. Norton.

Bradford, A. (2023). 'Exporting China's Digital Authoritarianism through Infrastructure', in *Digital Empires: The Global Battle to Regulate Technology*, New York: Oxford Academic. https://doi.org/10.1093/oso/9780197649268.003.0009

Breckenridge, K. (2018). 'The Failure of the "Single Source of Truth about Kenyans": The NDRS, Collateral Mysteries and the Safaricom Monopoly', *African Studies*, 78(1): 91–111. https://doi.org/10.1080/00020184.2018.1540515

Burt, C. (2019, 7 October). 'NEC Facial Recognition Border Tech for Kenya as Airport Biometrics Rollouts Continue', Biometric Update. https://www.biometricupdate.com/201910/nec-facial-recognition-border-tech-for-kenya-as-airport-biometrics-rollouts-continue (accessed 20 October 2023).

Centre for Intellectual Property and Information Technology Law (CIPIT) (2017, March). 'Safaricom and Internet Traffic Tampering'. CIPIT. https://blog.cipit.org/wp-content/uploads/2017/03/Final-March-Brief-pages.pdf (accessed 19 October 2023).

Cheruiyot, K. (2023). 'Digital ID: Government Switches from Huduma to Maisha Number at a Cost of Sh1 billion', *Nation*, 12 September. https://nation.africa/kenya/news/digital-id-government-switches-from-huduma-to-maisha-number-at-a-cost-of-sh1-billion-4366788 (accessed 20 October 2023).

Clarke, V., Braun, V. and Hayfield, N. (2015). 'Thematic Analysis', *Qualitative Psychology: A Practical Guide to Research Methods*, 3: 222–48.

Crabtree, C. (2018). 'Cambridge Analytica, Facebook, and the Revelations of Open Secrets', *Social Media + Society*, 4(3): 205630511879760.

Defenders Coalition (2020). 'Perception Survey Impact of Communication Surveillance on Human Rights Defenders in Kenya'. https://defenderscoalition.org/wp-content/uploads/2021/03/Coalition-Perception-Survey-English-1.pdf (accessed 9 June 2024).

*The East African* (2020, 28 July). 'Kenya to Monitor Social Media During Elections'. *The East African*. https://www.theeastafrican.co.ke/tea/news/east-africa/kenya-to-monitor-social-media-during-elections-1360384 (accessed 10 June 2024).

Foucault, M. (1995). *Discipline and Punish: The Birth of the Prison*, New York: Vintage.

Gravett, W. (2021, 8 October). 'The Impact of Chinese Digital Neocolonialism on Human Rights and Civil Liberties in Africa', Democracy in Africa. https://democracyinafrica.org/the-impact-of-chinese-digital-neocolonialism-on-human-rights-and-civil-liberties-in-africa/ (accessed 20 October 2023).

Hersey, F. (2023, 1 March). 'Kenya Huduma Number Funding Almost Entirely Cut as UPI, Digital Birth Registration Begins', Biometric Update. https://www.biometricupdate.com/202303/kenya-huduma-namba-funding-almost-entirely-cut-as-upi-digital-birth-registration-begins (accessed 20 October 2023).

Human Rights Watch (1991). 'Human Rights Watch World Report 1990 – Kenya', 1 January 1991, UNHCR refworld. https://www.refworld.org/reference/annualreport/hrw/1991/en/41286 (accessed 9 June 2024).

Jili, B. (2022b, August 25). 'The Rise of Chinese Surveillance Technology in Africa (part 4 of 6)', EPIC – Electronic Privacy Information Center. https://epic.org/the-rise-of-chinese-surveillance-technology-in-africa-part-4-of-6/ (accessed 20 October 2023).

KICTA. (2023). *Legal Challenges to the New ID System in Kenya: Insights from the Haki na Sheria Initiative*. Kenya ICT Action Network (KICTA).

Kiplagat, S. (2023). Regulator Allowed to Install Mobile Phone Spying Gadget, The Computer Society of Kenya, https://www.cskonline.org/about-us/kenya-ict-press/1335-regulator-allowed-to-install-mobile-phone-spying-gadget.

Kombo, S. (2023, 29 May). 'Kenya's Unique Personal Identifier (UPI): What You Need to Know', Techweez. https://techweez.com/2023/05/29/kenya-unique-personal-identifier-id/ (accessed 20 October 2023).

Land, M., Meier, P., Belinsky, M. and Jacobi, E. (2012). *Information and Communication Technologies for Human Rights*, Washington, DC: World Bank Institute.

*Law Society of Kenya v Communications Authority of Kenya & 10 others* (Petition 8 of 2020) [2023] KESC 27 (KLR) (Civ) (21 April 2023) (Judgment). Available at: Kenya Law Reports.

The Markup. (2022). *China's Role in Global Surveillance Projects: Implications and Concerns*. https://themarkup.org

Marczak, B., Scott-Railton J., McKune, S., Razzak, B. A. and Deibert, R. (2018). 'Hide and Seek: Tracking NSO Group's Pegasus Spyware to Operations in 45 Countries', University of Toronto: *The Citizen Lab*. https://citizenlab.ca/2018/09/hide-and-seek-tracking-nso-groups-pegasus-spyware-to-operations-in-45-countries/ (accessed 20 October 2023).

Marczak, B., Scott-Railton, J., Prakash Rao, S., Anstis, S. and Deibert, R. (2020). 'Running in Circles: Uncovering the Clients of Cyberespionage Firm Circles', University of Toronto: *The Citizen Lab*. https://citizenlab.ca/2020/12/running-in-circles-uncovering-the-clients-of-cyberespionage-firm-circles/ (accessed 20 October 2023).

Marquis-Boire, M., Dalek, J., McKune, S., Carrieri, M., Crete-Nishihata, M., Deibert, R., Khan, S. O., Noman, H., Scott-Railton, J. and Wiseman, G. (2013a). 'Planet Blue Coat: Mapping Global Censorship and Surveillance Tools', Citizen Lab Research Report No. 13, University of Toronto: *The Citizen Lab*. https://citizenlab. ca/2013/01/planet-blue-coat-mapping-global-censorship-and-surveillance-tools/ (accessed 20 October 2023).

Maundu, C. (2021, 7 October). 'Kenyan Government's Use of Surveillance Technologies to Tackle COVID-19 Raises Human Rights Concerns'. *Global Voices*. https://globalvoices.org/2021/10/07/kenyan-governments-use-of-surveillance-technologies-to-tackle-covid-19-raises-human-rights-concerns/ (accessed 23 October 2023).

Moss, S. (2019, 30 April). 'Huawei to Build Konza Data Centre and Smart City in Kenya, with Chinese Concessional Loan', Data Center Dynamics.https://www. datacenterdynamics.com/en/news/huawei-build-konza-data-center-and-smart-city-kenya-chinese-concessional-loan/ (accessed 23 October 2023).

Mungai, C. (2019). 'Kenya's Huduma: Data Commodification and Government Tyranny', *Al Jazeera*. https://www.aljazeera.com/opinions/2019/8/6/kenyas-huduma-data-commodification-and-government-tyranny (accessed 9 June 2024).

Namwaya, O. (2017). 'Not Worth the Risk', in *Human Rights Watch*. https://www.hrw. org/report/2017/05/30/not-worth-risk/threats-free-expression-ahead-kenyas-2017-elections (accessed 24 October 2023).

*Nation* (2017). 'Big Brother Could Start Tapping Your Calls, Texts from Next Week', *Nation*. https://nation.africa/kenya/news/big-brother-could-start-tapping-your-calls-texts-from-next-week-362204 (accessed 9 June 2024).

Nyabola, N. (2019). 'Platform Governance of Political Speech', *Models for Platform Governance*, 63. Centre for International Governance Innovation. https://www. cigionline.org/articles/platform-governance-political-speech/ (accessed 24 October 2023).

Ocobock, P. (2012). 'Spare the Rod, Spoil the Colony: Corporal Punishment, Colonial Violence, and Generational Authority in Kenya, 1897–1952', *The International Journal of African Historical Studies*, 45(1): 29–56.

Ogara, E. A. and Odhiambo-Otieno, G. W. (2003). *Challenges of Implementing Telemedicine Initiatives in Kenya*, Kenya: Ministry of Health. http://www.health. go.ke

Omolo Ochilo, P. (2013). 'Press Freedom and the Role of Media in Kenya', *Africa Media Review*, 7(3): 19–33.

*Ondieki v Maeda* (Petition E153 of 2022). High Court of Kenya.

Open Society Justice Initiative (n.d.). *Nubian Rights Forum et al. v. the Honourable Attorney General of Kenya et al. ('NIIMS case')*. https://www.justiceinitiative.org/litigation/nubian-rights-forum-et-al-v-the-honourable-attorney-general-of-kenya-et-al-niims-case (accessed 9 June 2024).

Privacy International (2017). 'Track, Capture, Kill: Inside Communications Surveillance in Kenya'. https://privacyinternational.org/reports/2307/communications-surveillance-kenya (accessed 9 June 2024).

Privacy International. (2022, 27 January). 'Data Protection Impact Assessments and ID Systems: The 2021 Kenyan Ruling on Huduma Number'. Privacy International. http://privacyinternational.org/news-analysis/4778/data-protection-impact-assessments-and-id-systems-2021-kenyan-ruling-huduma (accessed 9 June 2024).

Roberts, T., Mohamed Ali, A., Farahat, M., Oloyede, R. and Mutung'u, G. (2021). *Surveillance Law in Africa: A Review of Six Countries*, Brighton: Institute of Development Studies. https://doi.org/10.19088/IDS.2021.059

Sen, A. (1999). *Development as Freedom*, London: Alfred A. Knopf.

Shaffer, R. (2019). 'Following in Footsteps: The Transformation of Kenya's Intelligence Services Since the Colonial Era', *Studies in Intelligence*, 63(1): 23–40.

*The Standard* (2017). 'Is Someone Listening in on Your Calls? Here's Why You Should Be Worried', *The Standard*. https://www.standardmedia.co.ke/article/2001229876/is-someone-listening-in-on-your-calls-heres-why-you-should-be-worried (accessed 9 June 2024).

Uhuru, P. (2023). 'Nairobi's Watchful Eyes: How Reliable are the CCTV Cameras?' Edgelands Institute. https://www.edgelands.institute/blog/nairobis-watchful-eyes-how-reliables-are-the-cctv-cameras (accessed 9 June 2024).

UN Kenya. (2021, 10 September). 'Strengthening Estonia–UN Relation for Digital Transformation', United Nations in Kenya. https://kenya.un.org/en/144998-strengthening-estonia-un-relation-digital-transformation (accessed 11 June 2024).

United Nations (n.d.). *Digital Human Rights*, Office of the Secretary-General's Envoy on Technology, https://www.un.org/techenvoy/content/digital-human-rights (accessed 10 June 2024).

Wangari, N. (2024, 6 June). 'In Africa's First "Safe City", Surveillance Reigns', Coda Story. https://www.codastory.com/authoritarian-tech/africa-surveillance-china-magnum/ (accessed 21 June 2024).

Woodhams, S. (2022). 'Huawei Says Its Surveillance Tech Will Keep African Cities Safe but Activists Worry It'll Be Misused', *Quartz*, 21 July. https://qz.com/africa/1822312/huaweis-surveillance-tech-in-africa-worries-activists (accessed 24 June 2024).

# 7

# Digital surveillance in Nigeria

Nana Nwachukwu

## Introduction

Over the last decade, Nigeria has witnessed a substantial increase in the adoption of digital surveillance technologies, with an estimated investment of at least $1.2 billion. Adopting these technologies has brought about both positive and negative impacts, leading to a complex interplay between the pursuit of enhanced security and concerns over privacy and government overreach. Faced with challenges such as terrorism, banditry, kidnapping, and armed robbery, the Nigerian government has turned to technology to enhance intelligence gathering, improve law enforcement capabilities, and maintain public order. These technologies include surveillance cameras, facial recognition systems, biometric databases, and advanced internet and mobile interception systems. However, while the government frames digital surveillance as a crucial tool for addressing serious crime, critics argue that, in practice, surveillance is not being targeted at these issues exclusively (Ibezim-Ohaeri et al. 2021). Instead, it is often directed at citizens exercising their constitutional and civil rights to assembly and expression, as well as journalists and civil society actors.

Surveillance technologies have a complex history within Nigeria, evolving from colonial-era population control tools to modern digital tracking methods. Today, the widespread adoption of smartphones, growing internet penetration, and the increasing sophistication of surveillance tools offer unprecedented opportunities for state and corporate actors to monitor citizens. While digital surveillance technologies have undoubtedly contributed to some successes in crime prevention and detection, they have also raised concerns among civil society groups, human rights organizations, and privacy advocates. One of the primary concerns is the abuse of power and the infringement of individual privacy rights. Critics argue that the government uses these technologies to monitor and control citizens, suppress dissent, and stifle political opposition. Another concern is Nigeria's need for a comprehensive legal framework governing digital surveillance technologies. The country currently lacks specific legislation that explicitly addresses government agencies' collection, storage, use, and disclosure of personal data. This legal vacuum leaves room for arbitrary and unchecked surveillance practices with little recourse for citizens whose rights are violated.

This chapter will review the available evidence about the procurement, use, and oversight of digital surveillance technologies in Nigeria. It will analyse the impact on citizen agency, human rights, and competing power interests. The remaining sections of this chapter will be organized in the following way. The next two sections will first provide some historical context on surveillance in Nigeria before then presenting a descriptive overview of current digital surveillance practices. I will then review the existing conceptual literature on power, agency, and rights to explain the framework that I use in the analysis section to assess digital surveillance practices. The final section will draw some conclusions and make some tentative recommendations for policy, practice, and future research.

## Background

Nigeria, the most populous country in Africa, has a complex surveillance history shaped by its colonial past, shifting political landscapes, and the rapid adoption of digital technologies.

### Colonial foundations (1900–60)

British colonial rule in Nigeria relied heavily on a system of 'indirect rule' where local intermediaries, known as Warrant Chiefs, were appointed to administer their communities. Established in the early 1900s, this system positioned

Warrant Chiefs as vital enforcers of colonial policy. Intelligence gathering was key to their role – monitoring their communities, reporting on taxation compliance, potential dissent, and resistance to the colonial administration. These chiefs acted as the eyes and ears of the colonial administration, collecting taxes, maintaining order, and, most importantly, gathering intelligence. This system embedded information gathering and monitoring of potential dissent, laying the foundation for state surveillance in Nigeria (Afigbo 1972). In 1948, a formal structure was created within the Nigerian Police as a 'Special Branch', which later grew to become today's State Security Service (DSS n.d.).

## Post-independence evolution (1960–present)

After Nigeria's independence in 1960, the new government retained elements of the surveillance apparatus established during the colonial era. The tools were reoriented, often targeting political rivals and voices of dissent, a pattern mirrored in other post-colonial African states. Targeting dissent has been a recurring theme in the surveillance practices of many post-colonial African states, including Nigeria. In the early years following Nigeria's independence, the country was fraught with regional tensions and power struggles. Governments during this period often used surveillance to suppress political opposition, whether real or perceived, viewing it as necessary to maintain national unity (Falola 1999).

The Nigerian Civil War, from 1967 to 1970, marked a significant escalation in these efforts. The government intensified its surveillance to maintain control and identify those who might sympathize with separatist causes, illustrating the lengths to which it would go to safeguard the state's integrity. The origins of the Biafran War lay in a complex mix of ethnic tensions and political grievances. The Igbo people of southeastern Nigeria, feeling marginalized by a federal government dominated by the northern regions, declared the independence of Biafra in 1967, leading to a devastating civil war. According to researchers Heerten and Moses (2017: 134), the aftermath of the war entrenched a narrative within Nigeria's security apparatus that associated the Igbo people with secessionism and potential rebellion. This led to a long-standing practice of ethnic profiling, where Igbo individuals were frequently viewed through the lens of their ethnicity and the historical context of the Biafran secession, rather than as citizens with equal rights and status in the Nigerian state.

Nigeria experienced long periods of military rule post-war, during which surveillance was heavily used to suppress dissent and perceived threats. Military coups were common and created paranoia among leaders. Military regimes, such as General Sani Abacha's, expanded surveillance capabilities to consolidate power, often using ruthless methods.

During these regimes, surveillance took various forms, including infiltrating civil society. Reports from human rights groups noted instances of government agents embedding themselves within student unions, labour movements, and other groups critical of the government. The control over the media and the monitoring of communications, such as phone calls, were strategies used to suppress dissent (Osaghae 2018). Furthermore, the regimes were marked by practices such as detention without trial, creating a pervasive climate of fear and self-censorship among the populace. The absence of transparency and robust legal frameworks around these surveillance practices made it exceedingly difficult for citizens to challenge their use or to hold the government accountable for any abuses (Osaghae 2018).

Throughout these periods, the surveillance apparatus operated with weak oversight, featuring limited legal safeguards and a lack of transparency. This environment facilitated potential abuses, allowing for the targeting of government critics without accountability. Even after Nigeria returned to multiparty democracy in 1999, the legacy of surveillance and its implications for human rights remained a concern. Human rights organizations have continued to document instances where journalists, activists, and opposition figures were monitored and potentially intimidated, underscoring the enduring challenges of surveillance in a democratic Nigeria (Osaghae 2018).

## The digital surveillance landscape

With the investment of $1.2 billion, the rise of digital technologies has supercharged Nigeria's surveillance landscape (Allam and Oboh 2023). The widespread use of mobile phones, increasing internet penetration, and the popularity of social media offer unprecedented opportunities for the state to track and monitor citizens. These tools are often presented as necessary for combating crime and terrorism, yet raise significant concerns about privacy infringement and the potential for suppressing dissent in the digital sphere. The expansion of digital surveillance in Nigeria must be understood in the context of its historical legacies. The colonial past established a foundation of using surveillance for social control, while post-independence administrations continued and adapted these practices. Today's advanced digital tools build upon this long-standing pattern, fuelling concerns about the balance between security and individual freedoms in Nigeria's evolving democracy.

## Internet interception

Internet interception in Nigeria involves monitoring and capturing internet traffic, including emails, browsing histories, and social media activities. This form of surveillance is primarily conducted by government security agencies, including the State Security Service (SSS) and the Nigerian Communications Commission (NCC). The primary justification for internet interception is national security, targeting threats such as terrorism and cybercrime. However, the lack of robust legal frameworks and oversight mechanisms has led to concerns about arbitrary surveillance practices and potential human rights violations. Critics argue that internet interception could be used to monitor and suppress political dissent, infringing on citizens' rights to privacy and freedom of expression (Ogala 2016).

Studies have highlighted the risks of internet interception, emphasizing its impact on privacy and freedom of expression (EFF 2014; Ibezim-Ohaeri et al. 2021). According to Fortin (2013), a Freedom of Information request lodged by digital rights activist 'Gbenga Sesan revealed that the Nigerian government had issued a $40 million contract for internet monitoring technologies from Israeli company, Elbit Systems.

## Mobile interception

Mobile interception encompasses monitoring phone calls and text messages, and location tracking. This surveillance method is widely used by various government bodies, including the SSS, the National Intelligence Agency (NIA), and the Nigerian Police. Mobile interception is justified as a tool for combating crime and ensuring national security. Telecommunications companies and internet service providers play a significant role by providing the necessary technical infrastructure to facilitate mobile interception. However, similar to internet interception, the absence of transparency and proper regulatory oversight has raised significant human rights concerns. The potential for abuse, including targeting political opponents and activists, poses a threat to individual privacy and civil liberties. A study carried out by Marczak et al. (2020) reported that the Nigerian government has been identified as a likely client of Circles, a surveillance firm known for exploiting vulnerabilities in the global mobile phone system to monitor and intercept phone communications and traffic. Two state governors in Nigeria reportedly acquired Circles systems at a reported cost of $3.2 million and $4.9 million, respectively, and used them to spy on political opponents, with installations allegedly placed in their residences (Mojeed 2015; Ogundipe 2017, quoted in Allam and Oboh 2023).

Circles' technology is a significant example of mobile interception. This method is widely used by various government bodies, including the SSS, NIA, and the Nigerian Police. Mobile interception is justified as a tool for combating crime and ensuring national security. Telecommunications companies and internet service providers play a significant role by providing the necessary technical infrastructure. However, the absence of transparency and proper regulatory oversight raises significant human rights concerns. Research shows that mobile interception can lead to abuses, including the targeting of political opponents and activists (Roberts et al. 2021; CIPESA 2021).

## Social media monitoring

Social media monitoring involves tracking activities on platforms such as Facebook, Twitter, and WhatsApp. This surveillance is primarily conducted by government security agencies to identify and suppress dissent. Social media monitoring is often justified under the guise of maintaining public order and national security. However, this practice can lead to self-censorship among users, as individuals may fear being monitored and targeted for their online activities. Cambridge Analytica played a controversial role in social media monitoring in Nigeria during the 2015 presidential election. Hired by a

Nigerian billionaire to aid the re-election campaign of then-president Goodluck Jonathan, the firm was paid approximately £2 million. Their strategy included orchestrating a fierce campaign against Jonathan's rival, Muhammadu Buhari. It is reported that Cambridge Analytica was offered hacked personal data of Nigerian politicians by Israeli hackers (Cadwalladr 2018). The deployment of social media monitoring technologies raises concerns about freedom of expression and the right to privacy, as it can be used to stifle political opposition and control public discourse.

Government security agencies primarily conduct this surveillance to identify and suppress dissent. Social media monitoring is often justified under the guise of maintaining public order and national security. However, this practice can lead to self-censorship among users, as individuals may fear being monitored and targeted for their online activities. In Nigeria, the authorities employed digital surveillance tactics to suppress dissent and monitor communications. One prominent example was the seven-month ban on the social media platform Twitter, which was lifted on 13 January 2022 after a court ruling declared the ban unlawful. Also, the Nigerian Broadcasting Commission (NBC) suspended a Vision FM radio programme for criticizing the head of the National Intelligence Agency and sanctioned media outlets for broadcasting content perceived to promote terrorism. In July, five staff members of the *Peoples Gazette* were arrested for publishing an allegedly defamatory report about the former Chief of Army Staff. Furthermore, social media celebrities were detained and punished for defaming state officials in comedy sketches, exemplifying the state's use of digital surveillance and punitive actions to control the narrative and silence critical voices (Amnesty International 2021). Studies indicate that social media monitoring can significantly impact freedom of expression and privacy, potentially stifling political opposition and controlling public discourse (Nyabola 2018; Duncan 2022).

## Public space surveillance

CCTV cameras and facial recognition systems are employed by government agencies, particularly in urban areas, allegedly to enhance public safety and combat crime. Private sector companies often collaborate with the government to provide and manage these surveillance systems. As documented by Allam and Oboh (2023) as early as 2008, the Nigerian government awarded a $470 milllion contract to the Chinese company ZTE to install thousands of CCTV cameras in Lagos and Abuja (*Punch* 2021). More recently, in 2019 the government invested another $113 million with Chinese company Huawei on border surveillance cameras (Akintaro 2022).

While public space surveillance is promoted for its potential to deter criminal activities, it also poses significant risks to privacy. The deployment of facial recognition technology, in particular, raises concerns about profiling and discrimination. The lack of comprehensive data protection laws exacerbates these issues, leaving citizens vulnerable to privacy violations (Norris and Armstrong 1999; Browne 2015).

## Biometric digital-ID systems

Biometric digital-ID systems involve the collection and storage of biometric data, such as fingerprints and facial images. The National Identity Management Commission (NIMC) is responsible for managing Nigeria's biometric data. In 2012 Nigeria secured $433 million from the World Bank and international donors to build a biometric digital-ID system provided by the French weapons and surveillance company Thales Solutions (Adepetun 2020).

Nigeria's biometric identity system landscape is fragmented, with the Bank Verification Number (BVN) and the National Identification Number (NIN) being the primary identifiers, managed by separate entities. While these systems are promoted for enhancing service delivery and curbing crime, their duplication and the centralization of biometric data under the NIMC raise significant privacy concerns. The absence of robust legal frameworks and oversight mechanisms to safeguard biometric information creates vulnerabilities for potential misuse and surveillance. As critics argue, the widespread adoption of biometric digital-ID systems, without adequate safeguards, can lead to mass surveillance and infringement of individual privacy rights (Breckenridge 2019; Jili 2022).

Having provided an overview of the Nigerian digital surveillance landscape, the next section reviews concepts of power, agency, and rights to frame the chapter's analysis.

## Power, agency, and rights

### Power

Power is a multifaceted concept widely studied across various disciplines, including political science, sociology, and philosophy. At its core, power refers to the ability or capacity to influence or control behaviour and outcomes in a given context. Max Weber defines power as the probability that one actor within a social relationship can carry out their own will despite resistance (Weber 1947), emphasizing the relational and coercive aspects of power.

Michel Foucault offers a more nuanced view, highlighting the pervasive and diffuse nature of power. He argues that power is not just held by institutions or individuals but is distributed throughout society and embedded in everyday practices and discourses (Foucault 1978). Foucault introduces the concept of 'biopower', which refers to the regulation of populations through various techniques and institutions that manage life, health, and bodies.

In the context of digital surveillance, power dynamics are evident in how governments and corporations collect, analyse, and use data to monitor and influence citizens' behaviour. This surveillance extends Foucault's notion of biopower, where technological advancements enable more sophisticated and pervasive forms of control. In Nigeria, the use of surveillance technologies is deeply intertwined with the state's ability to monitor and control the population. The deployment of these technologies allows the government to exert significant influence over its citizens. Foucault's concept of biopower is particularly relevant here, as it describes how modern states use various techniques to manage populations (Foucault 1978). These techniques include not only traditional forms of surveillance but also digital tools to collect and analyse data on citizens' activities. This form of power is pervasive and extends beyond mere coercion, embedding itself in the fabric of everyday life.

The Nigerian government justifies the use of surveillance technologies under the guise of national security. However, substantial evidence indicates that these technologies are also used to suppress dissent and control political opposition. For instance, the government has employed digital surveillance tools to monitor social media and track individuals critical of the regime (Ibezim-Ohaeri et al. 2021). This aligns with Weber's definition of power as the ability to enforce one's will despite resistance (Weber 1947), highlighting the coercive aspect of state power in the digital age.

In conclusion, power is a pivotal concept in understanding social dynamics. Weber defines it as the probability of achieving one's will despite resistance, while Foucault describes it as pervasive and embedded in societal structures and practices. Foucault's concept of biopower illustrates how power operates through the regulation of populations, managing life, health, and bodies (Foucault 1978). In Nigeria, digital surveillance technologies serve as tools for exercising power, used not only for security but also for political control. This demonstrates Foucault's notion of power as ubiquitous and instrumental in regulating society (Ibezim-Ohaeri et al. 2021).

## Agency

Agency refers to the capacity of individuals to act independently and make their own choices. It is a critical concept in understanding human behaviour and social structures. Agency contrasts with structure, which refers to the recurrent patterned arrangements that influence or limit the choices and opportunities available to individuals.

Anthony Giddens's theory of structuration posits that agency and structure are interdependent; structures are both the medium and outcome of the practices they recursively organize (Giddens 1984). This interplay suggests that while individuals are constrained by social structures, they also have the capacity to alter these structures through their actions. In the digital age, agency is manifested in how individuals engage with technology. While surveillance technologies can constrain agency by monitoring and influencing behaviour, individuals can also exercise agency by using digital tools to resist surveillance, advocate privacy rights, and mobilize for political action. Thus, understanding agency in the context of digital surveillance involves examining both the limitations imposed by surveillance systems and the potential for resistance and empowerment through technology.

In Nigeria, citizens have shown remarkable resilience and agency in the face of pervasive surveillance. Activists and civil society organizations use digital tools to mobilize, advocate for rights, and challenge state overreach. For example, despite the risks, platforms such as Twitter and WhatsApp are extensively used for organizing protests and spreading awareness about government misconduct (Ibezim-Ohaeri et al. 2021). This demonstrates how individuals can navigate and contest the power structures imposed by digital surveillance, exercising their agency within constrained environments.

Giddens's theory of structuration is useful here, as it posits that while social structures constrain individual actions, they are also produced and reproduced by those very actions (Giddens 1984). This dynamic interplay means that while surveillance technologies impose limitations on individual freedom, they also create opportunities for resistance and subversion. Agency refers to the capacity of individuals to make choices that are not wholly determined by social structures. In Nigeria, civil society groups have used digital platforms to campaign against repressive surveillance measures, demonstrating the exercise of agency within a constrained environment (Ibezim-Ohaeri 2021).

## Rights

Rights are fundamental principles that protect individuals' freedoms and entitlements within a society. Human rights, as defined in the Universal Declaration of Human Rights (UDHR), encompass privacy, freedom of expression, and protection from arbitrary interference. The right to privacy is critical in the context of digital surveillance. Article 12 of the UDHR emphasizes that 'no one shall be subjected to arbitrary interference with his privacy, family, home, or correspondence', highlighting the importance of safeguarding personal information and communications.

In Nigeria, the right to privacy is enshrined in Section 37 of the 1999 Constitution, which guarantees the privacy of citizens, their homes, correspondence, telephone conversations, and telegraphic communications (Constitution of the Federal Republic of Nigeria 1999). However, state surveillance practices, justified by national security and public order concerns, often challenge the implementation and enforcement of these rights. Balancing rights with security concerns is a critical issue in the digital age. Governments may justify surveillance measures as necessary to prevent crime and terrorism, yet these practices can infringe on individuals' privacy and freedom of expression. Rights provide a normative framework for evaluating the legitimacy and impact of surveillance practices.

The Lawful Interception of Communications Regulation 2019 provides a legal basis for state interception of communications in Nigeria, ostensibly for national security purposes (Federal Republic of Nigeria 2019). While intended to prevent crime and terrorism, this regulation risks potential abuses, such as stifling dissent and infringing on privacy and freedom of expression. The Nigerian government's use of surveillance technologies to monitor political opponents and civil society activists exemplifies this tension (Ibezim-Ohaeri et al. 2021).

## Why is this important?

The concept of rights is essential in evaluating the ethical and legal implications of digital surveillance. It offers a framework for assessing whether surveillance practices are justifiable, considering the balance between security needs and the protection of individual rights. One notable gap is the limited empirical research on the specific mechanisms through which surveillance technologies are deployed and their direct impact on civil liberties. While studies such as those by Spaces for Change (Ibezim-Ohaeri et al. 2021) have explored the broader implications of surveillance on civic space, detailed analyses of how these technologies function in practice and their nuanced effects on different segments of the population remain sparse.

A recurring theme is the tension between national security and individual privacy rights. Many governments, including Nigeria's, justify the use of extensive surveillance measures by citing the need to combat terrorism and maintain public order. However, this rationale often leads to an expansion of state powers at the expense of personal freedoms, raising critical concerns about the balance of power. The legal frameworks governing surveillance, such as the Nigerian Communications Commission's regulations and the Lawful Interception of Communications Regulation, provide the state with considerable leeway to monitor communications, often without adequate oversight or accountability mechanisms (Oloyede 2021).

Another significant theme is the concept of biopower as articulated by Michel Foucault, which is particularly relevant in the Nigerian context. The state's ability to regulate and control the population through digital means extends

Foucault's ideas on how power operates, not just through direct coercion but through more subtle forms of discipline and surveillance embedded in societal institutions. This pervasive surveillance affects not only political dissidents but also ordinary citizens, creating a climate of self-censorship and fear that stifles democratic engagement and public dissent (Foucault 1978).

Existing research in this area also highlights the critical role of agency in resisting and negotiating the impacts of surveillance. Giddens's structuration theory suggests that while individuals are constrained by surveillance systems, they also possess the capacity to act and potentially alter these structures (Giddens 1984). In Nigeria, instances of digital activism and the use of encrypted communication tools illustrate how individuals and civil society groups seek to reclaim agency and protect their privacy. However, these efforts are often met with increased state repression, underscoring the ongoing struggle between state control and individual freedom.

Regarding the concept of rights, there is the foundational importance of privacy as a human right, enshrined in both international declarations and Nigeria's Constitution. Yet, the enforcement of these rights is frequently undermined by state practices and legislative loopholes that allow for extensive surveillance under the guise of national security. The tension between legal provisions for privacy and the realities of state surveillance practices points to a significant gap in the legal and institutional frameworks designed to protect citizens' rights (Ibezim-Ohaeri et al. 2021).

Studies have shown that surveillance disproportionately affects marginalized groups, amplifying existing inequalities and fostering a sense of exclusion. This dimension of digital surveillance in Nigeria, where ethnic and regional divisions are pronounced, suggests that surveillance technologies may be used not only for security but also as tools of political control and social stratification (Ajala 2009; Suberu 1996).

## Key players and power dynamics in expanding surveillance in Nigeria

The Nigerian government is the primary entity wielding power in the realm of digital surveillance. The enactment of the Cybercrimes Act of 2015 significantly bolsters the government's authority, enabling them to intercept internet traffic, including emails, browsing histories, and social media activities. This law, while intended to combat cybercrime, provides the government with broad surveillance powers that can potentially be abused to target journalists, activists, and political opponents, thereby undermining democratic principles (OAL 2023; Al Jazeera 2020).

Key agencies like the Defence Intelligence Agency (DIA) play a crucial role, evidenced by the substantial budget allocated for surveillance activities. In 2023, the DIA was allocated N33.30 billion, with N11.90 billion dedicated to capital projects, including surveillance equipment procurement (Vanguard 2023). Foreign companies, especially from Israel and China, supply significant technological support. For example, Israeli firms like Elbit Systems and Circles have provided sophisticated cyber-defence tools and telecommunication surveillance equipment, enhancing the DIA's capacity to monitor digital communications (Johnson 2013; Al Jazeera 2020).

Often, state governments participate in these activities, sometimes acquiring surveillance tools through clandestine means. For instance, in 2015, the Bayelsa State governor procured hacking tools from the Italian firm Hacking Team using forged End-User Certificates, underscoring the pervasive and often secretive nature of these operations (Emmanuel 2015).

## Nigerian government's active role in surveillance

The Nigerian Communications Commission (NCC) facilitates mobile interception practices, using technologies like Stingrays, which mimic mobile phone towers to intercept call logs, text messages, and location data. This practice, lacking transparency and oversight, exacerbates privacy concerns and the potential for abuse, particularly against political opponents and activists. The justification for these practices often revolves around national security and crime prevention, but the broad application and inadequate regulatory framework raise significant human rights issues (Infosec Institute 2023; Allam and Oboh 2023; Efani 2023).

The government's reaction to the #EndSARS protests in 2020, where increased surveillance efforts were used to identify and intimidate protest organizers and participants, highlights the use of surveillance for social control. This led to the banning of Twitter in June 2021, reflecting the government's discomfort with social media's power to amplify dissent (Dahir 2021; Eweniyi 2021).

Public space surveillance has also been enhanced through the deployment of CCTV cameras in major cities, with technology provided by Chinese companies Huawei and ZTE. The National Identity Number (NIN) system, managed by the National Identity Management Commission (NIMC), extends surveillance capabilities by mandating the linkage of SIM cards to NINs, integrating telecommunications data with the national identity database (Roberts et al. 2023). While this system aims to enhance security, it faces criticism due to issues like data duplication and privacy concerns (Macdonald 2023; Idehen 2023).

## Impact on citizens' rights and resistance

Digital surveillance in Nigeria significantly impacts citizens' rights, particularly privacy and freedom of expression. Citizens often consent to surveillance under duress or as a requirement for accessing essential services. For instance, the NIN system necessitates linking NINs to SIM cards and bank accounts, compelling compliance despite privacy concerns (Macdonald 2023). Similar coercion is seen with the requirement for BVNs for banking services (Emejo 2024).

Opposition to surveillance is robust, particularly when measures are perceived as overreaching or directly threatening civil liberties. The #EndSARS protests illustrated significant resistance, with social media monitoring and the subsequent Twitter ban drawing widespread criticism. Citizens and activists viewed these measures as attempts to stifle dissent and control the narrative, infringing on free expression and assembly (Dahir 2021; Eweniyi 2021).

The impact of surveillance extends to various sectors of society, creating a climate of fear and self-censorship, particularly among journalists, activists, and political opponents. Surveillance technologies enable extensive monitoring of personal communications, suppressing political activism and free expression. This environment has driven many Nigerians, especially the youth, towards decentralized finance and cryptocurrencies as a means of resisting surveillance and avoiding harassment from security agencies (Salako 2022; Baydakova 2021).

Resistance efforts are spearheaded by civil society groups, privacy advocates, and investigative journalists. Organizations like Paradigm Initiative and Spaces for Change advocate for stronger data protection laws and oversight mechanisms (Paradigm Initiative 2021). Investigative journalism has played a crucial role in exposing the misuse of surveillance technologies, with media outlets like Premium Times and the International Centre for Investigative Reporting (ICIR) highlighting the ethical and legal implications of these practices (Yusuf 2023; ICIR 2021). These efforts underscore the need for transparency, accountability, and robust regulatory frameworks to protect citizens' rights in the digital age.

# Power interests advanced by digital surveillance in Nigeria

The deployment of digital surveillance technologies in Nigeria serves various power interests, primarily revolving around political control, social stability, economic gain, and international alliances. These interests are driven by both state and non-state actors, resulting in a complex landscape of power dynamics.

## Political control

One of the foremost power interests advanced by digital surveillance in Nigeria is the consolidation of political control. The Nigerian government has utilized surveillance technologies to monitor and suppress political dissent. During the #EndSARS protests, digital surveillance was employed to identify and intimidate protest organizers and participants, reflecting the government's intent to stifle opposition and maintain political dominance (Global Voices 2021). This use of surveillance to target activists, journalists, and political opponents underscores a broader strategy of retaining power by curtailing the ability of citizens to mobilize and challenge governmental authority (Marczak et al. 2020).

## Social stability

Surveillance is also justified as a means to ensure social stability and security. Nigeria faces significant threats from terrorist groups like Boko Haram and ISWAP, necessitating robust security measures. Surveillance technologies, such as Stingrays and sophisticated cyber-defence tools provided by companies like Elbit Systems and Circles, are used to monitor and disrupt terrorist activities (Johnson 2013). While these tools can enhance national security, their broad application often extends beyond legitimate security concerns to encompass monitoring of the general populace, thereby reinforcing state control over society under the guise of maintaining order (Allam and Oboh 2023).

## Economic interests

The expansion of digital surveillance in Nigeria is also driven by economic interests. The implementation of the National Identity Number (NIN) system, which mandates the linkage of SIM cards to NINs, integrates telecommunications data with the national identity database. This initiative not only aims to streamline government services and enhance security but also opens avenues for data monetization. The creation of vast databases of personal information presents significant economic opportunities for both the government and private entities involved in the surveillance ecosystem (Roberts et al. 2023).

Foreign companies, particularly from Israel and China, play a crucial role in supplying surveillance technology to Nigeria, thereby establishing lucrative economic relationships. These partnerships often involve substantial financial investments, such as the $40 million contract awarded to Elbit Systems for internet communications monitoring (Johnson 2013). Such economic engagements highlight the financial incentives underpinning the proliferation of surveillance technologies (Amnesty International 2021).

## International alliances

Digital surveillance in Nigeria is also influenced by international alliances and geopolitical considerations. The procurement of surveillance technologies from countries like Israel and China reflects strategic partnerships that extend beyond mere economic transactions. These alliances facilitate the transfer of advanced technologies and expertise, thereby enhancing Nigeria's surveillance capabilities. For instance, Chinese companies like Huawei and ZTE have been instrumental in providing the infrastructure for public space surveillance, further solidifying Sino-Nigerian relations (Roberts et al. 2023).

Moreover, the involvement of foreign technology providers in Nigeria's surveillance apparatus aligns with broader geopolitical interests, where countries seek to expand their influence through technological dominance. This dynamic is evident in the provision of surveillance tools that not only serve the immediate security needs of Nigeria but also embed the country within a network of international dependencies and alliances (OHCHR 2022).

## What rights are violated by the powers that wield digital surveillance as a tool?

The implementation of digital surveillance in Nigeria has led to significant violations of several fundamental human rights. The primary rights infringed upon include the right to privacy, the right to freedom of expression, and the right to freedom of assembly. These violations occur within a broader context of weak regulatory frameworks and the misuse of surveillance technologies by both state and private actors.

### Right to privacy

The right to privacy is enshrined in numerous international human rights instruments, including Article 12 of the UDHR and Article 17 of the International Covenant on Civil and Political Rights (ICCPR), both of which Nigeria has ratified. However, digital surveillance practices in Nigeria severely undermine this right. The use of sophisticated surveillance tools such as Pegasus spyware enables the government and other entities to intrude into individuals' private communications and data without their consent or knowledge. This intrusive monitoring extends to intercepting phone calls, reading text messages, tracking location data, and accessing social media accounts (OHCHR 2022; Amnesty International 2021).

The Nigerian government's extensive use of digital surveillance technologies, such as those provided by Circles and NSO Group, has facilitated widespread and clandestine monitoring of citizens, journalists, and political opponents. These actions often occur without judicial oversight or transparency, making it difficult for individuals to seek redress or hold perpetrators accountable (Amnesty International 2021).

## Right to freedom of expression

The right to freedom of expression is protected under Article 19 of the UDHR and the ICCPR. In Nigeria, this right is frequently violated through the use of digital surveillance. The government has leveraged surveillance technologies to monitor and suppress dissenting voices, particularly during periods of political unrest. For instance, during the #EndSARS protests in 2020, surveillance was intensified to identify and intimidate protest organizers and participants. This crackdown included monitoring social media activity and, in some cases, led to the arrest and harassment of activists and journalists (Global Voices 2021).

Also, reports indicate that surveillance tools have been used to target individuals critical of the government, thereby stifling free speech and creating a climate of fear among those who wish to express dissenting opinions. This practice is contrary to Nigeria's obligations under international human rights law, which mandates the protection of free expression even in digital spaces (OHCHR 2022; International Bar Association 2022).

## Right to freedom of assembly

The right to freedom of assembly is guaranteed by Article 20 of the UDHR and Article 21 of the ICCPR. Digital surveillance infringes upon this right by deterring individuals from participating in protests and public demonstrations. The surveillance of social media platforms and mobile communications during events such as the #EndSARS protests has led to the targeting and arrest of activists, which in turn discourages public participation in assemblies and movements critical of the government (Global Voices 2021).

Moreover, the lack of a comprehensive data protection and privacy law in Nigeria exacerbates these violations. Despite several attempts to pass legislation that would safeguard digital rights, such as the digital rights and freedom bill, political will to enact and enforce such laws remains weak. Consequently, surveillance practices continue unabated, and the fundamental rights of Nigerian citizens remain at risk (OHCHR 2022).

# Citizen agency to mitigate and overcome digital surveillance in Nigeria

The pervasive use of digital surveillance in Nigeria raises significant concerns about the erosion of civil liberties and the entrenchment of authoritarian governance. Combating the pervasive surveillance in Nigeria requires a multifaceted approach that leverages legal challenges, advocacy, technological solutions, international collaboration, grassroots activism, and policy advocacy.

## Legal challenges

Legal challenges represent a crucial form of citizen agency in combating unlawful surveillance. Civil society organizations and individuals can file lawsuits to challenge the legality of surveillance practices that violate constitutional rights. For instance, lawsuits have been filed challenging the mandatory linkage of SIM cards to NINs on the grounds of privacy violations (Techpoint Africa 2021). Leveraging existing legal frameworks, such as the Freedom of Information Act, can compel transparency and accountability from government agencies involved in surveillance (Allam and Oboh 2023).

## Advocacy and public awareness campaigns

Advocacy and public awareness campaigns are essential for mobilizing public opinion and pressuring the government to enact and enforce robust data protection laws. Organizations like Paradigm Initiative and Spaces for Change play a pivotal role in educating the public about the dangers of unchecked surveillance and advocating for stronger privacy protections (Paradigm Initiative 2021). These campaigns can also highlight instances of surveillance abuse, thereby fostering a more informed and engaged citizenry capable of demanding accountability from their leaders (Global Voices 2021).

## Technological countermeasures

Technological countermeasures offer individuals practical tools to protect their privacy against digital surveillance. Encryption technologies, for instance, can safeguard communications from unauthorized access. Utilizing secure messaging apps, virtual private networks (VPNs), and encrypted email services can help citizens maintain their privacy online (OHCHR 2022). Digital literacy programs can also empower citizens with the knowledge to use these technologies effectively and recognize potential security threats (Infosec Institute 2023).

## International collaboration

International collaboration can amplify efforts to mitigate surveillance abuses by holding governments and corporations accountable on a global scale. Human rights organizations, such as Amnesty International and the Committee to Protect Journalists (CPJ), can exert pressure on international bodies to scrutinize and sanction countries that engage in unlawful surveillance practices (Amnesty International 2021). Collaborative efforts can also involve advocating stricter export controls on surveillance technologies and promoting international standards for digital rights protection (OHCHR 2022).

## Grassroots movements and civil disobedience

Grassroots movements and acts of civil disobedience can draw attention to the adverse impacts of surveillance and galvanize public support for policy changes. The #EndSARS protests exemplify how decentralized social movements can resist state surveillance and demand reforms. By organizing through secure and anonymous channels, such movements can continue to advocate for human rights despite government efforts to monitor and suppress them (Global Voices 2021).

## Strategic litigation and policy advocacy

Strategic litigation involves using the legal system to achieve broader societal change. By challenging specific instances of surveillance abuse in court, activists can set legal precedents that protect privacy rights more broadly. Policy advocacy, on the other hand, involves lobbying for legislative changes that limit the scope of surveillance and enhance protections for personal data. These efforts can be supported by producing research and reports that highlight the negative impacts of surveillance and propose concrete policy solutions (Allam and Oboh 2023).

# Bibliography

Adepetun, A. (2020). 'Why Identity Matters for Nation's Development', in T. Roberts, J. Gitahi, P. Allam, L. Oboh, O. Oladapo, G. Appiah-Adjei, A. Galal, J. Kainja, S. Phiri, K. Abraham, S. Klovig Skelton and A. Sheombar (eds) (2023). *Mapping the Supply of Surveillance Technologies to Africa: Case Studies from Nigeria, Ghana, Morocco, Malawi, and Zambia.* The Institute of Development Studies and Partner Organisations. Online resource. https://hdl.handle.net/20.500.12413/18120 (accessed 5 June 2024).

Afigbo, A. E. (1972). *The Warrant Chiefs: Indirect Rule in Southeastern Nigeria 1891–1929,* London: Longman.

Ajala, A. (2009). 'Ethnic Relations and the Federal Structure in Nigeria', *Journal of Modern African Studies,* 47(2): 251–75.

Akintaro, S. (2022). 'FG to Deploy Surveillance Cameras for Security at Nigerian Borders', *Nairametrics,* https://nairametrics.com/2022/05/25/fg-to-deploy-surveillance-cameras-for-security-at-nigerian-borders/ (accessed 5 June 2024).

Al Jazeera (2020). https://www.aljazeera.com/news/2020/12/8/nigerias-defence-agency-acquires-spy-equipment-says-report (accessed 8 June 2024).

Allam, P. and Oboh, L. (2023). 'Nigeria Country Report', in T. Roberts, J. Gitahi, P. Allam, L. Oboh, O. Oladapo, G. Appiah-Adjei, A. Galal, J. Kainja, S. Phiri, K. Abraham, S. Klovig Skelton and A. Sheombar (eds) (2023). *Mapping the*

*Supply of Surveillance Technologies to Africa: Case Studies from Nigeria, Ghana, Morocco, Malawi, and Zambia*. The Institute of Development Studies and Partner Organisations. Online resource. https://opendocs.ids.ac.uk/articles/online_resource/Mapping_the_Supply_of_Surveillance_Technologies_to_Africa_Case_Studies_from_Nigeria_Ghana_Morocco_Malawi_and_Zambia/26431414?file=48182842 (accessed 5 June 2024).

Amnesty International (2021). 'Nigeria: Authorities Must Stop Crackdown on Media and Free Expression'. https://www.amnesty.org/en/latest/news/2021/07/nigeria-authorities-must-stop-crackdown-on-media-and-free-expression/ (accessed 10 June 2024).

Baydakova, A. (2021). 'Nigerians Turn to Crypto to Resist Surveillance and Censorship', *CoinDesk*. https://www.coindesk.com/markets/2021/07/26/nigerians-turn-to-crypto-to-resist-surveillance-and-censorship/ (accessed 10 May 2024).

Breckenridge, K. (2019). *Biometric State: The Global Politics of Identification and Surveillance in South Africa, 1850 to the Present*, Cambridge: Cambridge University Press.

Browne, S. (2015). *Dark Matters: On the Surveillance of Blackness*. Durham, NC: Duke University Press.

Cadwalladr, C. (2018). 'Cambridge Analytica Was Offered Politicians' Hacked Emails, Say Witnesses', *The Guardian*. https://www.theguardian.com/uk-news/2018/mar/21/cambridge-analytica-offered-politicians-hacked-emails-witnesses-say (accessed 9 June 2024).

CIPESA (2021). 'State of Internet Freedom in Africa 2021: Charting Patterns in Government Internet Controls'. https://cipesa.org/?wpfb_dl=425 (accessed 13 May 2024).

Constitution of the Federal Republic of Nigeria (1999). http://www.nigeria-law.org/ConstitutionOfTheFederalRepublicOfNigeria.htm (accessed 27 June 2024).

Dahir, A. L. (2021). 'Nigeria Suspends Twitter After Company Deletes President's Tweet', *The New York Times*. https://www.nytimes.com/2021/06/04/world/africa/nigeria-twitter-suspended.html (accessed 10 June 2024).

Duncan, J. (2022). *Disabling Dissent: The Pervasive Use of Digital Surveillance in Africa*, Johannesburg: Wits University Press.

Efani (2023). 'The Impact of Digital Surveillance on Privacy and Human Rights in Nigeria'. https://www.efani.com/blog/digital-surveillance-nigeria (accessed 10 June 2024).

EFF (2014). '13 Principles Week of Action: Human Rights Require a Secure Internet'. https://www.eff.org/deeplinks/2014/09/human-rights-require-secure-internet (accessed 8 June 2024).

Emejo, J. (2024). 'The Role of BVN in Enhancing Banking Security and Surveillance in Nigeria', *Business Day Nigeria*. https://businessday.ng/ (accessed 10 June 2024).

Emmanuel, O. (2015). 'Bayelsa Governor Acquires Hacking Tools from Italian Firm', *Premium Times*. https://www.premiumtimesng.com/ (accessed 10 June 2024).

Eweniyi, I. (2021). 'EndSARS: How the Movement Protests Police Brutality and Advocates for Human Rights in Nigeria', *TechCabal*. https://techcabal.com/2021/10/20/endsars-one-year-later/ (accessed 13 May 2024).

Falola T. (1999). *The History of Nigeria*. Westport, CT: Greenwood Press. Chapter 4. https://archive.org/details/historyofnigeria00falo (accessed 8 June 2024).

Federal Republic of Nigeria (2019). *Lawful Interception of Communications Regulation*. https://www.ncc.gov.ng/docman-main/legal-regulatory/regulations/874-lawful-interception-of-communications-regulations-2019/file (accessed 3 June 2024).

Fortin, J. (2013). 'Nigerian Citizens Call for Transparency amid Suspicions of Shady Government Deal for Internet Surveillance', *International Business Times*. https://www.ibtimes.com/nigerian-citizens-call-transparency-amid-suspicions-shady-government-deal-internet-surveillance (accessed 8 June 2024).

Foucault, M. (1978). *The History of Sexuality, Volume 1: An Introduction*, New York: Random House.

Giddens, A. (1984). *The Constitution of Society: Outline of the Theory of Structuration*, Cambridge: Polity Press.

Global Voices (2021). 'The Role of Digital Surveillance in Suppressing Dissent in Nigeria'. https://globalvoices.org/2021/10/25/the-role-of-digital-surveillance-in-suppressing-dissent-in-nigeria/ (accessed 10 June 2024).

Heerten, L. and Moses, A. D. (2014) 'The Nigeria–Biafra War: Postcolonial Conflict and the Question of Genocide', *Journal of Genocide Research*, 16(2–3): 169–203. https://doi.org/10.1080/14623528.2014.936700

Ibezim-Ohaeri, V., Lawal, R. A., MacHarry, C., Kingsley, G., Gbagir, J., Nwanguma, O., Juba-Nwosu, N., Fyneface, D., Olufemi, J., Unumeri, G., Ibezim-Ohaeri, V., and Nwodo, L. (2021). *Surveillance and the Future of Civic Space: Nigeria*. Spaces for Change.

ICIR (2021). https://www.icirnigeria.org/nigerian-security-agencies-use-israeli-us-technology-for-forensic-surveillance-of-journalists-phones/ (accessed 8 June 2024).

Idehen, F. (2023). 'NIN–SIM Linkage: Privacy Concerns and the Way Forward', *TechEconomy.ng*. https://techeconomy.ng/ (accessed 6 June 2024).

Infosec Institute (2023). 'Stingray Surveillance: How It Works and How to Protect Yourself'. https://resources.infosecinstitute.com/topic/stingray-surveillance/ (accessed 10 June 2024).

International Bar Association (2022). 'Human Rights in the Digital Age: Challenges and Opportunities'. https://www.ibanet.org/Human-Rights-in-the-Digital-Age (accessed 10 June 2024).

Jili, B. (2022). 'Digital Authoritarianism in Africa: Surveillance, Suppression, and Resistance', *African Affairs*, 121(484): 123–45.

Johnson, R. (2013). 'Israel's Role in Nigeria's Surveillance Apparatus', *Haaretz*. https://www.haaretz.com/ (accessed 13 May 2024).

Lawal, R. A., MacHarry, C., Kingsley, G., Gbagir, J., Nwanguma, O., Juba-Nwosu, N., Fyneface, F. D., Ogbeche, O., Olufemi, J., Unumeri, G., Ibezim-Ohaeri, V., and Nwodo, L. (2022). *Shrinking Civic Space in the Name of Security: Nigeria*. Action Group on Free Civic Space. https://www.business-humanrights.org/documents/37293/NIGERIA-SHRINKING-CIVIC-SPACE-IN-THE-NAME-OF-SECURITY-3.pdf (accessed 8 July 2024).

Macdonald, H. (2023). 'Challenges in Nigeria's Biometric Data Integration', *African Security Review*, 32(1): 45–60.

Marczak, B., Scott-Railton, J., Prakash Rao, S., Anstis, S., and Deibert, R. (2020). 'Running in Circles: Uncovering the Clients of Cyberespionage Firm Circles', *Citizen Lab*. https://citizenlab.ca/2020/12/running-in-circles-uncovering-the-clients-of-cyberespionage-firm-circles/ (accessed 3 June 2024).

Mojeed, M. (2015). 'EXCLUSIVE: Nigerians Beware! Jonathan Procures N11 Billion Equipment to Tap Your Phones', *Premium Times*, 26 February 2015. https://www.premiumtimesng.com/news/headlines/177557-exclusive-nigerians-beware-jonathan-procures-n11-billion-equipment-to-tap-your-phones.html (accessed 8 June 2024).

Norris, C. and Armstrong, G. (1999). *The Maximum Surveillance Society: The Rise of CCTV*, New York: Berg.

Nyabola, N. (2018). *Digital Democracy, Analogue Politics: How the Internet Era is Transforming Kenya*, London: Zed Books.

OAL (2023). 'Cybercrimes Act 2015: Legal Implications and Enforcement Challenges in Nigeria'. https://www.oal.com.ng/cybercrimes-act-2015-legal-implications-and-enforcement-challenges/ (accessed 10 June 2024).

Ogala, E. (2016). 'Nigeria's Internet Interception Bill Sparks Privacy Concerns', *The Guardian Nigeria*. https://guardian.ng/ (accessed 2 June 2024).

Ogundipe, S. (2017). 'INVESTIGATION: Two Years After, Niger Delta States Continue Controversial Spying Programmes', *Premium Times*, 30 June 2017. https://www.premiumtimesng.com/news/headlines/235396-investigation-two-years-after-niger-delta-states-continue-controversial-spying-programmes.html (accessed 5 June 2024).

OHCHR (2022). 'Privacy in the Digital Age: Report of the United Nations High Commissioner for Human Rights'. https://www.ohchr.org/en/documents/reports/privacy-digital-age (accessed 10 June 2024).

Oloyede, R. (2021). 'Nigeria Country Report', in T. Roberts (ed.), *Surveillance Law in Africa: A Review of Six Countries*, Brighton: Institute of Development Studies. https://doi.org/10.19088/IDS.2021.059

Osaghae, E. (2018). 'The Long Shadow of Nigeria's Military Epochs, 1966–79 and 1983–99', in Carl Levan and Patrick Ukata (eds), *The Oxford Handbook of Nigerian Politics*, 170–88, Oxford: Oxford University Press. https://doi.org/10.1093/oxfordhb/9780198804307.013.10

Paradigm Initiative (2021). 'Digital Rights in Nigeria: Advancing Privacy and Freedom of Expression'. https://paradigmhq.org/ (accessed 10 June 2024).

*Punch* (2021). https://punchng.com/on-fgs-new-nationwide-cctv-project/ (accessed 8 June 2024).

Roberts, T., Mohamed Ali, A., Farahat, M., Oloyede, R. and Mutung'u, G. (2021). *Surveillance Law in Africa: A Review of Six Countries*, Brighton: Institute of Development Studies. https://opendocs.ids.ac.uk/opendocs/handle/20.500.12413/16893 (accessed 8 June 2024).

Salako, A. (2022). 'Decentralized Finance: A Means to Resist Surveillance in Nigeria', *Crypto Africa*. https://cryptoafrica.org/ (accessed 9 June 2024).

Suberu, R. (1996). *Federalism and Ethnic Conflict in Nigeria*, Washington, DC: United States Institute of Peace Press.

Techpoint Africa (2021). 'SIM-NIN Linkage: Legal Challenges and Citizen Responses'. https://techpoint.africa/2021/12/15/sim-nin-linkage-legal-challenges/ (accessed 10 June 2024).

Vanguard (2023). 'DIA Budget Allocation and Surveillance Projects'. https://www.vanguardngr.com/ (accessed 4 June 2024).

Weber, M. (1947). *The Theory of Social and Economic Organization*. Translated by A. M. Henderson and Talcott Parsons. New York: Free Press; London: Collier Macmillan.

Yusuf, K. (2023). 'Heightened Surveillance by Security Operatives Puts Nigerian Journalists under Climate of Fear'. *Premium Times* Special Report. premiumtimesng.com (accessed 13 May 2024).

# 8

# Who supplies digital surveillance technologies to African governments?

## Pathways for resistance

Anand Sheombar and Sebastian Klovig Skelton

## Introduction

African citizens are increasingly being surveilled, profiled, and targeted online in ways that violate their rights. African governments frequently use pandemic or terrorism-related security risks to grant themselves additional surveillance rights and significantly increase their collection of monitoring apparatus and technologies while spending billions of dollars to conduct surveillance (Roberts et al. 2023). Surveillance is a prominent strategy African governments use to limit civic space (Roberts and Mohamed Ali 2021). Digital technologies are not the root of surveillance in Africa because surveillance practices predate the digital age (Munoriyarwa and Mare 2023). Surveillance practices were first used by colonial governments, continued by post-colonial governments, and are currently being digitalized and accelerated by African countries. Throughout history, surveillance has been passed down from colonizers to liberators, and some African leaders have now automated it (Roberts et al. 2023).

Many studies have been conducted on illegal state surveillance in the United States, China, and Europe (Feldstein 2019; Feldstein 2021). Less is known about the supply of surveillance technologies to Africa. With a population of almost 1.5 billion people, Africa is a continent where many citizens face surveillance with malicious intent. As mentioned in previous chapters, documenting the dimensions and drivers of digital surveillance in Africa is essential to protect digital rights. With this chapter, we aim to identify the drivers of the proliferation of surveillance technologies in African countries and suggest ways to counter them. This chapter draws on the African Digital Rights Network report *Mapping the Supply of Surveillance Technology to Africa* (Roberts et al. 2023) and a follow-up paper on the drivers of state surveillance (Sheombar and Skelton 2023). It assesses the paths to resisting the uptake of this state surveillance. We thus aim to provide a way to move from observation to impactful actions to counter surveillance tech supplying states exporting to African countries where it is abused for human rights violations.

This chapter is structured as follows. First, we introduce the categorization of surveillance technologies. This is followed by articulating the theoretical concepts used to analyse the motives for the proliferation of surveillance technologies. This is followed by our findings on the main countries and firms we identified as supplying surveillance technologies to African governments. Then, we delve into the motives for supplying and deploying state surveillance. From there, we suggest countermeasures in customer and supply-side countries. We conclude with some reflections.

## Concepts for the analysis of surveillance

In this section, we define terms and review some concepts of power, rights, and agency in order to clarify the analytical lenses that we use to identify and analyse the motives for digital surveillance and ways of resisting.

### Digital and state surveillance

When states apply surveillance, we refer to this as state surveillance. For the purpose of this study, state surveillance is defined as any observing, listening, monitoring, or recording by a state or its agents to track citizens' movements, activities, conversations, communications, or correspondence, including the recording of metadata (Roberts et al. 2021). To organize our analysis, we used the five categories of digital surveillance technology developed in our previous study (Roberts et al. 2023):

1. Internet interception: surveillance of private internet communications
2. Mobile interception: surveillance of private mobile phone communications
3. Social media monitoring: surveillance of social media interactions
4. Safe city/smart city: surveillance of public spaces using CCTV facial recognition
5. Digital-ID: surveillance using biometric scanning of face, iris, and/or fingerprints.

Internet interception technologies allow governments or other users to read private emails or instant messages and search for phrases like 'bomb' or 'protest'. Mobile interception technologies allow actors to intercept mobile phone calls and capture private information from mobile phones. Social media monitoring technologies are used to capture what users post, who they 'friend', and what they 'like' on social media. CCTV, facial recognition, and other digital sensors are used in smart city technology to collect information about people's movements and behaviours. Biometric digital identification technologies give each citizen a unique identification number validated via biometrics (iris scan, fingerprint, facial recognition). Identification data for all population members is recorded on a central registry and then integrated with data from mobile phones, bank accounts, driving licences, store cards, passports, medical records, and so on. In practice, these categories of surveillance technology may slightly overlap in functionalities.

## Multi-actor framework for surveillance and resistance analysis

To study the supply of surveillance technologies to Africa, we analysed actors and their power interests. Schuster et al. (2017) in their study of mass surveillance distinguish three main groups of actors with different interests. These are (1) state agencies and law enforcement authorities (LEA), (2) surveillance sector companies, and (3) citizens. Schuster et al. (2017) summarize the interests per group. State actors prioritize national security over privacy. Surveillance sector companies' primary interest is sales and income over national security or privacy. Some citizens may be willing to accept privacy-invasive technologies, while others will refuse erosion of their privacy or anonymity.

This list of actors is expanded by Wright et al. (2015), who argue that consultancies that advise governments on implementing surveillance should be included, as well as those who aim to regulate, oversee, or critique surveillance, like policymakers and civil society organizations. A further addition to the list of actors was made by Martin et al. (2009) who propose a multi-actor framework to examine the dynamics between the surveyors, the surveilled, and others involved. They distinguish between the governments and law enforcement agencies that are implementing surveillance, the surveillance technology companies, international governmental and non-governmental agencies, and the (non-human) surveillance technologies themselves. In Table 8.1, we adapt the approaches of Martin et al. (2009), Wright et al. (2015) and Schuster et al. (2017), and from our own analysis add two additional actors: media and academia. We will return to this disaggregation of surveillance actors later in this chapter when we provide recommendations for resisting the proliferation of surveillance practices targeting citizens toward the end of this chapter.

**Table 8.1** Multi-actor framework for surveillance and resistance actors

| Actor | Power interests | Assumed role |
|---|---|---|
| 1) Government (potentially both Northern-based supply-side and Global South (African) client-side country) | National security; digital governance | Surveillance authority (legal and illegal) |
| 2) State agencies and law enforcement authorities | National security | Conducting surveillance |
| 3) Private sector: i.e. Northern-based surveillance technologies firms | Sales and income generation | Provider of surveillance technologies and services |
| 4) Consultancies, lobby groups for surveillance | Lobbying and sales and income generation | Advocacy for surveillance capitalism interests |
| 5) Policymakers | Overseeing regulation | Regulating surveillance |
| 6) Internet and telecom service providers | Sales and income generation | Actor possibly involved in surveillance |
| 7) (Non-human) surveillance technologies | Surveillance data collection | Data collector |

| Actor | Power interests | Assumed role |
|---|---|---|
| 8) Citizens | Privacy, digital rights, convenience etc. | Subject to surveillance |
| 9) Civil society | Advocacy for citizen rights and freedoms | Subject to surveillance, but also a potential role in exposing surveillance and overseeing related regulation |
| 10) Media | News production – investigative journalism for scoops on surveillance stories | Subject to surveillance, but also a potential role in exposing surveillance and advocacy of citizens' rights |
| 11) Academia | Research – surveillance studies research gap | Subject to surveillance, but also role in exposing surveillance and advocacy of citizens' rights |

Source: Adapted from Martin et al. (2009), Wright et al. (2015) and Schuster et al. (2017).

## Surveillance technologies as panopticon

Surveillance reflects a power relationship in which the watcher covertly gains an advantage at the expense of the fundamental rights of those being watched (Roberts et al. 2021). Foucault utilizes Jeremy Bentham's 'panopticon' in which an invisible overseer (*surveillant* in French) has a panoptic view of every element of prisoners' or workers' lives. Some scholars trace this back to the colonial implementation of disciplinary mechanisms in Egypt, such as the model village or the army barracks, and therefore it has colonial roots (Mitchell 1991: 35). Giles Deleuze suggested that Foucault's 'disciplinary society' is increasingly being replaced by 'societies of control', meaning the ability to automate widespread surveillance across all communication media and digital platforms stands in for the panopticon's watchtower in this notion (Deleuze 1992). The concept of 'societies of control' has been increasingly used to describe modern societies characterized by 'surveillance capitalism', in which social media corporations and internet intermediaries are capable of real-time tracing and monitoring of users' digital footprints through the use of analytic tools and cookies (Zuboff 2019).

Using panoptic power as an analytics lens might help evaluate state agencies' growing digital surveillance capacity. However, the panoptic lens is less useful for analysing citizen evasion and resistance. It fails to account for everyday forms of surveillance resistance and novel ways in which surveillance targets try to beat the system (Munoriyarwa and Mare 2023). For this reason, we apply the powercube concept, which provides the instruments to overcome the shortcomings of the panoptic analytical lens.

## The powercube

For our analysis, we have used the powercube concept that interrogates three aspects of power (forms, spaces, levels) not only on their own but especially in the way they are related (Gaventa 2019). The powercube is used to ask questions about what forms of power are used, what spaces of power, or what levels of power.

The powercube describes how power operates across three dimensions: (1) Spaces: the arenas of power; (2) Forms: the degree of visibility of power; and (3) Levels: the places of engagement (Figure 8.1). The powercube is useful for analysing the dynamics of power in a particular context in order to inform action for change, including how to counter the rights-violating surveillance of citizens.

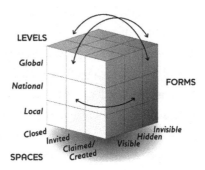

**Figure 8.1** Gaventa's three-dimensional powercube.
Source: Gaventa (2006).

We argue that the powercube can usefully inform the selection of viable strategies for countermeasures against creeping surveillance practices. Depending on the analysis of power operating in a particular space, action for change might vary. For example, in response to 'closed spaces' where decision making occurs behind closed doors, citizens might respond with monitoring projects and campaigns that insist on transparency and accountability. In 'invited spaces' where only selected actors are allowed to participate, lobbying for policy reforms might be viable. In 'claimed spaces' created by marginalized groups the emphasis may be to protect civic space and create alternative environments in which alternatives can be developed to support social movements.

Depending on the forms of power, citizens and civil society can take different actions. When dealing with a visible form of power, an approach to advocacy for policy change can be pursued. If the power is hidden, citizens and civil society, together with other actors, can organize or mobilize a coalition to introduce new voices and agendas to the table. Invisible power is often the most insidious form of power and involves 'the internalised, often unconscious acceptance of dominant norms, institutions, languages and behaviours as natural and normal, often desirable, even if they appear to be against the interests of the actors involved' (Oosterom and Scott-Villiers 2016: 2). Tackling the effects of invisible power often takes the form of critical awareness raising.

Furthermore, introducing another level of advocacy activities, such as opening a national coalition when initially working on a local level or jumping to a global level by collaborating internationally, can create useful strategies for change. Gaventa (2020) argues that strategies for action need to: '1) connect across all the spaces, levels and forms to build alignment, 2) link vertically, as well as horizontally, 3) build coalitions to do so, and 4) recognise the dynamic changing nature of power, adapt and support over time'. In this chapter we apply powercube analysis to interrogate the data about the surveillance technology suppliers and the stakeholders and interests involved.

## Method of research on suppliers of surveillance technologies

For this study, the researchers conducted desk research and used a combination of information sources in the public domain, such as open source databases, including news media articles; open government data on export licences; export and import licence portals, procurement notices, civil society research, and databases[1] into the spread of surveillance equipment, academic articles, and information openly published by digital surveillance companies, such as press releases and brochures (Table 8.2). We also analysed archival records of websites and publications on company websites via the Internet Archive Wayback Machine.[2]

A variety of data sources were used in this study including company reports, media articles, and reports and databases produced by civil society organizations. In many countries, companies are legally required to publish annual operations reports. Furthermore, exporting particular military and surveillance technologies often requires an export licence that is governed by the global Wassenaar Arrangement for arms and dual-use technologies. Accessing the database of military and surveillance technologies export licences also provided useful data (ArmsControlCenter 2023).

Investigative journalists and mainstream media have conducted extensive multi-country analyses of the most important surveillance technology stories.

**Table 8.2** Descriptive features of desk research data sources

| | |
|---|---|
| Types of sources | News media articles; open government data on export licences; export and import licence portals, procurement notices, civil society research, and databases into the spread of surveillance equipment; academic articles; information openly published by digital surveillance companies, such as press releases and brochures. Archival records |
| Northern Hemisphere supplier countries | China, European Union agencies, Germany, France, Italy, Israel, Russia, the United Kingdom, the United States (including UN agencies) |
| African customer countries | The project initially focused on case studies in Nigeria, Ghana, Morocco, Malawi, and Zambia. Additional information was collected from all other African countries found in the analysed sources |
| Surveillance technology categories | Internet interception technologies<br>Mobile phone interception technologies<br>Social media monitoring technologies<br>Safe city/smart city technologies<br>Digital/biometric-ID technologies |

Source: Authors.

The Pegasus Spyware story is a prime example, and we were able to use media stories to source evidence on the use of this surveillance technology in many African countries (Marczak et al. 2018).

We also analysed academic papers and NGO reports on surveillance technologies in Africa. For the document analysis, we applied guidelines from academic desk research, the checklist for 'Challenging Public Private Surveillance Partnerships' from Privacy International on data collection, as well as mapping stakeholders, cross-checking sources, and 'who, what, when, where, how, and why' questions to identify the surveillance technology firm, category of surveillance technology, exporting country, and importing African state (Ginés 2018; Privacy International 2022).

We noticed that publicly available information from governmental departments and surveillance technology suppliers is often partial and incomplete. Sometimes, we used the Internet Archive Wayback Machine to access information removed from the web. Even governments that provide elaborate export licence databases, like the United Kingdom, still obfuscate details of the surveillance technologies.

Using data from these sources we mapped the surveillance technology exports per supplier country and per surveillance technology category before using the powercube to analyse the motives for surveillance and possible counterstrategies.

## Summary of supplier countries of surveillance technologies

This section first summarizes the main findings of the *Mapping the Supply of Surveillance Technology to Africa* report (Roberts et al. 2023). Based on extensive desk research, we identified the following major countries exporting surveillance technologies to Africa: China, European Union agencies, Germany, France, Italy, Israel, Russia, the United Kingdom, and the United States. Table 8.3 provides a summary of supply-side countries of surveillance technologies and the main export categories of surveillance technologies.

We identified the following major Northern Hemisphere countries exporting surveillance technologies to Africa: China, European Union

**Table 8.3** Supplier countries of surveillance technologies

| Surveillance tech supply-side country/ institution summary | Main surveillance technology export category | African market focus | Examples of suppliers |
|---|---|---|---|
| China: China's exports of surveillance technology to Africa are rapidly increasing. China is currently the leading provider of 'safe city' surveillance technology for public areas. China has been offering billions of dollars in loans to purchase its 'safe city' package | All, with an emphasis on AI and safe city/smart city | Whole of Africa, with emphasis on African states involved with The Digital Silk Road (DSR), as a component of China's Belt and Road Initiative (BRI) | Nigeria has heavily invested in CCTV and safe city surveillance projects with Chinese companies ZTE and Huawei |
| European Union: The EU is the primary source of funding for border surveillance technology; this technology transfer is often accompanied by a downplaying of the surveillance element | Digital/biometric-ID (border control) | North and West Africa | The EU financed spyware surveillance software, hardware, and training for the Moroccan police out of the budget of the EU's order Management Programme for the Maghreb Region |
| France: In the slipstream of French government politics come French surveillance technology companies with a particular focus on francophone countries | Internet and mobile surveillance technologies | Mainly Francophone Africa | The company Altrnativ has allegedly sold surveillance technologies to the governments of Benin, Chad, Cameroon, Comoros, Gabon, and the Republic of the Congo |
| Italy has a large defence and security sector | Mobile phone spyware | Whole of Africa | Hacking Team's spyware 'Remote Control System' was sold to the Moroccan intelligence services. Other customers of this spyware were agencies of African governments of Egypt, Ethiopia, Morocco, Nigeria, and Sudan |

| Supplier country | Technology/service | Coverage | Examples |
|---|---|---|---|
| Germany is Europe's largest arms exporter, and many firms active in the high-tech surveillance industry | Mobile phone spyware | Whole of Africa | The now-bankrupt company FinFisher sold Command and Control servers to law enforcement in South Africa |
| Israel: The history of Israel is closely intertwined with the development of arms and digital surveillance technologies. In Israel's 'military-innovation ecosystem' the line between private and public space is blurred. Using military-grade surveillance tools for its spyware diplomacy | Mobile hacking software. A broad range of products and services, including spyware, psychological operations, and misinformation campaigns aimed at influencing elections | Most African countries except for adversaries | The NSO Group has state customers for Pegasus spyware in Algeria, Egypt, Ivory Coast, Kenya, Morocco, Rwanda, South Africa, Togo, Uganda, and Zambia |
| United Kingdom: The UK government has maintained close political and economic ties with many African governments of former colonies | Internet and mobile interception technologies. Social media surveillance and 'political marketing' consultancy | Nigeria is the largest customer, followed by Morocco, Ghana, Zambia, and Malawi | BAE Systems has sold a mobile and internet interception system called Evident to authorities in Morocco and Algeria |
| Russia: Not sufficient evidence that Russia is a prominent supplier of surveillance technologies to African countries | Intercept and monitor Internet and telecommunications network traffic | n/a | |
| United States of America: US surveillance companies are less visible than suppliers from other supplier countries in Africa | Social media surveillance and 'political marketing' consultancy | Most African countries except adversaries | Dataminr, which specializes in advanced real-time social media monitoring, provided services to public authorities in South Africa to monitor student demonstrations in Cape Town |

Source: Based on Klovig Skelton and Sheombar (2023).

agencies, Germany, France, Italy, Israel, the United Kingdom, and the United States. Publicly available information from governments and suppliers on their websites or from other online presence does not present much or only fragmented information, or even attempts to obfuscate these exports. Exporting governments tend to be focused on particular countries more than others, the European Union seemingly focusing on countries in the Northern region of Africa, particularly Morocco, whereas the United Kingdom and China are active in all regions of Africa. Each exporting country tends to have a focus area, within the five surveillance technology categories we used for this book. For example, China is a major provider of safe city technologies; mobile phone hacking spyware exporters include Germany, Italy, and Israel; the UK exports mobile and internet interception technology; the EU is an important funder of border surveillance technologies throughout North and West Africa. Of all of the main arms-exporting countries, Russia seems to be less active in the supply of surveillance technologies to African states at the moment. US surveillance companies are less visible than other countries' suppliers across the African countries, while some are deployed via UN agencies' programmes in Africa.

## Motives for state surveillance

For the analysis of the motives for state surveillance, we drew on our supply-side report of surveillance technologies exported to Africa, as well as the country reports (of the importing African countries), bundled in the publication 'Mapping the Supply of Surveillance Technologies to Africa' (Roberts et al. 2023). We have identified six – not mutually exclusive – motives for state surveillance, including the suppliers' perspective. These are: (1) surveillance as legitimacy for state security, (2) surveillance for political gain, (3) surveillance as diplomacy, (4) surveillance as a tool for development, (5) surveillance as neocolonialism, and (6) surveillance as business opportunity. These motives are not mutually exclusive and often complement each other in our analysed cases. A downplaying of the surveillance element often accompanies the transfer of surveillance technologies.

## Surveillance as state security

Automated widespread digital surveillance resembles the panopticon's watchtower (Deleuze 1992), for exerting power over citizens. African governments frequently use pandemic or terrorism-related security risks to grant themselves additional surveillance powers and to justify purchases of monitoring apparatus and surveillance technologies. Citizens' privacy and digital human rights are in danger from technologies being instrumentalized as tools for surveillance, control, and oppression (UNHCR 2022). A motive that further undermines civil rights is the exertion of authoritarian control over citizens by using digital surveillance technologies (Feldstein 2019; van der Lugt 2021).

For example, a main driver for digital surveillance in Morocco is the pursuit of national security. However, this comes at a cost. Morocco has a history of political repression and human rights violations, and digital surveillance is a tool for suppressing dissent, rights to privacy, and freedom of expression (Galal 2023). The European Union supplied Morocco with phone-hacking spyware (DISCLOSE 2022). They financed the surveillance software, the required hardware, and the training of the Moroccan police on how to use the spyware out of the budget of their Border Management Programme for the Maghreb Region.

Although EU institutions are under an obligation to conduct human rights risk and impact assessments prior to engaging in any form of surveillance transfer, the European Ombudsman found in December 2022 that the European Commission had failed to take necessary measures to ensure the protection of human rights in the transfer of surveillance technology to African governments (Klovig Skelton 2022). Another example we highlighted is the investments in Ghana in an all-encompassing 'intelligent video surveillance' system implemented by Huawei and ZTE (AIDDATA 2013).

## Surveillance for political gain

Another motive for acquiring surveillance technologies could be, as Hillman (2021) stated, 'a vanity project', capturing votes during elections for ruling politicians who introduce smart city projects to position themselves as innovative, modern, and forward-looking. There are indications that Israeli companies may have been involved in misinformation campaigns to influence elections or bring about regime change in certain African countries (Whittaker 2019). Israeli experts were involved in setting up a war room for the ruling party for the 2014 elections in Botswana or using information from hacked emails from the then-opposition candidate Muhammadu Buhari, in a WhatsApp influencing campaign at the elections in Nigeria in 2015 (Bob 2021; Mandela 2022). Although these interventions do not create a 'chilling effect' on citizens out of fear, their behaviour is influenced, and democratic spaces and people's agency are shrunk (Murray et al. 2023).

## Surveillance as diplomacy

For some countries, the export of surveillance technologies has become an instrument of spyware diplomacy – a mechanism for furthering their geopolitical power interests (Bergman and Mazzetti 2022). The NSO Group's Pegasus spyware revelations showed that the Israeli government, by allowing export licences through its Ministry of Defence, has been using military-grade surveillance tools for its 'spyware diplomacy', creating a diplomatic bargaining chip for the country's political goals (Bergman and Mazzetti 2022; Dadoo 2022). Some argue that spyware may have played a role in Israel being accredited observer status at the African Union (Mandela 2022). A similar approach is identified by China's strategic objectives by pushing for the adoption of Chinese surveillance technologies (Hicks 2022).

Using 'spyware diplomacy', Israel is seeking legitimacy in Africa, weakening solidarity with Palestine, increasing a pro-Israel stance among the African countries, and fighting Boycott, Divestment, and Sanctions (BDS) campaigns against the occupation of Palestine (Dadoo 2021; Mandela 2022). In the slipstream of French government politics there are some French surveillance technology companies that have hired former French officials to facilitate doing business in Francophone Africa (Braun 2022). While this 'diplomacy' may be effective in furthering the interests of powerholders, it has a negative impact on citizens' rights and democracy. Morocco, for example, has used Pegasus spyware to hack journalists, activists, and political dissidents at home and abroad (Fatafta 2023).

## Surveillance as a tool for development: Smart or safe cities

Surveillance technologies have been exported as part of developmental or infrastructure projects. This motive of surveillance is tied to a trend from 'disciplinary society' to 'societies of control' by automated widespread surveillance via the 'Smart' or 'Safe' city (Deleuze 1992). Attractive loans by the exporting state sometimes incentivize the acquisition of surveillance technologies. These surveillance packages branded variously as 'Safe City' by the Chinese company Huawei or as 'Smart City' by rival Chinese company ZTE transmit these multiple streams of surveillance data to a central command and control 'data centre' where citizens can be monitored and tracked in public spaces and online.

Furthermore, this surveillance as a tool for the development motive is aligned with a neoliberal development paradigm for digital transformations, in which 'the state acts to support market-driven development', in this case, securitization of cities and privatization of public services (Galič and Schuilenburg 2020; Heeks et al. 2022).

## Surveillance as neocolonialism: Border externalization or data extraction

This motive resonates with surveillance practices initially used by colonial governments, and now, post-colonial governments are tasked with surveillance duties by former colonizing states. The chief guard has delegated the digital watch tower operations to a state guard on African soil. The European Union has funding mechanisms for controlling migration (EuropeAid 2008). These EU activities are aimed at migration management via border externalization, 'by both relocating the border outside the state's territory (externalization) and delegating border control functions to non-state and third-state actors (outsourcing)' (Pacciardi and Berndtsson 2022: 4010). Border externalization has colonial roots and reflects a colonial disciplinary mechanism outsourced to (former colonial) African states – assigned as guards – outside the European Union, with the task of controlling migration (Mitchell 1991: 35).

## Surveillance as a business opportunity

The extraction and trading of surveillance data is the business model of 'surveillance capitalism' (Zuboff 2019). There are economic benefits for surveillance sector firms in exporting to willing governmental clients in the Global South, sometimes stimulated by intensive marketing campaigns or proving 'battle-tested' capabilities: surveillance capitalism by a state-corporate surveillance model (Loewenstein 2023). For example, the Israeli surveillance industry sees growth potential in the African market, with follow-up sales for upgrading of Israeli surveillance technologies sold to African countries (Salman 2021).

# Pathways to resistance

From our findings and analysis, a list of recommendations emerges about how any surveillance abuse can be effectively resisted, mitigated, and abolished and what tactics are viable for expanding the agency and building citizens' power to resist rights-violating surveillance. Feldstein (2021) suggests four pressure points for approaches to consider in these tactics: reputational costs, economic costs, political factors, and supply-side considerations, which we have adapted to calls-to-action per relevant actor group involved in or affected by the transfer of surveillance technologies. The original supply-side considerations from Feldstein (2021) have been merged with the other existing factors (reputational, economic, and political) because our study already deals with the supply-side of surveillance technologies. Furthermore, we have included an additional consideration: technological actions that can be taken to counter harmful state-enabled surveillance. We argue that these tactics may be applied to several actors, including both supply-side exporting states and the African states that are the customers of surveillance technologies. Identification of the motives for state surveillance enables us to see which pressure points to use to target certain actors and what strategies for action to follow, derived from the powercube analysis.

## Reputational

When discussing reputational pressure points, we mean actions intended to affect the positive reputation certain actors are pretending to have. This pressure point could be applied in situations where motives for state surveillance occur, such as surveillance as legitimacy for state security, or surveillance for political gain, or surveillance as diplomacy. With this pressure point we are ultimately targeting the governments involved in exporting and importing the surveillance technologies and the providers of these technologies.

Following Gaventa's powercube assessment, an intervention for dealing with visible forms of power like that of governments would be advocacy for a policy change. Furthermore, actions that create cooperation on a national or international level would create the capacity for revealing hidden forms of power, such as deals made behind closed doors between governments and surveillance technology providers.

Governments that have imported and adopted surveillance technologies may feel pressure when their alleged noble intentions for using these technologies are exposed and called out on a national or international stage. They have implemented these technologies under the pretext of national security, safe cities, and otherwise improving security for citizens. The exposure of over-policing outside their mandate and for purposes that do not cover security may pressure governments to adjust their actions. Civil society organizations, both local and international, are in a position to organize themselves for this task. Witness statements from citizens (often anonymized) provide evidence of atrocities inflicted by the surveillance practices. Civil society, especially human rights organizations, can launch awareness and education campaigns about the issue of digital surveillance. On an international level, pressure campaigns against surveillance technology companies may be effective. Civil society can call out the human rights violations caused by the exports of the exporting government. This may seem daunting in an authoritarian environment, but connective action among civil society and citizens has been shown to be a formidable power. Human rights organizations can create archival records of surveillance cases and push for litigation against suppliers of surveillance technologies that are likely to be abused.

To expose these abuses of surveillance, civil society actors should cooperate with media actors (CIPESA 2023). Investigative journalism investigates, documents, and reveals surveillance practices to a broader audience. Other actors that may need support from civil society when refusing to collaborate with illegal surveillance practices are the internet and telecom service providers. We have seen the international collaboration of investigative journalists in exposing the use of Pegasus spyware against journalists and civil society across the world. These revelations were damaging to the reputation of governments that had closed deals with the Israeli NSO Group, the supplier of the Pegasus spyware. This story was exposed by an international investigative journalism initiative of more than eighty reporters from seventeen media organizations in ten countries (Amnesty International 2022).

## Economic

The economic pressure point could be applied in situations where motives like surveillance as a business opportunity or surveillance as a tool for development (e.g., smart or safe cities) occur. This could target all actors financially benefiting from the exports, purchase, and deployment of these citizen rights-violating surveillance technologies.

Some governments that have imported surveillance technologies argue these benefit the country's socio-economic development. For example, safe or smart city implementations are hailed as a solution for increasing citizens' safety and reducing crime rates. The mass surveillance of citizens in many public spaces and the contested claims by some technology providers who promote the crime prediction capabilities of those smart city systems are ignored. A war on crime is used as an argument for massive investments instead of interventions to alleviate poverty and improve healthcare or education. Protecting human rights in smart cities 'requires law, governance and political action – the tools available depend on the context and jurisdiction', Wernick and Artyushina (2023: 13) argue.

Following Gaventa's powercube analysis approach, an intervention for dealing with closed spaces of power, like those of governments, is by holding actors involved accountable and insisting on transparency and accountability. Furthermore, these actions should target the implicated surveillance technology providers. This holding to account is a role that human rights organizations could fulfil by creating archival records of surveillance cases and pushing for litigation against suppliers of surveillance technologies that are likely to be abused. For example, victims of Pegasus spyware and their relatives are suing the Israeli NSO group for spyware abuse (Madureira 2023).

Another strategy following the powercube assessment is supporting 'claimed spaces' by mobilizing for direct action to economically hit suppliers and protect civic space. Instruments for these are demands for economic pressure campaigns or corporate boycotts. For example, the restrictive measures taken against the NSO Group by the US government came into place after public pressure (Suderman 2021).

## Political

The political pressure point could be applied in situations where motives like surveillance for political gain, surveillance as diplomacy, or surveillance as neocolonialism occur. This intervention could target governmental actors on the supplying state side as well as the receiving/demand governmental state side.

For example, many Global North governments present themselves as guardians of democratic values or technology innovation for development, but have double standards for violating digital rights as part of human rights. We see these double standards in the case of EU institutions' efforts in border externalization programmes in Northern Africa. The European Ombudsman concluded that these EU institutions fail to protect human rights in the transfer of surveillance technologies in these collaboration programmes with African governments. Any export of surveillance technology should require a government export licence and human rights assessment.

Following Gaventa's powercube assessment, an intervention for deepening 'invited spaces' would be to ensure inclusion and capacities for negotiation and deliberation. Civil society organizations can help map surveillance technologies and their supply chains. They must insist on being consulted and having their voices heard, ensuring legislation based on human rights. Academics and researchers in the country must research digital and communication surveillance and its implications for citizens. This ensures capacity building in knowledge of surveillance and a push for a legal framework guided by international human rights standards and principles, including the rights to privacy and freedom of expression.

In the study, *Mapping the Supply of Surveillance Technologies to Africa*, the African Digital Rights Network recommends the following actions (Roberts et al. 2023): to influence the reform of surveillance law and practice; a call to defund mass surveillance; increasing public awareness about the constitutional right to privacy of communication and violations of these rights; and greater civil society capacity.

**Technological**

Following Gaventa's powercube assessment, an intervention for dealing with invisible forms of power like the surveillance firms' technological capabilities could lie in building awareness of the dangers of rights-violating surveillance and creating an alternative (safer) digital environment to protect citizens.

For this reason, to counter intrusive surveillance technologies irrespective of the motives for state surveillance, civil society, in collaboration with actors in the technology sector focusing on using tech for good, digitally capable human rights organizations, and universities, could develop technical solutions that protect citizens' privacy and security. For example, the use of encryption technologies, such as virtual private networks (VPNs) and privacy-preserving secure messaging apps, help prevent unauthorized access to digital information and protect sensitive data from theft or misuse. Furthermore, the development of anti-spyware tools could be a countermeasure, thus becoming a sousveillance actor, circumventing internet shutdowns (Feldstein 2022). Encouraging citizens to download anticensorship or anti-spyware apps may be a useful and effective way to pressure governments to stop abusing surveillance technologies.

**Recommendations for resistance to digital surveillance proliferation**

We have discussed four pressure points for approaches to consider in tactics for resistance to digital surveillance proliferation: reputational, economic, political, and technological. Table 8.4 presents suggestions to counter, grouped per pressure point for motives.

# Conclusion

This chapter addresses how citizens and civil society can counter the deployment of right-violating digital surveillance by understanding the drives for their proliferation. There are many actors involved in the transfer of rights-violating digital surveillance technologies, and multiple actors could play a

**Table 8.4** Recommendations for resistance to digital surveillance proliferation

| Pressure points for motives | Target surveillance and resistance actors | Approach(es) and examples for actions |
|---|---|---|
| **Reputational:**<br>• surveillance for political gain<br>• surveillance as legitimacy for state security | • Governments (both importing and exporting/supply-side)<br>• surveillance technologies suppliers | • Government should engage in **dialogue with citizens** to build trust and confidence in digital surveillance systems to ensure transparency and accountability. For example, the creation of the Digital Rights Group in Malawi is evidence that resistance is also emergent. Public participation in the development of surveillance policies will amplify the democratic process<br>• Calling for the establishment of an **independent watchdog** would strengthen accountability<br>• **Awareness building:** Civil society, especially human rights organizations: launch **awareness and education campaigns** about the issue of digital surveillance<br>• **Naming and shaming** in international forums<br>• **Media strategies** (traditional and social media) by civil society, especially human rights defence organizations and (independent) journalists<br>• Citizens' **documentation of repression** |
| **Economic:**<br>• surveillance as a tool for development (e.g. smart or safe cities)<br>• surveillance as a business opportunity | • Governments<br>• Surveillance technologies suppliers | • Governments and civil society: find a **balance between national security and the protection of citizens' rights**<br>• **Economic pressure campaigns**<br>• Pressure campaigns against companies<br>• **Protect civic space:** Human rights organizations: create archival records of surveillance cases and push for litigation against suppliers of surveillance technologies that are likely to be abused.<br>• Corporate boycotts |

| Pressure points for motives | Target surveillance and resistance actors | Approach(es) and examples for actions |
|---|---|---|
| **Political:**<br>• surveillance as legitimacy for state security<br>• surveillance for political gain<br>• surveillance as diplomacy<br>• Surveillance as neocolonialism | • Government (potentially both supply- and demand-side country) | • **Advocacy for policy change:** Governments and policymakers need to establish clear and transparent legal frameworks that govern the use of digital surveillance for legitimate reasons<br>  Civil society organizations can help **mapping** surveillance technologies and their **supply chains:** in Nigeria, Action Group on Free Civic Space (AGFCS) uses the diversity and expertise of their network to initiate joint action research projects<br>  Electoral challenges to incumbents<br>• **Mobilize for direct action: sanctions**<br>• **Monitor to hold actors accountable:** academics and researchers in the country must research digital and communication surveillance and its implications for citizens<br>• Civil society: capacity building in knowledge of surveillance, and **push for legal framework** guided by international human rights standards and principles, including the rights to privacy and freedom of expression. For example, in Nigeria, groups like SERAP use public interest litigation as a strategy for demanding surveillance contract transparency. Another example, is the Kenyan civil society took the government to court for illegal surveillance practices through Huduma number biometric ID and won<br>  Call for government **restrictions** (e.g., export controls) |
| **Technological:**<br>• surveillance as a business opportunity | • Surveillance technologies suppliers<br>• Every actor being surveilled | • Civil Society and Tech for good actors: Develop **technical solutions** that protect citizens' privacy and security, such as anti-spyware tools, thus becoming a sousveillance actor<br>• Collaborating with companies or **digitally capable actors** from civil society on technical counter and protection solutions and anti-repression tools |

Source: authors.

role in resisting these transfers. Our mapping of a multi-actor framework for surveillance and resistance actors revealed at least ten key players, ranging from governments (potentially both supply- and demand-side country) to the private sector, i.e. Northern-based surveillance technologies firms, to citizens, civil society, and the media. Combined with the identified six non-exclusionary motives for state surveillance, this provides recommendations for resisting the deployment of rights-violating digital surveillance. By applying the powercube, we suggest various pathways for resistance that can be grouped into reputational, economic, political, and technological actions to target actors involved in the transfer of surveillance technologies to change the power, agency, or rights dynamics to favour the rights of citizens.

Surveillance technologies, tools, and tactics, which are mostly non-African, are undermining democracy and human rights in Africa by enabling mass surveillance and disinformation that manipulates and undermines political discourse (Mwesigwa 2019). So, what should be done to limit the effects of surveillance? There is a need to raise awareness in African countries about both privacy rights and surveillance abuses by the transfer and deployment of surveillance technologies. Because of a lack of a clear regulatory framework, many African countries are vulnerable to the misuse of surveillance technologies (Roberts et al. 2021).

Each country should develop a country-specific advocacy capabilities and capacity approach to effectively monitor and mitigate the abuse of surveillance powers and their effects on citizens' rights and create viable paths to overcoming injustice. For the country-specific approaches, pro-digital rights actors can derive inspiration from each other. International, regional, and local collaboration and knowledge transfer are essential for successfully countering shrinking online civic space and ensuring digital rights for citizens.

# Notes

1    Special acknowledgement to Edin Omanovic from Privacy International who created and maintained an open-source repository of surveillance contracts worldwide, and made available data about the African countries included in this study.

2  The Wayback Machine is a digital archive of the World Wide Web founded by
the Internet Archive; it allows the user to go 'back in time' to see how websites
looked in the past.

# Bibliography

AIDDATA (2013). Project ID: 30956 *China Eximbank provides $123.4 million
preferential buyer's credit for Phase 2 of Dedicated Security Information System
Project (linked to #1862).* https://china.aiddata.org/projects/30956/ (accessed 7
September 2023).

Amnesty International (2022). 'The Pegasus Project: How Amnesty Tech Uncovered
the Spyware Scandal'. https://www.amnesty.org/en/latest/news/2022/03/the-
pegasus-project-how-amnesty-tech-uncovered-the-spyware-scandal-new-video/
(accessed 7 September 2023).

ArmsControlCenter (2023). 'Fact Sheet: The Wassenaar Arrangement'. https://
armscontrolcenter.org/fact-sheet-the-wassenaar-arrangement/#:~:text=At%20
a%20Glance,the%20proliferation%20of%20such%20items (accessed 29
September 2023).

Bergman, R. and Mazzetti, M. (2022, 28 January). 'The Battle for the World's
Most Powerful Cyberweapon', *The New York Times.* https://www.nytimes.
com/2022/01/28/magazine/nso-group-israel-spyware.html (accessed 7 September
2023).

Bob, Y. J. (2021, 8 April). 'How Are Israelis Involved in African Elections?', *The
Jeruaselem Post.* https://www.jpost.com/international/how-are-israelis-involved-
in-african-elections-664548 (accessed 7 September 2023).

Braun, E. (2022, 7 December). 'Destination Africa: The Scramble to Sell
Cyberweapons to Dictators'. *Politico.* https://www.politico.eu/article/destination-
africa-scramble-sell-cyberweapons-dictators-qwant-eric-leandri/

CIPESA (2023). 'How Enhanced State Surveillance Is Hurting Digital Rights in Africa
Brief'. https://cipesa.org/wp-content/files/How_Enhanced_State_Surveillance_is_
Hurting_Digital_Rights_in_Africa_Brief.pdf

Dadoo, S. (2021, 24 February). 'African Governments Are Crushing Opposition
Using Israeli Spyware'. Middle East Monitor. https://www.middleeastmonitor.
com/20210224-african-governments-are-crushing-opposition-using-israeli-
spyware/ (accessed 7 September 2023).

Dadoo, S. (2022, 12 September). 'Israel's Spyware Diplomacy in Africa'. https://
orientxxi.info/magazine/israel-s-spyware-diplomacy-in-africa,5859 (accessed 7
September 2023).

Deleuze, G. (1992). 'Postscript on the Societies of Control', *October*, 59: 3–7.

DISCLOSE (2022). 'How the EU Supplied Morocco with Phone-Hacking Spyware'.
https://disclose.ngo/en/article/how-the-eu-supplied-morocco-with-phone-
hacking-spyware (accessed 21 August 2024).

EuropeAid (2008). 'Aeneas Programme'. https://download.taz.de/migcontrol/eu/
EU_AENAS_%20projects%20funded%20to%20third%20countries%202004%20
-%202006_eng.pdf (accessed 7 September 2023).

Fatafta, M. (2023). 'Normalizing the Surveillance State – Cybersecurity Cooperation
and the Abraham Accords'. https://merip.org/2023/09/the-abraham-accords-
cybersecurity/ (accessed 7 September 2023).

Feldstein, S. (2019). *The Global Expansion of AI Surveillance* (Vol. 17), Washington,
DC: Carnegie Endowment for International Peace.

Feldstein, S. (2021). *The Rise of Digital Repression: How Technology is Reshaping
Power, Politics, and Resistance*, New York: Oxford University Press.

Feldstein, S. (2022). 'Government Internet Shutdowns Are Changing: How
Should Citizens and Democracies Respond?'. Carnegie Endowment. https://
carnegieendowment.org/files/Feldstein_Internet_shutdowns_final.pdf (accessed 7
September 2023).

Galal, A. (2023). 'Morocco Country Report', in T. Roberts, J. Gitahi, P. Allam, L.
Oboh, O. Oladapo, G. Appiah-Adjei, A. Galal, J. Kainja, S. Phiri, K. Abraham,
S. Klovig Skelton and A. Sheombar (eds), *Mapping the Supply of Surveillance
Technologies to Africa*, Brighton: Institute of Development Studies.

Galič, M. and Schuilenburg, M. (2020). 'Reclaiming the Smart City: Toward a New
Right to the City', in J. C. Augusto (ed.), *Handbook of Smart Cities* (pp. 1–18),
Cham: Springer Nature Switzerland.

Gaventa, J. (2006). 'Finding the Spaces for Change: A Power Analysis', in R. Eyben, C.
Harris and J. Pettit (eds), *Exploring Power for Change*, IDS Bulletin 37.6, Brighton:
Institute of Development Studies.

Gaventa, J. (2019). 'Applying Power Analysis: Using the "Powercube" to Explore
Forms, Levels and Spaces', in R. McGee and J. Pettit (eds), *Power, Empowerment
and Social Change* (pp. 117–38), London: Routledge.

Ginés, R. (2018). 'Eight Breakable Rules of Investigative Writing'. https://kit.
exposingtheinvisible.org/en/investigative-storytelling.html (accessed 29
September 2023).

Heeks, R., Ezeomah, B., Iazzolino, G., Krishnan, A., Pritchard, R. and Zhou, Q. (2022). 'Development Transformation as the Goal for Digital Transformation', *ICTs for Development*. https://ict4dblog.wordpress.com/2022/12/13/development-transformation-as-the-goal-for-digital-transformation/ (accessed 26 November 2023).

Hicks, J. (2022). 'Export of Digital Surveillance Technologies from China to Developing Countries', Institute of Development Studies, K4D. https://doi.org/10.19088/K4D.2022.123

Hillman, J. E. (2021). *The Digital Silk Road: China's Quest to Wire the World and Win the Future*, London: Profile Books.

Klovig Skelton, S. (2022). 'EU Fails to Protect Human Rights in Surveillance Tech Transfers', *Computer Weekly*.https://www.computerweekly.com/news/252528048/EU-fails-to-protect-human-rights-in-surveillance-tech-transfers (accessed 10 December 2023).

Klovig Skelton, S. and Sheombar, A. (2023). Mapping the Supply of Surveillance Technologies to Africa. *Supply-side report*. In T. Roberts (ed.), *Mapping the Supply of Surveillance Technologies to Africa: Case Studies from Nigeria, Ghana, Morocco, Malawi, and Zambia* (pp. 136–67). Brighton, UK: Institute of Development Studies.

Loewenstein, A. (2023). *The Palestine Laboratory: How Israel Exports the Technology of Occupation Around the World*, London and New York: Verso Books.

Madureira, V. (2023). 'Journalists File US Lawsuit Against Pegasus Spyware Producer'. https://www.occrp.org/en/daily/17109-journalists-file-us-lawsuit-against-pegasus-spyware-producer (accessed 10 December 2023).

Mandela, Z. (2022, 20 April). 'Israel Uses Spyware, Weapons and Agritech to Buy Influence in Africa', *Mail & Guardian*. https://mg.co.za/opinion/2022-04-20-israel-uses-spyware-weapons-and-agritech-to-buy-influence-in-africa/ (accessed 10 December 2023).

Marczak, B., Scott-Railton, J., McKune, S., Abdul Razzak, B. and Deibert, R. (2018). *Hide and Seek: Tracking NSO Group's Pegasus Spyware to Operations in 45 Countries*. https://catalog.caida.org/paper/2018_b_marczak_tr_univ_toronto (accessed 9 December 2023).

Martin, A. K., Brakel, R. v. and Bernhard, D. J. (2009). 'Understanding Resistance to Digital Surveillance: Towards a Multi-disciplinary, Multi-actor Framework', *Surveillance and Society*, 6(3): 213–32.

Mitchell, T. (1991). *Colonising Egypt: With a New Preface*, Berkeley, CA: University of California Press.

Munoriyarwa, A. and Mare, A. (2023). *Digital Surveillance in Southern Africa: Policies, Politics and Practices*, Cham: Springer.

Murray, D., Fussey, P., Hove, K., Wakabi, W., Kimumwe, P., Saki, O. and Stevens, A. (2023). 'The Chilling Effects of Surveillance and Human Rights: Insights from Qualitative Research in Uganda and Zimbabwe', *Journal of Human Rights Practice*, 16(1): 397–412. https://doi.org/10.1093/jhuman/huad020

Mwesigwa, D. (2019, 9 December). 'Africa in the Crosshairs of New Disinformation and Surveillance Schemes That Undermine Democracy', CIPESA.https://cipesa.org/2019/12/africa-in-the-crosshairs-of-new-disinformation-and-surveillance-schemes-that-undermine-democracy/ (accessed 7 September 2023).

Oosterom, M. and Scott-Villiers, P. (2016). *Power, Poverty and Inequality*. https://opendocs.ids.ac.uk/articles/report/Power_Poverty_and_Inequality/26476270/1/files/48249664.pdf

Pacciardi, A. and Berndtsson, J. (2022). 'EU Border Externalisation and Security Outsourcing: Exploring the Migration Industry in Libya', *Journal of Ethnic and Migration Studies*, 48(17): 4010–28. htts://doi.org/10.1080/136918 3X.2022.2061930

Privacy International (2022). *Challenging Public Private Surveillance Partnerships: A Handbook for Civil Society*. https://privacyinternational.org/sites/default/files/2022-07/Challenging%20Public-Private%20Partnerships%3A%20A%20Handbook%20for%20Civil%20Society_0.pdf (accessed 29 September 2023).

Roberts, T. and Mohamed Ali, A. (2021). 'Opening and Closing Online Civic Space in Africa: An Introduction to the Ten Digital Rights Landscape Reports', *Digital Rights in Closing Civic Space: Lessons from Ten African Countries*, Brighton: Institute of Development Studies.

Roberts, T., Mohamed Ali, A., Farahat, M., Oloyede, R. and Mutung'u, G. (2021). *Surveillance Law in Africa: A Review of Six Countries*, Brighton: Institute of Development Studies. https://opendocs.ids.ac.uk/opendocs/handle/20.500.12413/16893

Roberts, T., Gitahi, J., Allam, P., Oboh, L., Adekunle Oladapo, O., Appiah-Adjei, G., Galal, A., Kainja, J., Phiri, S., Abraham, K., Klovig Skelton, S. and Sheombar, A. (2023). *Mapping the Supply of Surveillance Technologies to Africa: Case Studies from Nigeria, Ghana, Morocco, Malawi, and Zambia*, Brighton: Institute of Development Studies. https://doi.org/10.19088/IDS.2023.027

Salman, Y. (2021). 'The Security Element in Israel-Africa Relations', *Strategic Assessment*, 24(2): 38–53.

Schuster, S., van den Berg, M., Larrucea, X., Slewe, T. and Ide-Kostic, P. (2017). 'Mass Surveillance and Technological Policy Options: Improving Security of Private

Communications', *Computer Standards & Interfaces*, 50: 76–82. https://doi.org/10.1016/j.csi.2016.09.011

Sheombar, A. and Skelton, S. K. (2023). 'Follow the Surveillance: A Breadcrumb Trail of Surveillance Technology Exports to Africa', Paper presented at After Latour: IFIP WG 8. 2 and WG 9. 4 Joint Working Conference, IFIPJWC 2023, Hyderabad, India, December 7–8, 2023, Proceedings. https://link.springer.com/chapter/10.1007/978-3-031-50154-8_19 (accessed 10 December 2023).

Suderman, A. (2021). 'US Puts New Controls on Israeli Spyware Company NSO Group'. https://apnews.com/article/technology-business-united-states-spyware-e15abad12084154b873765b420ae5f05 (accessed 7 September 2023).

UNHCR (2022). 'Spyware and Surveillance: Threats to Privacy and Human Rights Growing, UN Report Warns'. https://www.ohchr.org/en/press-releases/2022/09/spyware-and-surveillance-threats-privacy-and-human-rights-growing-un-report (accessed 7 September 2023).

van der Lugt, S. (2021). 'Exploring the Political, Economic, and Social Implications of the Digital Silk Road into East Africa: The Case of Ethiopia', in S. Florian (ed.), *Global Perspectives on China's Belt and Road Initiative* (pp. 315–46). Amsterdam: Amsterdam University Press.

Wernick, A. and Artyushina, A. (2023). 'Future-proofing the City: A Human Rights-based Approach to Governing Algorithmic, Biometric and Smart City Technologies'. *Internet Policy Review*, 12(1): 1–26. https://doi.org/10.14763/2023.1.1695

Whittaker, Z. (2019, 18 September). 'Documents Reveal How Russia Taps Phone Companies for Surveillance'. *TechCrunch*. https://techcrunch.com/2019/09/18/russia-sorm-nokia-surveillance/?guccounter=1 (accessed 7 September 2023).

Wright, D., Rodrigues, R., Raab, C., Jones, R., Székely, I., Ball, K., Bellanova, R., and Bergersen, S. (2015). 'Questioning Surveillance', *Computer Law & Security Review*, 31(2): 280–92. https://doi.org/10.1016/j.clsr.2015.01.006

Zuboff, S. (2019). *The Age of Surveillance Capitalism: The Fight for a Human Future at the New Frontier of Power*, London: Profile Books.

# Index